A Natural and Unnatural

History of Cannibalism

A Natural and Unnatural

History of Cannibalism

BILL SCHUTT

PROFILE BOOKS

First published in Great Britain in 2017 by
PROFILE BOOKS LTD
3 Holford Yard
Bevin Way
London
WC1X 9HD
www.profilebooks.com

**wellcome
collection**

Published in association with Wellcome Collection
Wellcome Collection
183 Euston Road
London NW1 2BE
www.wellcomecollection.org

1 3 5 7 9 10 8 6 4 2

Typeset in Sabon by MacGuru Ltd
Printed and bound in Great Britain by Clays, St Ives plc

ISBN 978 1 78125 397 7
eISBN 978 1 78283 130 3

FSC
www.fsc.org
MIX
Paper from
responsible sources
FSC® C018072

For Janet and Billy Schutt

And for my best friend, Robert A. Adamo (1953–2011)

CONTENTS

PROLOGUE

'A census taker tried to quantify me once. I ate his liver with some
fava beans and a big Amarone.'

Hannibal Lecter in Thomas Harris, *The Silence of the Lambs*

TO MARK ITS ONE-HUNDRED-year anniversary in 2003, the
American Film Institute polled its members to determine
the fifty greatest screen villains of all time. Topping the AFI
list was the ultimate in fictionalised cannibals, Dr Hannibal Lecter, while second place went to Norman Bates, the
mother-fixated hotel manager of Alfred Hitchcock's 1960
classic *Psycho*.

While Bates's link to man-eating may not be immediately
clear, it turns out that he too had his roots in the cannibal
tradition. From the film's opening scene, Hitchcock invited
audiences to confront some long-held taboos. Filmgoers tit-
illated the previous year by the first of the Rock Hudson/
Doris Day bedroom comedies suddenly found themselves
transformed into voyeurs, peering into shadowy corners
previously unseen by mainstream movie audiences. *Psycho*
soon became a sensation with the public and remains so
today. More than a half-century after its release, Bernard
Herrmann's strings-only score is perhaps the most instantly
recognisable music ever written for a film. Less well known
was the fact that Joseph Stefano's screenplay for *Psycho*
had been adapted from a Robert Bloch pulp novel about

Wisconsin native Edward Gein (pronounced Geen), a real-life murderer, grave robber, necrophile and cannibal.

Born in 1906, Gein lived a solitary and repressed life under the thumb of a domineering mother. The family owned a 160-acre farm, seven miles outside the town of Plainfield, but when his brother died in 1944 Gein abandoned all efforts to cultivate the land. Instead, he relied on government aid and the occasional odd job to support himself and his mother. When she died in 1945, Gein found himself alone in the large farmhouse. He sealed off much of it and left his mother's room exactly as it looked when she was alive. The house itself fell into such serious disrepair that the neighbourhood kids began claiming that it was haunted.

On the night of 17 November 1957, things began to unravel for the recluse known as 'Weird Old Eddie'. The police were investigating the disappearance of local shopkeeper Bernice Worden when they got a tip that Gein had been seen in her hardware store several times that week. They picked him up at a neighbour's house, where he was having dinner, and questioned him about the missing woman. 'She isn't missing,' Gein told them, 'she's down at the house now.'

Gein's dilapidated farmhouse had no electricity, so the cops used torches and oil lamps to pick their way through the debris-strewn rooms. In a shed in the back yard, one of the men bumped into what he assumed to be the remains of a dressed-out deer hanging from a wooden beam. But the fresh carcass hanging upside down was no deer; it was the decapitated body of Mrs Worden. As the stunned lawmen moved through the gruesome crime scene it became clear that the neighbourhood kids had been right. The Gein house was haunted. Each room they entered presented a new nightmare: soup bowls made from human skulls, a pair of lips attached to a window shade drawstring, a belt made from human nipples. In the kitchen, the police reportedly found Bernice Worden's heart sitting in a frying pan on the stove and an icebox stocked with human organs.

Soon after Gein's arrest, media correspondents from all over the world began descending on the town and its shocked populace. Reporters poked around the Gein farm and interviewed neighbours. Some of the locals recounted how they'd been given 'venison' by Gein, who later told authorities that he had never shot a deer in his life. Perhaps surprisingly, the Plainfield Butcher had also been a popular babysitter.

With the publication of a seven-page article in *Life* magazine (and a two-page spread in *Time*), millions of Americans became fascinated with Ed Gein and his crimes. Plainfield became a tourist attraction with bumper-to-bumper traffic crawling through the narrow streets.

The following year, Robert Bloch drew on the Gein crimes in his novel, relocating his tale to Phoenix and concentrating on the mother fixation while playing down the mutilation and cannibalism. An assistant gave Alfred Hitchcock the book and he procured the film rights soon after reading it. The director also had his staff buy up as many copies of the novel as they could find. He wanted to prevent readers from learning about the plot and revealing its secrets. After some initial resistance from Paramount Pictures, the 'Master of Suspense' directed his most famous and financially successful film – one that would never have been made if not for Ed Gein, a quiet little cannibal who explained to the authorities, 'I had a compulsion to do it.'*

---

* When *Psycho* opened, on 16 June 1960, it was an instant hit, with long lines outside theatres and broken box office records all over the world. Over fifty years later the film is remembered best for its famous shower scene, one which reportedly caused many of our Greatest Generation to develop some degree of ablutophobia, the fear of bathing (from the Latin *abluere*, 'to wash off'). Few theatregoers realized that the 'blood' in *Psycho* was actually the popular chocolate syrup Bosco (a fact the company somehow neglected to mention in their ads and TV commercials).

Perhaps it shouldn't come as a surprise, though, that our greatest cinematic villain is a man-eating psychiatrist while the mild-mannered runner-up is based on a real-life cannibal-killer. Particularly if we consider that many cultures share the belief that consuming another human is the most heinous act a person can commit. As a result, real-life cannibalistic psychopaths like Jeffrey Dahmer (another Wisconsin native) and his Russian counterpart Andrei Chikatilo have attained something akin to mythical status in the annals of history's most notorious murderers. These tales feed our obsession with all things gruesome – an obsession that is now an acceptable facet of our society.

Psychopaths aside, perhaps those most commonly associated with the word 'cannibal' are the so-called 'primitive' social or ethnic groups who historically have engaged in ritual man-eating. In colonial times, these 'savages' were at best pegged as souls to be saved, but only if they repented. If they failed to do so, they were brutalised, enslaved and murdered. The most infamous period of such ill treatment began during the last years of the fifteenth century when millions of people indigenous to the Caribbean and Mexico were summarily reclassified as cannibals for reasons that had little to do with people-eating. Instead, it paved the way for them to be robbed, beaten, conquered and slain, all at the whim of their new Spanish masters.

However, although defining someone as a cannibal became an effective way to dehumanise them, it's also worth remembering that there is evidence of ritual cannibalism, as embodied in various customs related to funerary rites and warfare, occurring throughout history.

As I began studying the subject, I sought to determine not only the perceived function, significance and consequences of cannibalism, but also the extent of the practice, both temporally and geographically. This was complicated by general disagreement among anthropologists: some deny that ritual cannibalism ever occurred, others claim that it was a rare exception and still others assert that it was a relatively common practice in many cultures – including Western society – throughout history and in a variety of forms.

As a zoologist, I was intrigued at the prospect of documenting cases of non-human cannibalism too, and I have made this my starting point in the book. Looking back now, I can see that I'd begun my inquiry with something less than a completely open mind. Part of me reasoned that since cannibalism is an uncommon behaviour in humans, it would likely be similarly rare in the animal kingdom. Once I dug further, though, I discovered that cannibalism is far from unknown in the animal kingdom, although it differs in frequency between major animal groups, being nonexistent in some and widespread in others. It also varies from species to species and even within the same species, depending on local environmental conditions. Animal cannibalism serves a variety of functions, depending on the cannibal. There are even examples it benefits the cannibalised individual.

In several instances animal cannibalism appears to have arisen only recently, and largely due to human activity. The false claim that polar bears are now eating their own young owing to climate change and the shrinking of Arctic ice is one high-profile instance of this phenomenon that hasn't escaped the scrutiny of the press.

The real story behind polar-bear cannibalism turned out to be just as fascinating, though it would also serve as a perfect example of how many stories about cannibalism have turned out to be untrue, unproven or exaggerated – distorted by sensationalism, deception or a lack of scientific knowledge. With the passage of time, these accounts too often become part of the historical record, their errors long forgotten. Part of my job would be to expose those errors.

I was also extremely curious to see if the origin of cannibalism taboos could be traced back to the natural world. Might it be that an aversion to consuming our own kind is hardwired into the human brain and thus part of our genetic blueprint? I reasoned that if such a built-in deterrent existed, then humans and most non-humans (with the exception of a few well-known anomalies such as black widow spiders and praying mantises) would avoid cannibalism at all costs.

Conversely, was it possible that the revulsion most of us feel at the very mention of cannibalism might stem solely from our culture? Of course, this led to even more questions. What are the cultural roots of the cannibalism taboo and how has it become so widespread? I also wondered why, as disgusted as we are at the very thought of cannibalism, we're so utterly fascinated by it. Might cannibalism have been more common in our ancestors, before societal rules turned it into something abhorrent? I looked for evidence in the fossil record and elsewhere.

Finally, I considered what it would take to break down the biological or cultural constraints that prevent us from eating each other on a regular basis. Could there ever be a future in which human cannibalism becomes commonplace? And, for that matter, is it already becoming a more frequent occurrence? The answers to these questions are far from clear cut but, then again, there is much about the topic of cannibalism that cannot be neatly labelled either black or white. Likely or not, though, the circumstances that might lead to outbreaks of widespread cannibalism even in the present century are grounded in science, not science fiction.

In researching these questions I have looked at the iconic cases of human cannibalism through history alongside animal behaviours, approaching each from a scientific viewpoint, delving into aspects of anthropology, evolution and biology. What, in biological terms, happens to our bodies and minds under starvation conditions? Why are women better equipped to survive starvation than men? And what physiological extremes would compel someone to consume the body of a friend or even a family member?

As you read on, you will encounter everything from cannibalism *in utero* to placenta-eating mothers who uphold a remarkably rich tradition of medicinal cannibalism. I hope you'll find this journey as fascinating and surprising as I have – a journey whose goal is to allow us better to understand the complexity of our natural world and the long and often blood-spattered history of our species.

With this in mind, why not grab that big Amarone (or, if you're more cinematically inclined, a nice Chianti) and let's get started.*

---

* For suitable background music, try 'Timothy', the catchy one-hit wonder by The Buoys. The song, written by Rupert Holmes of 'The Piña Colada Song' fame, tells the tale of three trapped miners, two of whom survive by eating the title character. In 1971 'Timothy' reached number 17 on the Billboard Top 100 even though many major radio stations refused to play it. In an unsuccessful attempt to reverse the ban, executives at Scepter Records began circulating a rumour that Timothy was actually a mule.

ANIMALS

1

ANIMAL THE CANNIBAL: NATURE'S WAY?

Cannibals prefer those who have no spines.

Stanislaw Lem, *Holiday*

I WAS KNEE-DEEP in a pond that seemed to be composed of equal parts rainwater and cowpats when I felt a nibbling on my leg hair.

'If you stand still for long enough, they'll definitely nip you,' I was informed.

The 'they' were spadefoot toad larvae (commonly known as tadpoles) and the warning had come from Dr David Pfennig, a biology professor at the University of North Carolina who had been studying these toads in Arizona's Chiricahua Mountains for over twenty years.

At Pfennig's invitation, I had arrived at the American Museum of Natural History's Southwestern Research Station in mid-July – just after the early summer monsoons had turned cattle wallows into nursery ponds, and newly hatched tadpoles into cannibals. But the real reason I had come wasn't because the tadpoles were eating each other. It was because some of them *weren't* eating each other. In fact, when this particular brood had hatched about a week earlier they were all omnivores, feeding on plankton and general pond detritus.

Then, two or three days later, something peculiar had taken place. Some of the tiny amphibians experienced dramatic growth spurts, their bodies ballooning overnight. Now, as I waded, scoop-net in hand, through 'Sky Ranch Pond' (a slimy-bottomed mud hole with delusions of grandeur), these pumped-up proto-toads were four or five times larger than their peers. They looked like two different species. I also noted that the larger individuals were light tan in colour while the little guys had bodies flecked with dark green.

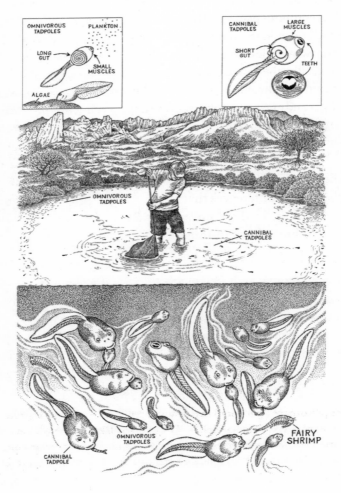

Pfennig explained that initially people had indeed thought they *were* different species, and as I used a magnifying glass to get a better look at my captives I saw that the differences went far beyond body size and colour. The larger tadpoles were also sporting powerful tails and sharp beaks.

'They're made of keratin,' Pfennig explained, referring to the beaks – the same tough, structural protein found in our nails and hair.

Later, while comparing the two tadpole morphs under a dissecting microscope, I saw that behind a set of frilly lips, the flat keratinous plates had been transformed into a row of sharp-edged teeth in the cannibalistic forms. It was also evident that the jaw muscles were significantly enlarged in the cannibals, especially the jaw-closing *levator mandibulae*. Studies had shown that myofibres, the cells making up these muscles, were larger and greater in number in the large specimens – producing a more powerful bite. Of course, the extra bite force was necessary to subdue and consume their omnivorous pond-mates.

Not quite so obvious was a significant shortening of the gastrointestinal (GI) tract in the cannibals, as a result of the dietary differences that accompanied the tadpole transformations. In the omnivores, a long GI tract is required for the breakdown of tough-to-digest plant matter, while a shorter GI tract suffices for the meat-eaters.*

---

* A lengthy intestine is a hallmark of many herbivores since longer guts entail longer passage times for the food moving through them – allowing for additional chemical digestion and more thorough absorption of nutrients. In many animals, though (including all vertebrates and even invertebrates like termites), the digestive tract cannot digest cellulose, the polysaccharide that makes up plant-cell walls. The problem is solved by the presence of endosymbiotic bacteria or protozoans ('gut flora') that produce cellulases – enzymes capable of digesting polysaccharides. In 'foregut fermenters' like cows, a multi-chambered stomach serves as a homestead for the enzyme-generating microbial horde, while in 'hindgut fermenters' like horses, a pouch-like section of the intestine called the cecum houses the endosymbionts.

Over a three-day period, I watched and captured tadpoles. I learned a great deal about the three species of *Spea* that laid their eggs in such dangerously unpredictable conditions. Much of this information centred on their ecology, behaviour and evolution, and, of course, their cannibalism – something the local research teams seemed to view as perfectly normal.

Until relatively recently, cannibalism in nature would have been regarded as anything but normal. As a result, until the last two decades of the twentieth century, relatively few scientists spent any time studying a topic they regarded as biologically insignificant. The party line was that cannibalism, when it did occur, was the result of either starvation or the stresses related to captive conditions.

It was as simple as that.

Or so we thought.

IN THE 1970S Laurel Fox, a University of California Santa Cruz ecologist, took some of the first steps towards a scientific approach to cannibalism. She had been studying the feeding behaviour of predatory freshwater insects called backswimmers. Fox determined that, while the voracious hunters relied primarily on aquatic prey, cannibalism was also a consistent part of their diets.

I contacted Fox and asked her about the resulting transition that had taken place in the scientific community. She told me that her observations in the field had sparked her interest and that, soon after, she began compiling a list of research papers in which cannibalism had been reported. Although there turned out to be hundreds of references documenting the behaviour in various species, no one had linked these instances together or come up with any general rules. By the time Fox's review paper came out in 1975, she had concluded that cannibalism was not abnormal behaviour at all, but a completely normal response to a variety of environmental factors.

Significantly, Fox also determined that cannibalism was a far more widespread occurrence than anyone had previously imagined, and that it took place in every major animal group, including some that were long considered to be herbivores, such as butterflies. She emphasised that cannibalism in nature, which some researchers referred to as 'intraspecific predation', also demonstrated a complexity that seemed to match its frequency. Fox suggested that the occurrence of cannibalism in a particular species often depended on variables like population density and changes in local environmental conditions. Fox even followed cannibalism on the human branch of the evolutionary tree. After pondering reports that ancient cultures practising non-ritual cannibalism lived in 'nutritionally marginal areas', she proposed that consuming other humans might have provided low-density populations with 5–10 per cent of their protein requirements. Conversely, she suggested that cannibalism was rare in settlements where populations were dense enough to allow for the production of an adequate and predictable food supply.

In 1980 ecologist and scorpion expert Gary Polis picked up the baton and began looking at invertebrates that consumed their own kind. Like Fox, he noted that, while starvation could lead to increases in the behaviour, it was certainly not a requirement. Perhaps Polis's most important contribution to the subject was assembling a list of general rules under which most examples of invertebrate cannibalism could be placed, namely:

1. immature animals get eaten more often than adults;
2. many animals, particularly invertebrates, do not recognise individuals of their own kind, especially eggs and immature stages, which are simply regarded as a food source;
3. females are more often cannibalistic than males;

4. cannibalism increases with hunger and a
   concurrent decrease in alternative forms of
   nutrition; and
5. cannibalism is often directly related to the degree
   of overcrowding in a given population.

Polis emphasised that these general rules were sometimes found in combination, such as overcrowding and a
lack of alternative forms of nutrition (a common cause and
effect), both of which now fall under the broader banner of
'stressful environmental conditions'.*

In 1992 zoologists Mark Elgar and Bernard Crespi
edited a scholarly book on the ecology and evolution of cannibalism across diverse animal taxa. In it, they refined the
scientific definition of cannibalism in nature as 'the killing
and consumption of either all or part of an individual that
is of the same species'. Initially the researchers excluded
instances where the individuals being consumed were
already dead or survived the encounter – the former they
considered to be a type of scavenging. Eventually, though,
they decided these were variants of cannibalistic behaviour
observed across the entire animal kingdom. Although there
are certainly grey areas (encompassing things like breast
feeding or eating one's own fingernails), my fallback definition of cannibalism is this: The act of one individual of a
species consuming all or part of another individual of the
same species. In the animal kingdom this would include
scavenging (as long as the scavenged body was from the
same species as the scavenger) and maternal care in which
tissue (e.g. skin or uterine lining) was consumed. In humans,
cannibalism would extend beyond the concept of nutrition
into the realms of ritual acts, medicine and mental disorder.

---

* Tragically, Dr Polis drowned when his research vessel sank during a
storm in the Sea of Cortez in 2000, an accident that also claimed the
lives of a graduate student and three Japanese ecologists.

As the study of cannibalism gained scientific validity in the 1980s, more and more researchers began looking at the phenomenon, bringing with them expertise in a variety of fields. From ecologists we learned that cannibalism was often an important part of predation and foraging, while social scientists studied its relationship to courtship, mating and even parental care. Anatomists found strange structures to examine (like the keratinous beak of the spadefoot toad) and field biologists studied cannibalism under natural conditions, thus countering the previous belief that the behaviour was captivity-dependent.

By the 1990s, Polis's observations had been confirmed among widely divergent animal groups, both with and without backbones, supporting the conclusion that the benefits of consuming your own kind could outweigh the often substantial costs. Once these general rules were established, and as a new generation of researchers built upon foundations constructed by pioneers like Fox and Polis, cannibalism in nature, with all of its intricacies and variation, began to make perfect evolutionary sense.

Arizona's lowland scrub stood in stark contrast to the lush peaks and boulder-strewn valleys of the state's Chiricahua Mountains. These 'sky islands' provided a spectacular backdrop to examine yet another transient pond.

The air temperature had risen to ninety-five degrees Fahrenheit, which kept most of the area's land-dwellers hiding in shade or below ground, but the inhabitants of Horseshoe Pond reminded me of overexcited kids tearing around a playground. By this time, I had already begun to see distinct patterns of behaviour in the spadefoot tadpoles that motored hyperactively just below the water's surface.

I noticed that the smaller omnivores generally stuck to the shallows bordering the shoreline. They buzzed through the brown water in a non-stop, seemingly random quest for food, changing direction abruptly and often. One explanation for the patternless swimming became apparent as I waded further away from the shore, for here in the deeper water was the realm of the cannibals. I stood quietly and watched as hundreds of conspicuously larger tadpoles crisscrossed the pond, making frequent excursions from the deeper water toward the shore in a relentless search for prey.

'They remind me of killer whales hunting for seals,' said Ryan Martin, a former student of Pfennig's, now a professor at Case Western Reserve, who was also studying spadefoot toads here in Arizona.

The comparison was apt. But the question remained: why did the local spadefoot larvae exhibit cannibalistic behaviour? There certainly seemed to be enough organic matter suspended in these algae-tinted ponds to feed them all and more.

As I spoke to Pfennig and his team of researchers, I learned that the answer was directly linked to the aquatic environments where the parents deposited their eggs.* Formed by spring and early summer monsoons, the transient ponds frequented by the spadefoots (spadefeet?) are often little more than puddles, and as such they can evaporate quite suddenly in the hot, dry environment of south-eastern Arizona. Natural selection, therefore, would favour any adaptation enabling the water-dependent tadpoles to 'get out of the pool' as quickly as possible. In this instance, the phenomenon that evolved can be filed under the rather broad ecological heading of *phenotypic plasticity*: when changing environmental conditions allow multiple characteristics or traits to arise from a single genotype (the genetic makeup of an organism).

One (non-cannibalistic) example of this is the water flea (*Daphnia* spp.). Water fleas are tiny aquatic crustaceans,

---

* Toads and frogs belong to the amphibian order Anura (from the Greek for 'no tail'). Most anurans lay their eggs in fresh water, with hatchlings undergoing complete metamorphosis from gill-bearing tadpoles to lung-breathing juveniles.

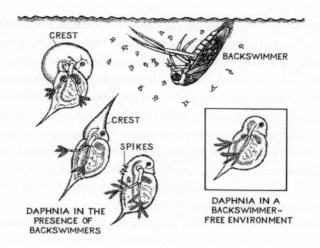

CREST

BACKSWIMMER

CREST

SPIKES

DAPHNIA IN THE
PRESENCE OF
BACKSWIMMERS

DAPHNIA IN A
BACKSWIMMER–
FREE ENVIRONMENT

named for a swimming style in which they appear to jump. In response to the appearance of backswimmers, they develop tail spikes and protective crests. Although the genetic potential for body armour is always there, it doesn't exhibit itself until a specific environmental change occurs, in this case the arrival of *Daphnia*-munching backswimmers.

Another example of this is the bluehead wrasse, a reef-dweller famous for its habit of removing parasites from much larger fish, even entering into their mouths. Here, however, it's the removal of a male wrasse from its harem of thirty to fifty females that alters their local environment. Rather than waiting for a new male to arrive, something extraordinary takes place in the harem. Within minutes, one of the females begins exhibiting male-typical behaviours. Relatively quickly, the former female transforms into a male. The opposite can also occur, as in the case of the clownfish, whose real-life behaviour could have offered an intriguing alternative resolution to *Finding Nemo*.

In spadefoot toads, though, it's not the appearance of a predator or the loss of a harem's personal sperm bank that initiates the alternate phenotype (the cannibalistic larvae). The selection pressure lies in the temporary nature of the ponds where the eggs are deposited and hatch, and where the tadpoles develop. The period from egg to juvenile toad usually takes around thirty days unless the pond dries out first, killing the entire brood. In response to this particular environmental selection pressure, spadefoot toads evolved a means by which some of the tadpoles can mature in about two-thirds of the time (twenty days). The increased growth rate occurs because the cannibal larvae are getting a diet high in animal protein as well as a side order of veggies, the latter in the form of nutrient-rich plant matter consumed by their omnivorous prey.

It's interesting to note that a related species of spadefoot, *Spea couchii*, does *not* have this ability to transform into cannibalistic morphs but has evolved an alternative solution to the transient-pond problem: they can go from egg to toad in only eight days – an amphibian record.

Though the spadefoot toad story has been well researched, it is not fully resolved. No one has been able to identify the precise stimulus within these brood ponds that triggers the appearance of the cannibal morphs. Until recently, the prime candidates were a pair of microscopic fairy shrimp species. David Pfennig and his colleagues proposed that the consumption of the shrimp by some of the spadefoot tadpoles served to trigger the cascade of genetically controlled developmental changes that transformed the shrimp-eaters into outsized cannibals.

But what was it that set this transformation into motion? Pfennig hypothesised that iodine-containing compounds found in the shrimp might cause the activation of specific genes in the tadpoles, genes that weren't turned on in the individuals that didn't consume shrimp. The most likely trigger substance turns out to be thyroxin: a thyroid hormone whose functions include stimulating metabolism and promoting tissue growth. However, this theory was undermined by experiments showing that even tadpoles not fed fairy shrimp could still undergo the transformation to cannibals, indicating that (at the very least) something besides thyroxin intake must initiate the changes.

'What if it's not what they're eating but the mechanism of chewing itself that serves as a tactile trigger?' I made the suggestion while brainstorming the problem with biologist Ryan Martin. 'What if chewing on something alive like a fairy shrimp, something larger or something that struggles when you clamp onto it, sets this developmental cascade into motion?'

Martin shot me a 'not bad for a bat biologist' look. 'Sounds like a good grad student project.'

'Hey, it's all yours,' I said with a laugh. We then set to work, drawing up an outline for a potential experiment to test the hypothesis.

Although the jury is still out, Pfennig and his co-workers have previously worked on a completely different cannibalism trigger in another amphibian. And this one happened to be one of North America's most spectacular species.

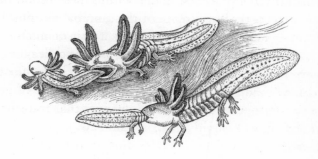

Tiger salamanders are the largest salamanders in the United States, reaching lengths of up to thirteen inches. These thick-bodied, sturdy-limbed urodelans are wide-spread across much of the country.* Their markings, yellow

---

* Urodela (Greek for 'conspicuous tail') is the order containing approximately 655 salamanders, lizard-shaped amphibians generally found in moist terrestrial environments.

blotches against a black body, make them easy to identify but they are rarely seen in the open except during annual marches to a nuptial pond. Tiger salamander eggs are laid in the late winter or early spring and, like other salamanders (and their cousins the frogs and toads), their larvae are fully aquatic with external gills and fish-like tails. They typically feed on zooplankton and other micro-invertebrates, but under certain environmental conditions a small percentage of them develop traits that include huge heads, wide mouths and elongated teeth. Consequently, these toothy individuals exploit larger prey, which includes other tiger salamander larvae.

Pfennig and his colleagues set up lab experiments on their fertilised eggs to investigate the stimuli that set these changes into motion. First, the researchers determined that the cannibal morphs only developed when larvae were placed into crowded conditions. Next, they used a variety of experiments to determine whether the larval transformation might be triggered by visual cues, smell, or touch. They concluded that the tactile cues were significant: the act of bumping into each other was key in the production of the cannibals.

Movement- and touch-related, I thought, remembering my suggestion about a possible tactile trigger for the spadefoot cannibals. But instead of speculating about my own half-formed ideas, the conversation turned toward the pros and cons of cannibalism, especially as it pertained to consuming kin.

As we have seen, one of Gary Polis's general rules about cannibalism is that immature animals get eaten far more often than adults. Ultimately, this makes larvicide (or infanticide) the most common form of cannibalism in the animal kingdom. Intuitively, it doesn't seem logical to eat the next generation, but the behaviour can make evolutionary sense for several reasons. Young animals not only provide a valuable source of nutrition but in most species are also relatively defenceless. As such, they present instant nutritional benefit but little or no threat to larger members of the same species, most of which are invulnerable to attacks from immature forms.

But beyond acquiring a meal, cannibalism enables individuals of species such as spadefoot toads to accelerate their developmental process, thus allowing them to quickly outgrow a stage where they might be preyed upon or perish due to unpredictable environmental conditions. In species like the flour beetle, this may also impart a reproductive advantage, since studies have shown that cannibalistic individuals produce more eggs than non-cannibals. Finally, many animals maintain specific territories, within which they are intolerant to the presence of conspecifics (i.e. members of the same species). According to Polis, crowding increases the frequency with which individuals violate the space of others. By reducing overcrowded conditions, cannibalism can serve to decrease the frequency of territory violations.

But, of course, there are also obvious and serious drawbacks to being a cannibal.

Perhaps the most significant of these is a heightened chance of acquiring harmful parasites or diseases from a conspecific. Both parasites and pathogens are often species-specific and many of them have evolved defences to defeat their host's immune system. As a result, predators that consume their own kind run a greater risk of picking up a disease or a parasite than predators that feed solely on other species. In the most famous example of cannibalism-related disease transmission, the Fore people of New Guinea were nearly driven to extinction by their ritualised consumption of brains and other tissues cut from the bodies of their deceased kin, kin who had themselves been infected by kuru, an incurable and highly transmissible neurological disease. More on that topic later, but the potential for disease transmission stands as a prime example that non-humans and humans alike share some of the negative consequences of cannibalism.

Cannibals can also experience decreases in a measure of evolutionary success known as 'inclusive fitness', in which the survival of an individual's genes, whether they're from an offspring or a collateral relative such as a brother, sister, or cousin, is the true measure of evolutionary success. A cannibal that consumes its own issue, siblings or even more distant relatives, removes those genes from the population, so it reduces its own inclusive fitness. Since this is disadvantageous, natural selection should favour cannibals that can discriminate between kin and non-kin.

As a result, it made perfect sense that David Pfennig and his colleagues had also worked on questions related to kin recognition. The researchers found that their study subjects could often identify their own relatives.

They do so by means of what's known as 'the armpit effect', Pfennig told me, whereby an individual forms a template for the scent of its kin based on its own smell. He cited a species of paper wasps that regularly raid the nests of other paper wasps to provide food for their own. In these species, individuals learn that if an individual smells like your nest or burrow ... you don't eat them.

Similarly, tiger salamander larvae are more likely to eat the larvae of unrelated individuals than they are to consume relatives. Pfennig explained that he and his colleagues determined this experimentally by preventing them from being able to smell by applying superglue to their nares.

In the wild, cannibal tadpoles have been found to release siblings unharmed yet consume non-relatives. However, in the lab, apparently all bets are off if the cannibals are deprived of food then placed in a tank with other tadpoles. In these cases, starvation becomes the great equaliser and both kin and non-kin are eaten. As I would learn from researchers, unearthing new evidence about the behaviour in humans, this particular aspect of cannibalism spans the *entire* animal kingdom.

On the plane ride back to New York, I thought a

great deal about the cannibalism I'd seen in the temporary ponds.

Cannibal morphs.

I wondered whether H. G. Wells knew about their existence when he wrote *The Time Machine* in 1895. In Wells's classic novel, the Time Traveller encounters two human species: the child-sized and docile Eloi and the brutish Morlocks, who raise the Eloi in order to feed upon them. Wells explained the Morlocks' cannibalistic behaviour by suggesting that they were once members of a worker class, toiling underground for lazy upper-class surface dwellers. The Time Traveller speculates that a food shortage (i.e. an environmental change) forced the subterraneans to alter their diets – at first rats but ultimately something a bit larger. Eventually, this behaviour resulted in a race of hulking cannibals, feeding on the surface-dwellers, whose own evolutionary path would produce the sheep-like Eloi, pampered, well fed and eventually slaughtered for food.

In his cautionary tale of class distinction, Wells imagined a biological phenomenon remarkably similar to what scientists like David Pfennig and his colleagues are working on today.

Many scientists now believe that phenotypic plasticity offers the perfect building blocks for the type of evolutionary change described by Wells over a century ago. These building blocks could be novel traits like the tiger salamander's jaws or the spadefoot tadpole's serrated beak – each having originated as an environment-dependent alternative to an already established ancestral trait. What these scientists hypothesise goes far beyond the realm of cannibalism and into the very mechanisms of evolution itself. Their claim is that the appearance of new traits in a population, generally regarded as a first step toward the evolution of new species, can occur by means other than the accumulation of micromutations, the classic mechanism by which new traits, and eventually new species, are thought to appear.

Some researchers now believe that in given generations, novel traits originating as examples of phenotypic plasticity even have the potential to produce separate species.

This idea originated with the German/American geneticist Richard Goldschmidt (1878–1958), infamous for his stance that micromutations accumulating over long periods of time were inadequate to explain the evolution of different species. He proposed two additional mechanisms; the first, speciation by macromutations (i.e. those causing a profound effect on the organism), eventually led to the derision associated with his name and the legacy-destroying label of 'non-Darwinian'. Less well known is Goldschmidt's suggestion (quite correct, it appears) that mutations can result in major changes during early development, and that these can lead to large effects in the adult phenotype. This hypothesis and the related concept of developmental adaptability are two of the key principles of the modern field of evolutionary developmental biology, informally known as 'evo-devo'.

Okay, so now that I'd captured and examined cannibalistic tadpole morphs and heard all about their outsized salamander cousins, it was time to look into other examples of cannibalism in nature and to determine why these creatures were eating each other. I decided that the best way to cover and divvy up the material was to look at what I considered to be the most dramatic examples of Gary Polis's cannibalism-related generalisations. Admittedly, some of what I uncovered was hard to categorise, thus leading me to the realisation that cannibalism can extend far beyond the realm of generalisation. I also learned that, normal behaviour or not, sometimes cannibalism in the animal kingdom can get downright weird.

2

IT'S ALL RELATIVE: FILIAL AND SIBLING CANNIBALISM

3rd Fisherman: I marvel how the fishes live in the sea.

1st Fisherman: Why, as men do a-land; the great ones eat up the little ones.

William Shakespeare, *Pericles* Act II, Sc. i

MANY INVERTEBRATES DO NOT recognise individuals of their own kind as anything more than food. As a result, a significant amount of cannibalism takes place within such groups as molluscs, insects and arachnids (spiders and scorpions). Clams, corals and thousands of other aquatic invertebrates have tiny, planktonic eggs and larvae, and these are often a major food source for the filter-feeding adults. Since the planktonic forms often belong to the same species as the adults feeding on them, by definition this makes filter-feeding a form of indiscriminate cannibalism.

Although both fertilised and unfertilised eggs are eaten by thousands of species, the practice of consuming conspecific eggs appears to have led to the evolution of an interesting take on the concept of the 'kids' meal'. Trophic eggs, for instance, are produced by some species of spiders, lady beetles and snails, and function solely as food. These often outnumber the fertilised eggs in a given clutch – a phenomenon exemplified by the rock snail. This species commonly lays around five hundred eggs at a time, but averages only sixteen hatchlings. The vast majority of the eggs are consumed.

In the black lace-weaver spider, this is only the beginning. One day after their young hatch, new mothers lay a clutch of trophic eggs, which they dole out to their hungry babies. The meal tides the young spiders over for three days, after which they're ready for their next stage of development.

Arthropods – the phylum that includes spiders, insects and crabs – are characterised by having their skeletons outside their bodies. To grow in size, they undergo a regular series of moults during which their jointed cuticle or exoskeleton is shed and replaced by a new one arising from beneath the old. After their first moult, and after the trophic eggs have been consumed, young black lace-weaver spiders are too large for their mother to care for, though they are in dire need of additional food. In an extreme act of parental devotion, she calls them to her by drumming on their web and presses her body down into the gathering crowd. The ravenous offspring swarm over their mother's body, then eat her alive, draining her bodily fluids and leaving behind a husk-like corpse.

Such a willing act of self-sacrifice is hardly the norm, however. Insects undergoing pupation, the quiescent stage of metamorphosis associated with the production of a chrysalis or cocoon, are particularly vulnerable to attack from younger peers. To counter this threat, the ravenous larva of the elephant mosquito not only consumes fellow pupae but also embarks on a killing frenzy, slaying but not eating anything unlucky enough to cross its path. The reason for this butchery appears to be the elimination of any and all potential predators before the larva enters the helpless pupal stage.

For some, cannibalism is only a juvenile phase. Certain snail species, for example, transform into vegetarian adults after a brief cannibalistic period. In one food preference test, hatchlings from a herbivorous species always chose conspecific eggs over lettuce, four-day-old individuals ate equal amounts of eggs and lettuce and sixteen-day-old individuals preferred the veggie option. When snails older than four weeks were denied the lettuce they starved to death, even in the presence of eggs. The reason for this gradual transition in feeding preference appears to be that these snails, like other herbivores from termites to cows, require a gut full of symbiotic bacteria before they can digest plant material. Since newly hatched snails have no gut bacteria, they're compelled to consume easily digested material, even if this turns out to be their own unhatched siblings.

Cannibalism also occurs in every class of vertebrates, from fish to mammals. For researchers, factors like relatively larger body size and longer lifespans have made these backboned cannibals easier to study than invertebrates. As a result, previously unknown examples of cannibalistic behaviour are being revealed on an increasingly frequent basis. Additionally, factors related to the increased size and longevity of vertebrates have made it easier for scientists to determine and track kin relationships, leading to a greater understanding of the complexities of cannibalism-related behaviours. One such result has been the classification of cannibalism into distinct forms, such as filial cannibalism (eating one's own offspring) and heterocannibalism (eating unrelated conspecifics), both of which have become vital to the concept of cannibalism as normal behaviour.

In most vertebrates, and specifically in mammals, filial

cannibalism has been reported in rodents (like voles, mice and wood rats), in rabbits and their relatives, as well as shrews, moles, and hedgehogs. These mammal mothers sometimes eat their young to reduce litter size during periods when food is scarce and cannibalism also occurs in other circumstances, such as when litter size exceeds the number of available teats or when pups are deformed, weak or dead.

In stark contrast, for fish, by far the largest of the traditional vertebrate classes, individuals in every aquatic environment and at every developmental stage are ambushed, chased, snapped up and gulped down on a scale unseen in terrestrial vertebrates. One reason that cannibalism occurs so frequently may be the fact that the group as a whole has more in common with the invertebrates (where cannibalism is often the rule and not the exception) than do the other vertebrate classes (reptiles, birds and mammals). Another way to consider this is to think of fish as a mosaic – composed of a suite of more recently evolved vertebrate traits (like a spinal column and larger brain) but still retaining some invertebrate characteristics. Here it is the production of high numbers of tiny offspring with little parental care, as well as a proclivity for indiscriminately consuming both eggs and young, that predisposes them to filial cannibalism.

At its most extreme, reproductive success in many fish species depends on a romantic-sounding technique known as broadcast spawning, during which females can release millions of eggs, while males simultaneously release clouds of sperm (milt). The end result is that *some* of the eggs get fertilised. Each female produces between four and ten million eggs in a single spawning, though the record is held by the ocean sunfish, which can broadcast up to 300 million.

But it's not just the abundance of eggs and young that makes fish such a popular menu item for members of their own species. Unlike most terrestrial vertebrates, which tend to produce few or single offspring of significant body size, most fish produce a huge number of extremely tiny young. This fact goes a long way towards explaining why the majority of them exhibit about as much individual recognition of their offspring as humans do for a handful of raisins. Fish eggs, larvae and fry are vast in number, minute in size and high in nutritional value. This makes them an abundant, non-threatening and easily collected food source. It's also why experts consider the absence of cannibalism in fish, rather than its presence, to be the exception not the rule.

Parental care occurs in only around 20 per cent of the 420 families of bony fish (a group composed of nearly all living fish species except sharks and their flattened relatives the skates and rays). The primary logic underlying this trend is the fact that the natural world is full of trade-offs. Here, it works like this: since females expend a tremendous amount of energy producing huge numbers of eggs, they can't afford to expend much energy caring for them or their young when they hatch. For this reason, the eggs and fry of most fish species exist in dangerous environments inhabited by a long list of potential predators.

Even in the ninety or so piscine families where parental care does occur, filial cannibalism is an extremely common practice, although it seems to depend on who is doing the babysitting. Among most land-dwelling vertebrates, females are the principal caregivers, while males take on support roles or simply make themselves scarce. In bony fish, though, it is often the males who guard the eggs, if they're guarded at all. But the male guardians often end up consuming some of the eggs (partial filial cannibalism), and sometimes all of them (total filial cannibalism).

One reason they engage in this seemingly counterproductive behaviour may be that generally they have much less invested in the brood than the females. It is less costly to produce a cloud of sperm than it is to produce, carry and distribute an abdomen full of eggs. Furthermore, with their ability to search for food seriously constrained by caregiving duties, males are forced to undertake at least some degree of fasting. This practice decreases their overall physical condition and thus the likelihood of future reproductive success. By consuming a portion of the eggs, males can increase their own survival chances and therefore produce additional offspring.

In some instances though, unrelated conspecific males will raid nests in order to consume or steal eggs. Egg theft can be explained by the females' preference to spawn at sites already containing eggs, even someone else's. In these instances, once a female has been lured in to deposit her own clutch, the male will selectively eat the eggs he previously stole and deposited there.

On the topic of parental care in fish, mouthbrooding cichlids certainly deserve a mention. Mouthbrooding occurs in at least nine piscine families, most famously in the freshwater Cichlidae. With over 1,300 species, cichlids have evolved extremely specialised lifestyles (including mouthbrooding) that serve to reduce competition with related species living in the same area. Typically, mouthbrooding refers to post-spawning behaviour in which parents (usually females) hold their fertilised eggs inside their mouths until they hatch, and sometimes even beyond. This provides the eggs and fry with a haven from predators, a point commonly portrayed in nature videos that depict young fish darting back into their parents' mouths at the first sign of danger. Less frequently reported is the fact that parents holding a mouthful of eggs usually eat a considerable portion of them, and sometimes the entire brood. Also unlikely to make it into family-friendly documentaries are shots showing the male cichlids' habit of fertilising the eggs in the females' mouth.

Mouthbrooders practise filial cannibalism primarily because, understandably, eating a regular meal is next to impossible while carrying around a mouthful of eggs.

The simplest way around this vexing problem? Cannibalism. Interestingly, scientists had thought that for the first
few days after spawning, female mouthbrooders selectively
consumed only unfertilised eggs. When researchers set out
to determine just how mothers were able to make the distinction, they were surprised to find that 15 per cent of
the consumed eggs were actually fertile. And should the
brood reach about 20 per cent of its original number, many
mothers will simply eat them all. As with similar examples
of total filial cannibalism, this usually occurs when the cost
of caring for the young becomes higher than the benefit of
producing a small number of offspring. In such cases, it
becomes more advantageous for the female to recover some
energy by consuming her remaining young and moving on
to find a new mate.

Perhaps the award for the most extreme example of
piscine cannibalism, however, goes to sand tiger sharks. In
their case the individuals doing the cannibalising haven't
even been born yet.

Sand tigers, like hammerheads and blue sharks, do not
deposit their eggs into the external environment. Instead
the eggs and young develop inside the females' oviducts,
a developmental strategy known as histotrophic viviparity.
Scientists who first looked at late-term sand tiger embryos
in 1948 noticed that these specimens were anatomically well
developed, with a mouthful of sharp teeth – a point driven
home when one researcher was bitten on the hand while
probing the oviduct of a pregnant specimen. Strangely,
these late-term embryos were found to have swollen
bellies, which were initially thought be yolk sacs – a form
of stored food. This was puzzling, though, since most of
the nutrient-rich yolk should have been used up by this late
stage of development. Further investigation showed that
the abdominal bumps weren't yolk sacs at all, they were
stomachs full of smaller sharks. These embryos (averaging
nineteen in number) had fallen victim to the ultimate in

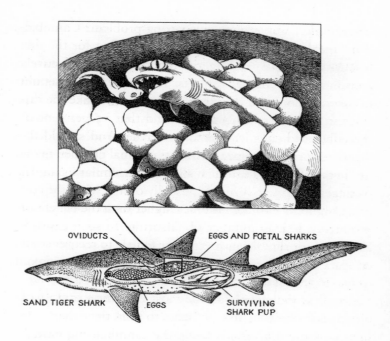

OVIDUCTS   EGGS AND FOETAL SHARKS

SAND TIGER SHARK   EGGS   SURVIVING SHARK PUP

sibling rivalry – a form of *in utero* cannibalism known as adelphophagy (from the Ancient Greek for 'brother eating') or sibling cannibalism.

This is possible because sand tiger shark oviducts contain embryos at different developmental stages, a characteristic that also evolved in birds. Once the largest of the shark embryos run through their own food supply, they begin consuming other eggs. And when the eggs are gone, the ravenous foetal sharks begin consuming their smaller siblings. Ultimately, only two pups remain, one in each oviduct. According to renowned shark specialist Stewart Springer, the selective advantage for the young sharks may extend beyond the obvious nutritional reward.

Springer, the first to study the phenomenon, believed that the surviving pups were born 'experienced young', having already killed for survival even before their birth. He hypothesised that this form of sibling cannibalism might afford the young sand tigers a competitive advantage during interactions with other predatory species looking for a meal.

Although the sand tiger is the only species known to consume embryos *in utero*, several other sharks exhibit a form of oophagy, in which the unborn residents of the oviduct feed on a steady supply of unfertilised eggs. Additionally, a form of adelphophagy occurs in some bony fishes in which broods mature at different rates. Once again, in these species it's the older siblings that cannibalise the younger.

Cannibalism of the young also occurs in many species of snakes, lizards and crocodilians, where, for example, it accounts for significant juvenile mortality in the American alligator. Although reptiles do not transition through larval stages like most fish and amphibians, the smallest and most defenceless individuals, namely eggs, neonates and juveniles, run the greatest risk of being eaten by their own.

Among birds, such behaviour is comparatively rare, a fact that may be related to one particular aspect of their anatomy – their beaks. These keratinous structures are responsible for the designation of most bird species as 'gape-limited predators'. In other words, their lack of teeth limits them to consuming prey small enough to be swallowed whole. Existing under this anatomical constraint, when cannibalism does occur in birds it falls more under the general heading of filial cannibalism, where eggs and younger siblings are consumed.

Cornell ornithologist Walter Koenig informed me that brood reduction is common among birds, and so it's likely that sibling cannibalism would be even more widespread if birds had beaks capable of tearing dying offspring to pieces, or could open their gapes wide enough to swallow them whole.

Heterocannibalism has been reported in seven of the 142 bird families and is most common in colonial seabirds. Here the practice of consuming eggs or young is an integral part of foraging strategy and it can have a significant effect on bird populations. In one study of a colony of 900 herring gulls, approximately one quarter of the eggs and chicks were cannibalised. This also occurs in acorn woodpeckers, as pairs of female woodpeckers will share a single nest and even feed and care for each other's young. But before this occurs, the nest mates will destroy and consume each other's eggs if one bird should lay first, presumably because the oldest hatchling would be the most likely to survive. To eliminate this advantage, the birds will keep eating each other's eggs until both lay their eggs on the same day, a process that can take weeks.

Sibling cannibalism is best known among the raptors – predatory birds like eagles, hawks, kestrels and owls, all of which possess strong eyesight, powerful beaks and sharp talons. As a result they are far better equipped than other birds to engage in cannibalism. In some species, sibling cannibalism is the end result of asynchronous hatching, in which two eggs are laid with one of them hatching several days before the other. The firstborn chick uses its extra bulk to win squabbles over food, or in instances where the parents are unable to provide enough to eat, the firstborn will kill and consume its younger sibling. Researchers sometimes refer to these types of victims as 'food caches', as sibling cannibalism becomes an efficient way to produce well-nourished offspring (albeit fewer of them) during times of stress.

Something similar happens in the snowy egret. Three eggs are laid, the first two having received a serious dose of hormones while still in the mother's body. The third egg receives only half the hormone boost, resulting in a less aggressive hatchling. If food is abundant the larger nestlings simply throw the passive chick out of the nest, but if alternative sources of nutrition become scarce, the smaller sibling is pecked to death and eaten.

According to Koenig and fellow ornithologist Mark

Stanback, filial cannibalism in birds has been reported in thirteen of 142 avian families but it is not well understood, perhaps because it is still infrequently observed. On rare occasions, birds like roadrunners will eat undersized chicks. Similarly, barn owls are reported to consume their own chicks during extreme environmental conditions. It has been suggested that filial cannibalism of dying or decayed offspring can prevent infection and deterioration of the entire clutch. Presumably there are also benefits to getting rid of dead chicks before they attract legions of carrion-eating flies and maggots. In most cases, however, it seems to be the lack of alternative forms of nutrition that initiates the behaviour.

3

SIZE MATTERS: SEXUAL CANNIBALISM

Whoever authorized the evolution of the spiders of Australia
should be summarily dragged out into the street and shot.

Mira Grant, *How Green This Land, How Blue This Sea*

WHILE IT'S FAIRLY COMMON KNOWLEDGE that the praying
mantis is the co-holder (along with the black widow spider)
of the title Nature's Most Infamous Cannibal, fewer people
realise that the name praying mantis is shared by nearly all
of the 2,200 species making up the order Mantodea.

The moniker comes from the curious manner in which
the insects hold their forelegs while resting. As a result of
this prayer-like attitude they've become some of the most
popular insects in mythology and folklore. Many of these
mantid myths have religious or semi-religious overtones. In
France, they're known as *prie dieu* and are said to point
lost children homeward. The Khoi people of South Africa
regard praying mantises as holy, while Arab and Turkish
folklore holds that the insects direct their prayers toward
Mecca. Americans once believed that praying mantises
blinded people and killed horses, this perhaps as a nod
to the fact that, rather than being used for prayer, the

31

anterior-most limbs are actually modified into lethal, spike-covered weapons. Often well-camouflaged, most species are ambush predators, lashing out with their 'raptorial legs' to capture, crush and secure their prey while a set of sharpened mouth parts slice, can-opener style, through the toughest exoskeleton.

Although mantises feed primarily on other insects, the largest species can reach around six inches in length and these giants will attack and consume small reptiles, birds and even mammals. It is likely that this type of predatory behaviour is responsible for the common misspelling 'preying mantis'.

As a child in America during the 1960s I was told that there would be a $50 fine for anyone caught killing a praying mantis (and my friends have the same recollections). Since I was unable to uncover a record of any such federal or state law, I can only assume that the story was a scare tactic designed to keep nasty little boys from slaughtering an uncommonly pious insect known to eliminate an array of less religiously inclined pests.

Many people are familiar with the praying mantis's supposed penchant for cannibalistic sexual encounters, reports of which began showing up in the scientific literature in the late nineteenth century. Back then, several authors claimed that female mantises regularly bit off the triangular heads of their partners during sex. It was claimed that the decapitated males continued to copulate, abdomens pulsing as if nothing much had happened, and several hours later the female would stride off, fully fertilised, leaving the male reduced to a tiny pile of wings. Similar tales about mantid mating continued into the early twentieth century, when members of a new generation of entomologists began investigating this rather puzzling behaviour.

One hypothesis reasoned that this occurred because the male mantis's brain actually inhibited sexual performance. With their heads removed, however, they became 'disinhibited', found the rhythm and eventually delivered a full load of sperm. Others suggested that getting oneself cannibalised made sense for praying mantis males that might have limited opportunities to mate over their lifetime. In these instances there would be selection pressure to fatten up the only female they might ever run into – especially one now carrying their sperm. Furthermore, headless males reportedly produced more sperm than those equipped with heads, leading to more fertilised eggs and more offspring. These accounts contributed to an overall impression that the decapitation of male mantises was a normal and necessary copulatory stage and, soon after, the concept became entrenched in textbooks and popular literature. Unfortunately, most observations of mantis cannibalism were made in laboratory settings and only after females had been deprived of food.

In reality, cannibalism varies across this large and diverse group. The behaviour has gone unobserved in most species, not necessarily because it doesn't happen, but because it hasn't been studied. Researchers such as biologists Eckehard Liske and W. Jackson Davis now believe that, rather than being a required component of mating, the consumption of males is more likely to be a foraging strategy employed by hungry females unable to wrap their forelegs around an alternative form of nutrition.

Support for this hypothesis comes from studies on a

wide variety of mantis species, including those in which worse-for-wear females exhibited improved body condition following the act of cannibalism, producing larger egg cases and more offspring. And, significantly, well-fed female mantises showed no cannibalistic tendencies during mating encounters.

Before we blame mantid cannibalism on captive conditions or starvation, though, the fact remains that both wild and captive males exhibit extreme caution as a normal preamble to copulation. Depending on the species, the males' initial approach can vary from the simple (slow and deliberate movement toward the female, followed by a flying leap onto her back) to the more complex (a series of ritualistic movements that include antennal oscillations and abdominal flexing, *then* a flying leap onto her back). Researchers believe that these movements serve to either circumvent or inhibit the females' aggressive, predatory response. It is, therefore, extremely unlikely that these forms of cautious behaviour by males would have evolved if there weren't at least some risk of attack by females.

What about the male's famous ability to 'keep the beat' even after losing its head? Liske and Davis have an explanation for that phenomenon as well. They believe that, rather than acting as a required stimulus for copulation by releasing sexual movements, decapitation artificially induces this process. This would be similar to the way that loping off a chicken's head artificially induces locomotor movements that can temporarily propel a headless bird around a barnyard. According to these researchers, from an evolutionary perspective, these reflexive abdominal contractions and the subsequent release of sperm may ensure that fertilisation takes place, even if the male is consumed.

AS FOR PRAYING MANTISES, so for certain notorious spiders has truth been masked by myth. After several papers in the thirties and forties reported that some female spiders devoured their mates after copulation, they became widely known as black widows. Although most of the initial observations turned out to be anecdotal, cannibalism and black widows became forever linked. The association continued through the seventies and eighties, even though researchers working with these spiders were beginning to discover that the behaviour was actually a rare occurrence. They determined not only that most male spiders depart unharmed after copulation, but also that some of them lived in the female's web for several weeks, even sharing her prey.

According to spider expert Rainer Foelix, the supposed aggressiveness of the female spider toward the male is largely a myth, and when a female is ready for mating, there is little danger for the male. However, if a male mistakenly showed up in the web of a hungry female, it would be quite another story.

What makes the black widow's notoriety even more unjust is the fact that sexual cannibalism has been reported in sixteen out of 109 spider families. But of these sixteen, one of the most interesting examples takes place in the black widow's Aussie cousin, the redback. In this species, males go to extreme lengths to guarantee not only their own demise but also their consumption.

The redback is common throughout Australia and, in a country renowned for its notorious creatures, it ranks among the most dangerous. The reasons behind their bad reputation start with a neurotoxic bite that can cause severe pain and swelling, and in rare instances seizures, coma and even death. Like the North American black widows, Australian redbacks are often found in close proximity to human residences, especially sheds and garages offering undisturbed areas full of clutter. Presumably because of the abundance of flies, both black widows and redbacks were once common in outhouses, where their fondness for living under toilet seats was almost as unpopular as their habit of biting anything that blocked their escape routes.

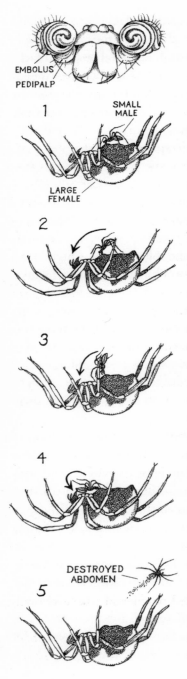

EMBOLUS
PEDIPALP

1
SMALL
MALE

LARGE
FEMALE

2

3

4

DESTROYED
ABDOMEN

5

Although encounters with humans are rarely fatal, the same cannot be said for male redback spiders attempting to mate. In the first stage of courtship, the male approaches the female's web and desperately tries to get her attention (it takes a bit of doing, since he is only about one fifth of her size). He does so by bouncing his body up and down, throwing some silk around and waving his front legs. As a point of information, as well as their eight legs, spiders have an additional pair of anteriorly located appendages called pedipalps. In male spiders, the pedipalps are modified for transferring sperm to the female's body, necessitated by the fact that spiders lack penises. Furthermore, there is no internal connection between the pedipalps and the testes, which are located within the abdomen. Instead, sperm is initially extruded from a furrow on the male's abdomen into a spun receptacle called a sperm web. As a male dips his pedipalps into the pooled sperm, a pair of coiled structures called emboli and their associated muscles work like tiny turkey basters to suck up the liquid and store it until copulation.

The next phase of redback courtship begins as the male initiates repeated bouts of physical contact with his potential mate, through a process of tapping, probing and nuzzling. The real heavy petting begins once the male locates the female's epigynal opening.

By now, if the female hasn't already eaten the male (which can put a serious dent in all this foreplay), the spiders briefly assume Gerhardt's position 3, a sort of missionary position for spiders. Gerhardt's position 3 appears to be favoured by all *Latrodectus* species except the Australian redback, where it is abandoned immediately after the male penetrates the female's epigynal opening with the tip of a sperm-charged embolus. The male then slowly performs a 180° somersault that ends with his abdomen resting against the female's mouthparts and she immediately expresses her gratitude by vomiting enzyme-laden gut juice onto the tiny acrobat. She then begins to consume the male's abdomen as they copulate, pausing from time to time to spit out small blobs of white matter. Upon the completion of the sex act, which takes anywhere from five to thirty minutes, the male crawls off a short distance, reportedly making repeated attempts to reel in his spent embolus by stretching it with his forelegs and then releasing it abruptly.

Approximately ten minutes later, rather than fretting over missing body parts, the male returns to the fray, this time wielding the second embolus. The half-eaten spider then proceeds to re-enact its earlier copulatory acrobatics. By way of a 'welcome back', the female resumes her meal, consuming more and more of the male's abdomen. At the end of this, though, rather than allowing him to crawl off, the female wraps her shredded partner in silk, eventually hoovering up his now liquefied innards.

While the benefits of a risk-free meal for the redback mum-to-be are fairly obvious, one has to wonder what is in it for the male, and the mating habits of the redback have indeed puzzled scientists. The only potential answer is that females that had recently eaten their mates were less receptive to the approach of subsequent suitors. Cannibalised males also copulated longer and fathered more offspring than non-cannibalised males. Ultimately, then, it seems that this rather extreme example of paternal investment optimises the likelihood that the cannibalised dad gets to pass his genes on to a new generation.

Things get dicey, though, when trying to determine the benefits for redback males eaten *before* mating takes place, a situation that has also been reported in orb-weaving spiders like *Araneus diadematus*. Mark Elgar and zoologist David Nash worked with this species and proposed that pre-mating cannibalism allows females to choose which male will get to inseminate them, with smaller males eaten more often than larger and presumably healthier individuals. The researchers also used modelling studies to propose that pre-mating cannibalism would occur only in instances where there was no shortage of males from which to choose.

Observations related to mantis and spider cannibalism serve to illustrate another of the general rules from Chapter 1: that among invertebrate cannibals, males get cannibalised far more frequently than females. This behaviour occurs particularly in species that exhibit sexual dimorphism, a condition in which there are marked anatomical differences between males and females of the same species.

The most common example of sexual dimorphism is body size, and among invertebrates females are often substantially larger than males. This appears to be related to the ability of larger mothers to better carry, protect and provide for their young. Relatively small body size can also provide males with a biomechanical advantage. Since gravity is less of a constraint on lightweight bodies than on heavier ones, this is especially evident in males that must climb in order to reach females. Likewise, tiny adult male spiders are able to 'balloon' like juveniles, using the wind as an energy-efficient means of travel to find a potential mate.

In those rare instances where male spiders are larger than females, the roles of cannibal and cannibalised are also reversed. This occurs in two species that exhibit some very un-spider-like traits. Among sand-dwelling wolf spiders, females undertake risky visits to burrows the larger males have built. Because these structures represent a high reproductive investment, male wolf spiders become extremely picky when females show up and initiate courtship – which they do by waving their forelegs around in the universal signal for 'Pick me! Pick me!' In many cases, though, researchers have noted that instead of attracting a mate, the females were often attacked and eaten.

To determine why, arachnologist Anita Aisenberg and her colleagues performed experiments in which twenty male spiders were consecutively exposed to one virgin and one previously inseminated female (in alternating order). Findings revealed that only 10 per cent of the virgin females were cannibalised compared with 25 per cent of the non-virgin females, especially those exhibiting lower body condition indices. In other words, male wolf spiders chose their mates based on looks and sexual history. The researchers concluded that by selecting younger, fitter females, male spiders maximised the likelihood that their mate would survive to produce successful offspring. Older, less fit females also served a purpose: food.

Cannibalism by males also occurs in water spiders, the only living arachnids that exist completely underwater. In this species, females spend most of their lives inside web-shrouded air bells, where their smaller bodies require less oxygen then their male counterparts. Natural selection may favour larger body size in male water spiders by providing them with enhanced swimming and diving abilities. While females are ambush predators, males are active hunters, and although their diets consist primarily of insect larvae, they

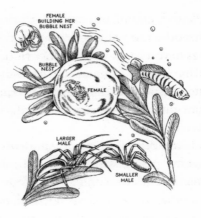

will kill and devour smaller males during intense competition for mates. The female water spiders' preference for larger males can also quickly become deadly, specifically during failed mating encounters.

These two examples illustrate that, when cannibalism occurs, it might well be size, rather than sex, that is the key determinant, with the smaller individuals ending up on the menu.

SPIDERS AND PRAYING MANTISES are far from the only animals who engage in cannibalistic copulation. When terrestrial snails cross paths (or, more accurately, slime trails), the potential for bizarre sexual encounters can rival any stag do. For the snails, the high hook-up ratio stems from the fact that most of the participants are simultaneous hermaphrodites, enabling them to exchange sperm while at the same time having their own eggs fertilised. And while this particular sexual orientation increases the likelihood that any two individuals that meet can mate, things can go downhill quickly once the lovers begin biting chunks out of each other.

Snails and slugs, their shell-challenged relatives, are molluscs, a biologically diverse invertebrate group that also contains the bivalves (clams, oysters and their relatives) and cephalopods (squid, octopi and cuttlefish). Known collect-ively as gastropods, the approximately 85,000 species of snails and slugs have a worldwide distribution, inhabiting a variety of marine, freshwater and terrestrial environments. To put this into perspective, there are approximately seven-teen times more gastropod species on the planet than there are mammals.

Gastropods are renowned for their slow-footed loco-motion – a point perennially celebrated at snail-racing championships. But what snails may lack in speed, they make up for in other ways: by devoting less energy to loco-motion, they can spend more of it involved in alternative behaviour – like mating.

Although snail sex can last for up to six hours in some herbivorous species this is definitely not the case in certain carnivorous gastropods, where foreplay can turn into can-nibalism in the blink of a turreted eye. In these species, since even copulating individuals will bite their mates, each potential sexual partner is also a potential predator. As a result, they often employ the wham-bam-scram approach during sexual encounters, which can sometimes linger on for as long as six seconds.

Even more shocking are banana slugs, which become so entwined during sex that they sometimes chew off their partner's corkscrew-shaped penis in an effort to disengage. During this process, known as apophallation, penises are slurped down spaghetti-style, occasionally by their owners. Although this usually puts an end to the tryst, the fact that the penis does not grow back presents fewer problems than one would expect. The hermaphrodite slugs simply carry on the remainder of their lives as females.

In some land snails, things get bizarre even before copulation starts: partners will shoot calcified 'love darts' at each other, an exchange initiated when the body of one snail touches that of a potential mate. This tactile stimula-tion triggers the release of built-up hydraulic pressure in a

sac surrounding the dart. As a result, the barbed projectile (also known as a gypsobelum) explodes outwards, embedding itself in the body wall of the second individual. In most instances, the skewered snail responds by shooting a dart of its own, and mating happens shortly thereafter.

Often, though, the exchange proceeds with something less than textbook precision. Since most snails are nocturnal, their visual systems are basic. They can differentiate between light and dark but an inability to determine details about their slimy targets (or anything else, for that matter) can lead to a serious lack of accuracy. As a result, headshots and similar misfirings are a common occurrence.

But why do some snails fire miniature harpoons at each other at all? The proposed function of this behaviour has undergone some revision. Earlier snail experts thought that love darts were the equivalent of an exchange of wedding gifts – in this instance calcium carbonate, a major component of the snails' shell and eggs. Another suggestion was that the projectiles might act as an aphrodisiac or that they somehow signalled the shooter's willingness to mate. But support for these hypotheses never materialised.

I posed the question to McGill University biologist Ronald Chase, whose work in the 1990s helped solve the mystery of this baffling behaviour. 'The darts serve to increase paternity,' he told me, since snails scoring love-dart hits on their partners before mating fathered twice as many offspring as those that didn't hit their targets. The key to the enhanced reproductive effect was apparently the tiny projectile's chemical coating. Chase and his colleagues showed that this hormone-like substance prevented digestive enzymes from destroying the majority of incoming sperm, something that occurred in non-skewered snails. Spared digestion, the snail sperm sped onward, eventually fertilising a greater number of eggs. A 2013 study by Japanese researchers also showed that snails skewered by love darts delayed re-mating with other individuals, an indication that something in the dart's mucous coating suppressed subsequent infidelity.

According to Chase, 'It's all basically sexual selection.' In other words, in any given population, some individuals outproduce other individuals because they're better at securing mates, usually by making themselves more attractive to the opposite sex or by beating back the competition. In land snails, explanations for who got the edge and how they achieved it are confounded just a bit by the fact that mating individuals exchange not only sperm but also explosive projectiles.

Before leaving the topic of snails, if all this talk about love darts has you thinking about one of the most endearing characters of ancient mythology, you aren't alone. Ronald Chase believes that Cupid, the Roman version of the Greek god Eros, had his origin in land snails and their love darts. According to Chase, the species of snail his group worked on is also found in Greece and – though no tangible evidence has been found – it certainly seems possible that the snails' romantic habits might have been a source of ancient inspiration for the famous arrow-shooting cherub.

4

UNDER PRESSURE: STRESS-RELATED CANNIBALISM

Hunger has its own logic.

Bertolt Brecht

OVERCROWDED CONDITIONS have long been known to increase cannibalism, as they often coincide with both hunger and a decrease in the availability of alternative forms of nutrition, a point that will become horribly clear once we begin our investigation of its human variant.

Carrying the banner (albeit a tiny one) for animal cannibalism due to overcrowding are the Mormon crickets. These insects are native to the North American West. Attaining a body length of nearly three inches, Mormon crickets are flightless, but like their winged cousins, the grasshoppers and locusts, they're renowned for their spectacular swarming behaviour and mass migrations. According to biologist and Mormon cricket expert Stephen Simpson, favourable warm and moist weather conditions in early spring can lead to the nearly simultaneous hatching of several million individuals. Almost immediately, the nymphs begin to march, and they do so in a spectacularly well-coordinated manner, swarming for self-protection.

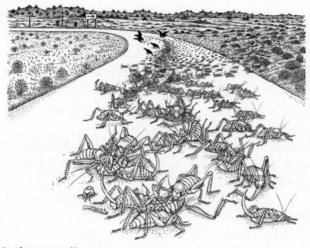

Seeking to illuminate principles of mass migration and collective behaviour, Simpson and his co-workers conducted food-preference tests on captive Mormon crickets. They determined that protein and salt were the limiting resources being sought by the swarming insect masses. Incidences of cannibalism began soon after these resources were depleted, the nearest source of protein and salt then being a neighbouring cricket. Simpson found that each insect chased the one in front, and was in turn chased by the cricket behind. In such circumstances, stopping to eat becomes risky, requiring individuals to fend off other members of the swarm with their powerful hind legs. 'Losing a leg is fatal,' he told me. 'The weak and the injured are most at risk.'

Simpson demonstrated the vulnerability of the weak and injured by glueing tiny weights to some of the crickets, thus causing them to lag behind their unencumbered swarm-mates. Almost immediately they were attacked and eaten by the hungry horde approaching from behind. In the end, Simpson and his colleagues determined that the massive migratory bands were actually forced marches.

WHILE AVIAN CANNIBALISM might be relatively rare in the wild, once birds are removed from their natural setting and packed shoulder-to-shoulder (or ruffled feather to ruffled feather) it's a different story. When thousands of stressed-out birds have little to occupy their time, the situation can deteriorate rapidly. In these instances the real meaning of the term 'pecking order' becomes gruesomely apparent as some individuals are pecked to death and eaten. Initially, cannibalism on poultry farms was thought to result from a protein-deficient diet, but researchers now believe that it's actually misdirected foraging related to cramped and inadequate housing conditions.

As the poultry and egg industries became established, feather pecking and cannibalism (known in the trade as 'pick-out') became two of the most serious threats faced by poultry farmers. To stop cannibalism and prevent the loss of their valuable egg-laying hens, farmers routinely clipped off the tip of the bird's beak. In the 1940s, however, the National Band and Tag Company came up with a far more humane method to deal with the problem. Their design team reasoned that if the birds couldn't see 'raw flesh or blood' then they wouldn't cannibalise each other, and so they came up with 'Anti-peck specks' – mini-sunglasses equipped with red celluloid lenses and aluminium frames and attached to the upper portion of the bird's beak near the base. Poultry farmers were informed that having their chickens see the world through rose-tinted glasses would 'make a sissy of your toughest birds'. Purchased in bulk ($27 per 1,000), apparently they worked.*

Currently, only seventy-five species of mammals (out of roughly 5,700) are reported to regularly practise some form of cannibalism. Although this number will likely increase as more researchers become interested in the topic, the overall low occurrence of cannibalism in mammals is

---

* Although Anti-peck specks are now collectors' items, the idea behind them lives on in plastic clips called 'Peepers', which can be attached via a pin through the nostrils of various commercially raised game birds.

probably related to relatively low numbers of offspring coupled with a high degree of parental care (compared to non-mammals).

The golden hamster, also known as the Syrian hamster, is a popular pet for children but is also known to display some nightmarish behaviour in captivity. The problems stem from major differences between the animals' natural habitats and the cramped captive conditions under which they are typically held. Native to northern Syria and southern Turkey, the hamster lives in dry, desert environments. Adults are solitary, highly territorial and widely dispersed. Individuals inhabit their own burrows and emerge for short periods at dawn and dusk to feed and mate. This crepuscular lifestyle is thought to help them avoid nocturnal predators like owls, foxes and feral dogs. The results of a study on golden hamsters in the wild emphasised the major differences between natural conditions and those imposed on pet hamsters. For example, the researchers determined that in the wild, the average time hamsters spent on the surface during a twenty-four-hour period was eighty-seven minutes.

The problems between natural and captive conditions often begin in pet shops, where male and female golden hamsters are often kept in unnaturally large groups and displayed in well-lit tanks. They are purchased singly or in pairs. As pets, these desert-dwellers are housed in cages or trendy modular contraptions of translucent plastic tubes linking 'rooms'. Unfortunately, the cages are often too small and golden hamsters have a hard time fitting through the plastic tubes, especially when pregnant or obese from overfeeding. Cage floors are usually covered in cedar shavings, hardly reminiscent of a desert environment. Regularly handled by children and often subjected to excessive noise and damp conditions resulting from soiled cage bedding or leaky water bottles, many pet hamsters spend their existence under the watchful gaze of dogs and cats: the hamster's natural enemies.

As a result of this catalogue of stresses in captivity, female golden hamsters, especially younger ones, frequently eat their own pups. Beyond over- or under-feeding and housing conditions, cannibalism can be triggered if hamsters are handled late in their pregnancy or if the babies are handled within ten days of their birth. The presence of additional individuals (even the father) can also lead females to consume their own, and heterocannibalism can occur if adult females encounter unrelated young. However, filial cannibalism can be prevented by isolating pregnant individuals, adequately meeting their nutritional requirements and refraining from handling female hamsters for a fortnight before and after they give birth.

Cannibalism of adults can also take place when several mature golden hamsters are kept in the same cage. This includes siblings, who reach sexual maturity at around four weeks of age. Under these conditions fighting is common, and serious injuries or even fatalities can result. In the latter instances, the survivor typically consumes the carcass of the loser.

Although mice, rats, guinea pigs and rabbits also occasionally cannibalise their young in captivity, primarily when food and water are scarce, there are several factors that appear to make golden hamsters even more prone to do so. Most significant is the fact that the hamster has the shortest gestation period (sixteen days) of any placental mammal and they can become pregnant again within a few days of giving birth. This means that females, already weakened and stressed out by the rigours of pregnancy, delivery and nursing, may be tending a new litter of eight to ten pups less than three weeks after their previous delivery.

When non-human primates are compared with other mammal groups, cannibalism is rare, having been observed in only eleven of 418 extant species, again under unnatural circumstances and often linked to overcrowding. Many examples of primate infanticide and/or cannibalism have been shown to be stress-related. Changes in location or deficient captive conditions play a role in most reports of primate cannibalism, with the latter blamed for incidences of infanticide in bush babies, lemurs, marmosets and squirrel monkeys. In each case, the victims were invariably neonates while the aggressors were either group members or relatives.

However, one primate group in which infanticide and cannibalism are relatively common practices is the chimpanzees. Descriptions of the behaviour among our closest relatives are both chilling and fascinating.

Initially, reports of chimpanzee cannibalism focused solely on adult males, who routinely killed and sometimes consumed infants belonging to 'strangers', i.e. adult females from outside their own groups. According to Dr Jane Goodall, female chimpanzees sometimes transferred from one community to another. 'A female who loses her infant during an encounter with neighbouring males is likely to come into oestrus within a month or so and would then, theoretically, be available for recruitment into the

community of the aggressors.' This behaviour is also seen in some types of bears and big cats.

Other attacks by male chimps on infant-bearing females occurred during 'inter-community aggression', for example when groups of male chimpanzees patrolling the outer edges of their territories encountered individuals from adjacent communities.

Then, in 1976, Goodall reported on three observations in which two female chimps were involved in within-group infanticide and cannibalism in Tanzania's Gombe National Park. What made these attacks unique was the absence of male involvement. Stranger yet was the fact that the individuals involved were a mother (Passion) and daughter (Pom) whose seemingly premeditated approach to somewhere between five and ten infant-bearing females provided researchers with a grim explanation for previously unexplained infant disappearances. Goodall believes that the attacks on the mothers functioned solely as a means to acquire food, since once they had established their claim over their prey they made no further aggressive attacks on the mothers.

Thirty years later, similar attacks by female chimp coalitions against infant-bearing mothers were observed in Uganda's Budongo Forest. A team led by comparative psychologist Simon Townsend concluded that the lethal attacks were triggered by an influx of females, leading to overcrowding and subsequent increased competition for resources.

Although acts of cannibalism in chimpanzees are not everyday occurrences, some researchers have suggested that the encroachment of humans into the areas surrounding preserves inhabited by chimps will eventually lead to population density issues and more competition for dwindling resources. If this occurs, incidences of cannibalism by our closest relatives may be expected to increase.

5

CARNIVORE CANNIBALS: FROM DINOSAURS TO POLAR BEARS

In Panama, I found a spider that eats its own limbs during lean times. I am told they grow back. But though the distinction is razor-thin, desperation is not the same thing as determination.

Taona Dumisani Chiveneko, *Sprout of Disruption*

Personally, I suspect that a whole pack of full grown *T. rex* would have a very hard time finding enough to eat.

Nicholas Longrich

THIS IS NOT A GOOD TIME to be a polar bear. Over the past several years, there has been a growing number of reports of cannibalism among the species, reflected in dozens of headlines such as 'Polar bears are turning to cannibalism as Arctic ice disappears', 'Is global warming driving polar bears to cannibalism?' and 'Polar bear cannibalism linked to climate change'.

As a vertebrate zoologist, I was interested in determining whether or not a transition in polar-bear diets had actually taken place. And if it had, I wondered whether humans were involved.

Polar bears are among the world's largest carnivores. They are, of course, famous for their meat-eating diets. Additionally, like many carnivores, they share a characteristic known as carnassial teeth. In the majority of mammal species, when the jaw closes, the premolar and molar teeth on the upper jaw fit snugly into those on the lower jaw. This facilitates the crushing of food items before they're swallowed. In most carnivore species, though, when the jaws close the last upper premolar and the first lower molar on each side shear past each other like blades, effectively slicing large pieces of meat. Carnassial dentition was lost in most bears as they evolved more omnivorous feeding habits. Here the hard-to-digest plant material required mashing up by more traditional molars, thus increasing its surface area and allowing for more efficient breakdown by enzymes like cellulase. In polar bears, however, fully functional carnassials have apparently re-evolved – a reflection of the species' strict meat-eating diet, which consists primarily of ringed seals and bearded seals. So, were polar bears – perfectly equipped natural killing machines – turning to cannibalism because they were under pressure from a changing environment? Or could there be another explanation?

Cannibalism has been recorded in at least fourteen species of carnivores. In pumas, lynx, leopards and sea lions it appears to occur for many of the usual reasons, including stress (due of lack of food), elimination of rivals and increased mating opportunities.

Heterocannibalism – in this case, eating cubs that another male sired – is clearly a reproductive strategy in male lions after taking over a pride. Through the practice of infanticide, the incoming males terminate the maternal investment in unrelated cubs. A lioness with cubs will not come into heat for a year and a half after giving birth but, similarly to what has been observed in other mammals, a lioness that loses her cubs becomes sexually receptive almost immediately.

So what can cannibal lions tell us about polar bears, many thousands of miles away on the Arctic ice cap? In 2009 stories started to emerge that polar bears were undergoing a serious change in dietary habits. With the accelerated shrinking of Arctic sea ice due to global warming, the hypothesis went, the bears had a shorter hunting season and fewer seal kills. As a consequence, the stressed-out bears were starving and resorting to cannibalism in order to survive.

One fact neglected in the sensational press coverage, however, was that, as discovered by wildlife biologist Mitchell Taylor, polar bears will readily eat other polar bears when they can do so without excessive risk of injury, and always have done.

In fact, males of most North American bear species will kill and eat conspecific cubs pretty much whenever they can get their paws on them. Researchers believe that infanticide during the breeding season may provide males with a reproductive opportunity as well as a nutritional reward since, like the previously described lionesses, female polar bears will come into oestrus more quickly if their offspring have been killed. Because of this, cannibalism has been and continues to be one of the greatest contributors to bear-cub mortality, especially just after leaving the maternity den. The threat from adult males is one of the key reasons that mother bears are so protective of their cubs and also explains why females give males such a wide berth when selecting den sites.

Not all polar-bear cannibalism relates to cubs, of course. In the mid-noughties, Arctic researcher Stephen Amstrup and his co-workers were alarmed by three incidences of cannibalism by polar bears in the southern Beaufort Sea which occurred during a two-and-a-half-month period. Two of the incidences involved the death and partial consumption of adult female bears. In one, the female's body was found inside a maternity den that collapsed during an attack by a predatory male bear. In the second case, the female polar bear was killed on the sea ice, presumably not long after emerging from its den with a cub. In the third case, a one-year-old male was killed and partially consumed by an adult male. According to Amstrup and his colleagues, these attacks were unique because they had taken place in areas not generally frequented by male polar bears. Each year, once the Arctic sea ice melts and polar bears are forced onto the land, males are usually found near the coast while females and their cubs venture further inland, away from the males.

In the cases documented by Amstrup, the researchers concluded that, 'The underlying causes for our cannibalism observations are not known.' They suggested that the incidents could have been 'chance observations of previously unobserved rare events, or even a single rogue bear that adopted a [hunting] strategy including cannibalism'. In other words, the researchers recorded an open verdict, though they advanced the hypothesis that these attacks and subsequent cannibalism might have resulted from male polar bears being 'the first population segment to show adverse effects of the large ice retreats of recent years ... We hypothesise that nutritional stresses related to the longer ice-free seasons that have occurred in the Beaufort Sea in recent years may have led to the cannibalism incidents we observed in 2004.' Despite the caution with which the researchers advanced their ideas, they found them heatedly challenged by climate-change sceptics, after sensationalised headlines in the media neglected to mention that cannibalism in polar bears was already known to be a naturally occurring event, with the first published report surfacing in 1897. This would be my first encounter with cannibalism-related sensationalism in the course of writing this book – but it would not be the last.

In fact, as I delved deeper into carnivore cannibalism, I found that the field was rife with controversy – and that the debate included even creatures that hadn't existed on earth for millions of years.

Coelophysis bauri was one of the earliest dinosaurs – a carnivorous and remarkably bird-like biped that lived approximately 200 million years ago across what is now the south-western United States. A fast runner, it stood about three feet tall at the hips and had a body that measured about ten feet from tip to tail. Equipped with a mouthful of recurved and blade-like teeth, *Coelophysis* was thought to feed on smaller animals such as lizards.

In 1947 a team from the American Museum of Natural History working at Ghost Ranch in New Mexico unearthed a huge bone bed composed of hundreds of *Coelophysis* skeletons. After examining the fossils, famed AMNH palaeontologist Edwin Colbert made the dramatic announcement that the abdominal cavities of some of the specimens contained the bones of smaller individuals of the same species. Thus was born the 'cannibal-*Coelophysis* hypothesis' and the subsequent portrayal of *Coelophysis* and other dinosaurs as cannibals. Reminiscent of the misconceptions concerning black widow spiders, the depiction of dinosaurs as cannibals remained unchallenged for decades.

In 2005, another group of researchers from the AMNH set out to determine whether or not these claims of dinosaur cannibalism could be supported. Led by palaeontologists Sterling Nesbitt and Mark Norell, they performed detailed morphological and histological analyses of the bones. Soon enough, the scientists uncovered a slight problem – not only were the bones in question not from juvenile specimens of *Coelophysis*, they weren't even dinosaur bones. Instead, the fragments recovered from the abdominal cavities belonged to crocodylomorphs, a group that includes crocodiles and their extinct relatives, but not dinosaurs.

I interviewed Mark Norell on a beautiful mid-September afternoon at the American Museum of Natural History. His lab is a dinosaur lover's dream – a remarkable fossil-filled space that opens onto one of the museum's famous turrets, with a view over a wide swath of Central Park.

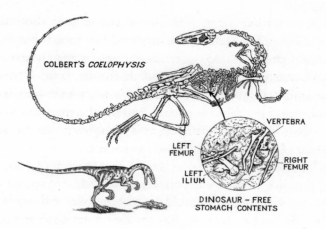

COLBERT'S *COELOPHYSIS*

VERTEBRA

LEFT
FEMUR

RIGHT
FEMUR

LEFT
ILIUM

DINOSAUR – FREE
STOMACH CONTENTS

'I think there's very little evidence at all for dinosaur cannibalism,' Norell told me. 'Although a lot of it really depends on what you'd call cannibalism. If a tyrannosaur dies and another tyrannosaur comes along and eats it, is that cannibalism? Or is that just scavenging a dead carcass? I have a picture around here someplace of a camel eating a dead camel that was lying there. Is that cannibalism?'

Using the example of besieged cities, where the victims of starvation or exposure were consumed, sometimes by their own relatives, I made the point that hunting and killing aren't necessarily prerequisites for cannibalism and therefore scavenging your own species would qualify.

But even allowing for a broad definition of cannibalism, in the case of dinosaurs, according to Norell the only compelling evidence appeared to have occurred in the late Cretaceous theropod *Majungasaurus crenatissimus*, uncovered by geologist Raymond Rogers in a Madagascan rock formation thought to be between 70.6 and 65.5 million years old.

In 2014, I interviewed Rogers to see how he had come to the conclusion that *Majungasaurus* was a cannibal. He explained that some of the *Majungasaurus* fossils bore distinctive cut marks. He also noted that there were only a few large carnivores living at the Madagascan site, which they named MAD05-42. One was a crocodile, which would have made no comparable traces on the bones, and the other a small theropod dinosaur, which had tiny teeth. The one remaining suspect was *Majungasaurus*, which had large teeth – and the denticle patterns matched.

'So there's no potential that you might be missing another large predator – something you just haven't dug up yet?' I asked.

'I don't think we're missing anything. And if we are missing something it would have to be big, and arguably it would have to be rare. But the bite marks are anything but rare. So … whatever it is, it would have to be really big, really cryptic, really rare, and it would have to bite everything, which doesn't make any sense.'

'So how do you know that these tooth marks on *Majungasaurus* bones weren't made during combat?'

Rogers pointed out that elements of the vertebral columns showed evidence of having been scraped and possibly gnawed. This type of 'late-stage scavenging' took place after the limb muscles and the guts had been consumed, and when the scavenger had to work hard to obtain any further nutrition from the carcass.

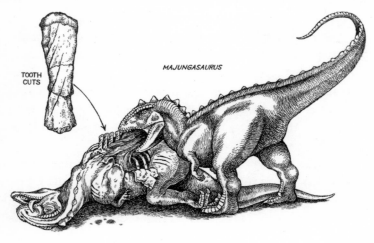

TOOTH CUTS

MAJUNGASAURUS

As seen in other species today, it sounded as if *Majungasaurus* had been following the pattern of cannibalism under stressful environmental conditions, in the absence of alternative food sources. Rogers explained that as the ancient ecological systems were devastated again and again, and a lot of things died, large meat-eating dinosaurs likely had to capitalise on whatever there was to feed upon, drawing on whatever resources were available. Despite the scarcity of evidence, Rogers believes that this behaviour would not have been uncommon. 'I have no doubts that cannibalism was widely practised by dinosaurs. The fact that there have only been two cases of dinosaur cannibalism ... that's just an artefact of palaeontology and the [scarcity of the] fossil record.'

So, knowing what we do about the prevalence of cannibalism in the animal kingdom, it makes sense that dinosaurs might have resorted to it for the same reasons other animals do – namely overcrowding, predation, competition and hunger.

6

SKIN DEEP: THE WEIRD
WORLD OF CAECILIAN
CANNIBALISM

Cannibalism is found in over 1,500 species.
Anthropophagusaphobia (fear of cannibals) is found in only one.
Which one seems unnatural now?

Unattributed internet picture caption

IS EATING ONE'S OWN FINGERNAILS or mucus an example
of auto-cannibalism? And what about breast-feeding? Is
this type of parental care yet another form of cannibalism?
These are examples of the grey area between what most
people consider cannibalism and other forms of behaviour.

Like breast-feeding, the following example is a form of
parental care, but one that extends further into the realm
of cannibalistic behaviour. It occurs in the Caecilians, a
small order of not-very-obvious amphibians, whose legless
bodies often get them mistaken for worms or snakes.
Caecilians inhabit tropical regions of Central and South
America, Africa and Southern Asia – a neat trick that lends
support to the theory of continental drift. (Although some
caecilians are aquatic, it is not believed that their ancestors
were strong enough swimmers to cross the Atlantic Ocean.

Instead, prehistoric caecilians were likely separated when the current continents of South America and Africa split apart between 100 and 130 million years ago.)

They also serve as great examples of convergent evolution, in which unrelated organisms evolve similar anatomical, physiological or behavioural characteristics because they inhabit similar environments. As a result of their subterranean lifestyles, caecilians share a number of anatomical similarities with moles and mole rats. In each, the eyes are either set deeply into the skulls or covered by a thick layer of skin, and as a consequence they are nearly blind.

Caecilians possess a pair of short 'tentacles' located between their nostrils and eyes. These chemosensors enable the subterraneans to 'taste' their environments without opening their mouths as they burrow through the soil or leaf litter in search of insects and small vertebrates. Similar sensory structures can be seen in other burrowing creatures, most notably the aptly named star-nosed mole.

Significantly, as a group, caecilians exhibit a fair degree of reproductive diversity. Approximately half of the 170 species are egg layers, and hatchlings either resemble miniature versions of their parents or pass through a brief larval stage. Other species are viviparous, giving birth to tiny, helpless young.

All caecilians do share one characteristic, namely, internal fertilisation, and during this process sperm is deposited into the female's cloaca by the male with the aid of a unique, penis-like structure called a phallodeum. In many vertebrates, the cloaca is a single opening shared by the intestinal, reproductive and urinary tracts.

Information about caecilian cannibalism first began emerging from Marvalee Wake's lab at the University of California, Berkeley. The herpetologist was looking at foetal and new-born individuals from several viviparous species and began investigating the function of their peculiar-looking baby teeth, known to scientist-types as deciduous dentition.

While some of the teeth were spoon-shaped, others were pronged or resembled grappling hooks, but none of them resembled adult teeth. Wake also performed a micro-scopic comparison of caecilian oviducts. She observed that in pregnant individuals, the inner lining of the oviduct was thicker and had a proliferation of glands, which she referred to as 'secretory beds'. These glands released a substance that fellow researcher H. W. Parker had previously labelled 'uterine milk'. He described the goo, which he believed the foetuses were ingesting, as 'a thick white creamy material, consisting mainly of an emulsion of fat droplets, together with disorganised cellular material'. Parker also thought that the caecilians' foetal teeth were used only *after* birth, as a way to scrape algae from rocks and leaves. Wake, however, had her doubts, especially since she noticed that these teeth were resorbed before birth or shortly after.

Pressing on with her study, Wake saw something odd. In sections of oviduct adjacent to early-term foetuses, the epithelial lining was intact and crowded with glands, while in females carrying late-term foetuses the lining of the oviduct was completely missing here, although it was intact in regions further away. Wake proposed that foetal caecilians used their teeth before birth to scrape fat-rich secretions and cellular material from the lining of their mother's oviduct. Although this couldn't be seen directly, she had gathered circumstantial evidence in the form of dif-ferences in the oviduct between early-term and late-term individuals. After an analysis of foetal stomach contents revealed cellular material, Wake had enough evidence to conclude that caecilian parental care extended beyond the production of uterine milk and into the realm of canni-balism. Unborn caecilians were eating the lining of their mothers' reproductive tracts.

But if the consumption of maternal cells gave this

admittedly strange behaviour a cannibalistic slant, it was in the egg-laying species that the story really took off.

In 2006 Alexander Kupfer, Mark Wilkinson and their co-workers were studying the oviparous African caecilian *Boulengerula taitanus* when they made a remarkable discovery. This species had been previously reported to guard its young after hatching and the researchers wanted to examine this behaviour in greater detail. They collected twenty-one females and their hatchlings, and set them up in small plastic boxes designed to resemble the nests they had observed in the field. Their initial observations included the fact that the mothers' skin was much paler than it was in non-mothers and that hatchlings also had a full set of deciduous teeth.

Intrigued, the researchers set out to film the parental care that had been briefly described by previous studies. On multiple occasions Kupfer and Wilkinson observed a female sitting motionless while the newly hatched brood, consisting of between two and nine young, slithered energetically over her body. Looking closer, they noticed that the babies were pressing their heads against the female's body, then pulling away with her skin clamped tightly between their jaws. As the researchers watched, the baby caecilians peeled

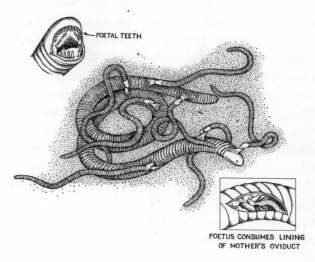

FOETAL TEETH

FOETUS CONSUMES LINING
OF MOTHER'S OVIDUCT

the outer layer of their mother's skin like a grape ... and then consumed it.

Scientists now know that these bouts of 'dermatophagy' recur on a regular basis and that the mothers' epidermis can serve as the young caecilians' sole source of nutrition for several weeks. Female caecilians are able to endure multiple peelings because their skin grows back at a rapid rate.

'The outer layer is what they eat,' Wilkinson said. 'When that's peeled off, the layer below matures into the next meal.'

In addition to the ability of the skin to quickly repair and replenish itself, the nutritional content of this material is yet another interesting feature in this bizarre form of parental care. The outermost epidermal layer, the *stratum corneum*, is usually composed of flattened and dead cells whose primary functions are protection and waterproofing. But when the researchers examined the skin of brooding female caecilians under the microscope they noticed that the *stratum corneum* had undergone significant modification. The layer was not only thicker but also heavily laden with fat-producing cells, which explained why the baby caecilians experienced significant increases in body length and mass during the week-long observations. It also explained why mothers of newly hatched broods experienced a concurrent decrease in body mass of 14 per cent. In short, dermatophagy is a great way to fatten up the kids but for mums on the receiving end of their gruesome attentions, the price is steep.

Scientists now believe that the presence of dermatophagy in both South American and African oviparous species offers strong support for the hypothesis that these odd forms of maternal investment originally evolved in the egg-laying ancestor of all modern caecilian species. Consequently, when the first live-bearing caecilians evolved, their unborn young were already equipped with a set of foetal teeth, which took on a new function, allowing them to tear away and consume the lining of their mothers' oviducts.

HUMANS

7

US AND THEM: EARLY HUMANS AND NEANDERTHALS

Here is a pile of bones of primeval man and beast all mixed together, with no more damning evidence that the man ate the bears than that the bears ate the man – yet paleontology holds a coroner's inquest in the fifth geologic period on an 'unpleasantness' which transpired in the quaternary, and calmly lays it on the MAN, and then adds to it what purports to be evidence of CANNIBALISM. I ask the candid reader, Does not this look like taking advantage of a gentleman who has been dead two million years ...

Mark Twain, *Life As I Find It*

IN 1856, THREE YEARS before publication of Charles Darwin's *On the Origin of Species*, a worker at a limestone quarry near Düsseldorf, Germany, uncovered the bones of what he thought was a bear. He gave the fossils to an amateur palaeontologist, who in turn showed them to Dr Hermann Schaaffhausen, an anatomy professor at the University of Bonn. The bones included fragments from a pelvis as well as arm and leg bones. There was also a skullcap – the section of the cranium above the bridge of the nose.

The anatomist immediately knew that while the bones were thick and strongly built, they had belonged to a human and not a bear. They were, though, unlike any human bones he had ever seen. Beyond the robust nature of the limbs and pelvis, the skullcap had a low receding forehead and a prominent ridge running across the brow. These anatomical differences led him to conclude that these were the remains of a 'primitive' human, 'one of the wild races of Northern Europe'.

The next year they announced the discovery in a joint paper, but the excitement they hoped to generate never materialised. This was, after all, a scientific community that had yet to reject the concept that organisms had not changed since God created them only five thousand years earlier. It was no real surprise then, when a leading pathologist of the day examined the bone fragments and pronounced them to be modern in origin, insisting that the differences in skeletal anatomy were pathological in nature, having been caused by rickets, a childhood bone disease. He blamed the specimen's sloping forehead on a series of heavy blows to the head.

By the early 1860s, following the publication of *On the Origin of Species*, there was increased interest in evolution, especially the topic of human origins. Now the concept of 'change over time' was no longer alien and in the newly minted Age of Industry, the idea of the survival of the fittest was not only palatable but also profitable. By 1864, the rickets/head-injury hypothesis had been overshadowed by the discovery of new specimens with identical differences in skeletal structure. 'Neanderthal man' became the first prehistoric human to be given its own name, a moniker derived from the Neander river valley, where the presumed first fossils had been uncovered.*

---

* In the early twentieth century, 'thal', the German word for 'valley', was changed to 'tal'. As a consequence, 'Neandertal' is a common

Thrust into the scientific and public eye, Neanderthal man became a Victorian-era sensation. Scientists like Darwin's contemporary and friend Thomas Huxley believed these particular remains were important because they established a fossil record for humans that supported Darwin's newly published theory. With none of his friend's famous restraint, Huxley announced that *Homo sapiens* had descended with modification from ape-like ancestors and the Neanderthals were just the proof he needed.

Huxley's rationale was that, although Neanderthals shared many characteristics with modern humans, they also exhibited primitive traits, thus serving as physical evidence that humans, like other organisms, had evolved gradually and over a vast time frame. Neanderthals, he reasoned, were a part of Darwin's branching evolutionary tree, with this particular branch leading to modern humans.

The most serious argument against Huxley's hypothesis was put forth in 1911. Pierre Marcellin Boule, a French anthropologist and scientific heavyweight, had been called upon to study and reconstruct a Neanderthal specimen that had been uncovered in France several years earlier. Once Boule was finished, anyone viewing the reconstruction would come away with some strong ideas about what Neanderthals looked like. Significantly, he gave the skeleton a curved rather than upright spine, indicative of a stooped, slouching stance. With bent knees, flexed hips and a head that jutted forward, Boule's Neanderthal resembled an ape. The anthropologist also claimed that the creature's intelligence matched its ape-like body.

Boule commissioned an artist to produce an illustration

---

alternative to 'Neanderthal'. Since the scientific name for the species (or subspecies) remained *Homo neanderthalensis*, most scientists do not use the new spelling. Soon after the name was coined, researchers determined that two other collections of strange bones found decades earlier in Belgium and Gibraltar (and unnamed by those who discovered them) were also the remains of Neanderthals.

of his reconstruction and the result depicted a hairy, gorilla-like figure with a club in one hand and a boulder in the other. The creature stood in front of a nest of vegetation, another obvious reference to gorillas. Boule's vision of Neanderthals, with their knuckle-dragging posture and ape-like behaviour, also left an indelible mark on a public eager to hear about its ancient ancestors. For decades to come, Neanderthals would become poster boys for stupidity. The epitome of a shambling, dim-witted brute, 'Neanderthal' became synonymous with 'bestial', 'brutal', savage' and 'animal'.* In 'The Grisly Folk', a short story written by H. G. Wells in 1921, the author stuck to the Boule party line, depicting 'Neandertalers' as cannibalistic ogres: '...when his sons grew big enough to annoy him, the grisly man killed them or drove them off. If he killed them he may have eaten them.' According to Wells, the grisly men also developed a taste for the modern humans who had moved into the neighbourhood, finding 'the little children of men fair game and pleasant eating'. Because of this type of behaviour ('lurking' was also a popular activity), Wells felt that the ultimate extermination of the Neanderthals was completely justified, allowing modern humans to rightfully inherit the Earth.

The only problem with Wells's character, according to palaeontologist Niles Eldridge, was that it was based on Boule's misconceptions. 'Every feature that Boule stressed in his analysis can be shown to have no basis in fact.'

Since the early twentieth century, Neanderthals have undergone a further series of transformations and today there are two main hypotheses.

That they were our direct ancestors (*Homo sapiens neanderthalensis*) became part of what is known as the

---

* Today, even among scientists and academics, calling someone a Neanderthal rarely implies that we're referring to a skilled hunter who uses his oversized brain to fashion and employ an array of sophisticated tools.

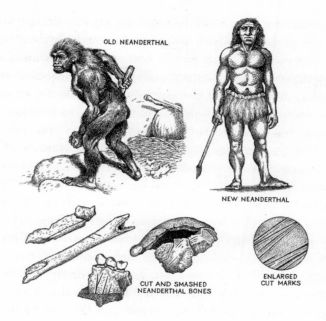

OLD NEANDERTHAL

NEW NEANDERTHAL

CUT AND SMASHED
NEANDERTHAL BONES

ENLARGED
CUT MARKS

Regional Continuity hypothesis. It is a view currently supported by palaeoanthropologist Milford Wolpoff, who believes that Neanderthals living in Europe and the Middle East interbred with other archaic humans, eventually evolving into *Homo sapiens*. According to Wolpoff, similar regional episodes took place elsewhere around the globe as other archaic populations intermingled, hybridising into regional varieties and even subspecies of humans. Importantly, though, there would be enough intermittent contact between these groups (Asians and Europeans, for example) so that only a single species of humans existed at any given time.

The Out of Africa hypothesis holds that modern humans evolved once, in Africa, before spreading to the rest of the world, where they displaced, rather than interbred with, *Homo neanderthalensis* and others who had been there previously. The groups driven to extinction by *Homo sapiens* had themselves evolved from an as of yet undiscovered species of *Homo* (perhaps *H. erectus*) that had originated in Africa and migrated out earlier.

But whatever hypothesis anthropologists choose to support concerning interactions between Neanderthals and modern humans, and the ultimate demise of the former, Neanderthals are no longer depicted as knuckle-dragging brutes. Instead, studies have shown that they were highly intelligent, with some specimens exhibiting a brain capacity 100–150ml greater than the 1,500ml capacity of modern humans! Researchers have also learned that Neanderthals used fire, wore clothing and constructed an array of stone tools, including knives, spearheads and hand axes.

The possibility that Neanderthals practised cannibalism was briefly argued in 1866 and again in the 1920s, after a fossil skull discovered in Italy was observed to have a gaping hole above and behind the right eye. The wound was initially interpreted as evidence that the skull had been broken open by another Neanderthal intent on extracting the brain for food, but researchers now believe that a hyena caused the damage.

More recent and significantly stronger evidence for Neanderthal cannibalism came from multiple sites in northern Spain, south-eastern France and Croatia. In each instance Neanderthal bones exhibited at least some of the characteristics interpreted by anthropologists as 'patterns of processing'. This term refers to the telltale damage found on the bones of animals that have been consumed by humans. This Neanderthal-inflicted damage includes some combination of cut marks, which result when a blade is used to remove edible tissue like muscle; signs of gnawing or peeling; percussion hammering (abrasions or pits that result from the bone being hammered against some form of anvil); burning; and the fracturing of long bones, presumably to access the marrow cavity.

But even when these patterns of processing are observed, researchers must proceed with caution before making claims about the occurrence of cannibalism. While these forms of bone damage can be strong indicators of human activity, they can also result from human behaviour or phenomena completely unrelated to cannibalism. According to anthropologist Tim White, 'Bodies may be buried, burned, placed on scaffolding, set adrift, put in tree trunks or fed to scavengers. Bones may be disinterred, washed, painted, buried in bundles or scattered on stones.' In what's called secondary burial, bodies that have already been buried or left to decompose are disinterred and subjected to additional handling. For the ancient Jews this involved placing the bones into stone boxes called ossuaries. For some Australian aboriginal groups and perhaps the ancient Minoans, secondary burial practices included the removal of flesh and cutting of bones. Rituals like these make it extremely difficult to distinguish between funerary rites and cannibalism, especially if the rites are no longer practised or if the group in question no longer exists.

Cut marks on bones may be the result of violent acts related to war or murder. If you can imagine someone unearthing the skeleton of a soldier killed by a bayonet or sword, they might misinterpret the cut marks on the bones as evidence of cannibalism.

Clearly, then, blade marks and other damage inflicted on Neanderthals by fellow Neanderthals and other ancient human groups may have been caused by a variety of actions. Archaeologists now consider this type of bone damage to be strong evidence for cannibalistic behaviour only when it can be matched to similar damage found on the bones of game animals uncovered at the same site. The implication is that if animal and human bodies were processed in the same manner, and if the remains were discarded together, it is reasonably certain that cannibalism took place.

This appears to have been precisely what happened at a Neanderthal cave site known as Moula-Guercy, in south-eastern France. An excavation begun there in 1991 revealed the remains of six Neanderthals and at least five red deer that date to approximately 100,000 years ago. The bones were distributed together and butchered in a similar fashion. The long bones and skulls were smashed and tell-tale cut marks on the sides of the skulls indicated that the large jaw closure muscles had been filleted. There were also characteristic patterns of modification on the lower jaws, providing evidence that the tongues had been removed. Both Neanderthal and deer bones also exhibited peeling and percussion pits. Lastly, there were distinctive patterns of cuts indicating that bodies from both species had been disarticulated at the shoulder, a process that would have made carrying and handling easier. According to Tim White, 'The circumstantial forensic evidence [for cannibalism at Moula-Guercy] is excellent.'

Of course, there is always the possibility that this type of damage to the animal bones took place during butchery but that the same types of stone tools were also used to deflesh and disarticulate human remains during non-cannibalistic mortuary practices. As in the case of dinosaurs, the only definitive evidence for prehistoric cannibalism would be the discovery of human remains inside fossil faeces or inside a human stomach.

But among anthropologists, even this type of evidence sparked a controversy.

In 2000, researchers working in the Four Corners region of the American south-west reported that human myoglobin (a form of haemoglobin found in muscles) had been identified from a single fossilised coprolite described as being consistent with human origin. The petrified faeces had evidently been deposited onto a cooking hearth belonging to archaic Puebloans (Anasazi) sometime around CE 1150. Together with defleshed human bones and butchering tools coated with human blood residue, the thirty-gram faecal fossil was used to support the claim that cannibalism had taken place at the south-western Colorado site known as Cowboy Wash. It is a finding that has been the subject of considerable debate, with some researchers insisting that the bone and blood evidence could also have resulted from corpse mutilation, ritualised executions or funerary practices.

These scientists also point out that, while the myoglobin in the coprolite was certainly human in origin, the animal that produced the faeces was never positively identified. This raises the possibility that a coyote or wolf consumed part of a corpse and subsequently defecated in the abandoned cooking hearth.

Even with a set of palaeoanthropological safeguards in place, mistakes can still occur. 'In many cases you're finding bones in the normal palaeontological environment,' renowned American Museum of Natural History palaeontologist Ian Tattersall explained. 'That is to say, they've all been scattered and they've been concentrated by water or whatever's happened to them, which had nothing to do with the actual human activities that may or may not have been carried out after they were deceased.'

To envision how this 'scattering' or concentration of fossils can occur, picture a stream cutting through a fossil-containing layer of rock. As the stream walls gradually wear away, fossils are exposed, washed out and deposited into the streambed randomly and over time. Similarly, different parts from the same organism might be exposed at different times, which can also lead to fragments from a single individual being scattered across a wide area.

This water-assisted movement can also take place *before* the specimens are fossilised. For example, the bodies of creatures that died along an ancient body of water (or in it) may have been carried away by currents and deposited together by gravity. If sediments covered the bodies rapidly enough they may have become fossilised, but their final location may have little or no relevance to what took place when the organisms were alive. For this reason, archaeologists must be cautious when animal and human bones are found mixed together, as it does not necessarily prove that humans did the mixing.*

One instance in which the evidence for human cannibalism remains solid involves *Homo antecessor* ('pioneering man'), the reputed ancestor of Neanderthals. The first fossils of this species were uncovered in the 1980s in Atapuerca, a region in northern Spain. Spelunkers found the bones of extinct cave bears at the bottom of a narrow fifty-foot-deep pit. Excavation of the pit, now known as Sima de los Huesos (the Pit of Bones), was initiated in 1984 by palaeontologist Emiliano Aguirre. After his retirement, Aguirre's students continued to work at the site and in 1991 they began emerging from the stifling heat and claustrophobic conditions with well-preserved hominid bones.

Since then, the site has yielded over 5,000 bone fragments from approximately thirty humans of varying age and sex. The researchers noted that some aspects of the skull and post-cranial skeleton appeared to be Neanderthal-like (including a large pelvis that someone christened 'Elvis'). Eventually, though, the remains from Atapuerca exhibited sufficient anatomical differences from Neanderthals to warrant placing them into a separate species.

According to Ian Tattersall, *Homo antecessor* was 'almost Neanderthal but not quite ... they were on the way to becoming Neanderthals.' To the surprise of researchers, the remains of *Homo antecessor* recovered from Sima de los Huesos were dated to a minimum of 530,000 years, indicating that the Neanderthal lineage had been in Europe 300,000–400,000 years before the first Neanderthals – far longer than anyone had imagined.

By 1994, researchers were claiming that *Homo*

---

* Similarly, cave collapses also appear to have caused the demise of a number of Neanderthals whose fossilised bones were initially thought to exhibit percussion pits.

antecessor remains showed evidence of having been cannibalised. In this case, the fracture patterns, cut marks and tool-induced surface modification were identical to the damage found on the bones of non-human animals that had presumably been used as food. All of the bones (human and non-human) were randomly dispersed as well. The researchers at Atapuerca concluded that the *H. antecessor* remains came from 'the victims of other humans who brought bodies to the site, ate their flesh, broke their bones, and extracted the marrow, in the same way they were feeding on the [animals] also preserved in the stratum.'

Interestingly, the presence of so many types of game animals led the same researchers to suggest that Atapuerca did not represent an example of stress-related survival cannibalism, and Ian Tattersall agreed. 'Sometimes the environment was pretty rich and you wouldn't necessarily need to practise cannibalism to make your metabolic ends meet, as it were.' It would be relatively easy to find alternative sources of protein.

Accordingly, the Neanderthal ancestors living at Atapuerca were likely not prehistoric versions of the group of nineteenth-century pioneers known as 'the Donner Party' (of whom more later) – stranded in horrible conditions and compelled by starvation to consume their dead. Instead *Homo antecessor*, like many species throughout the animal kingdom, may have simply considered others of their kind to be food. In other words, they may have eaten human flesh because it was readily available and because they liked it.

No one is absolutely certain when the transition from *Homo antecessor* to Neanderthal man took place, but it probably happened sometime around 150,000 years ago. If one does not subscribe to the idea that Neanderthal genes were eventually overwhelmed through interbreeding with their more intelligent cousins, then *Homo neanderthalensis* appears to have gone extinct approximately 30,000 years ago.

Ian Tattersall explained, 'Neanderthals and modern humans managed to somehow partition the Near East among themselves for a long, long period of time, at a time when modern humans were not behaving like they do today. They left no symbolic record [e.g. depictions of their behaviour and beliefs]. As soon as they started leaving a symbolic record, the Neanderthals were out of there.'

The significance of this, he explained, was that by the time the Neanderthals' homeland in Europe was invaded by modern humans, humans were behaving in the modern way and had become insuperable competitors.

Given what we know about modern humans and their treatment of the indigenous groups they encounter, it's difficult to argue against Tattersall's conclusions. In all likelihood, the Neanderthal homeland was indeed invaded by an advanced, symbolism-driven species, and, as we'll see in the following chapter, it would have been more of a surprise if *Homo sapiens* hadn't raped, enslaved, and slaughtered the Neanderthals and other groups they encountered there.

8

MYTHS OF THE OTHER: COLUMBUS, CARIBS AND CANNIBALISM

DURING HIS SECOND VOYAGE to the New World in 1493, Christoffa Corombo (aka Christopher Columbus) was accompanied by Dr Álvarez Chanca, a physician from Seville, who offered this description of events, after the landing party entered a small village on the island Columbus would name Santa María de Guadaloupe.

> The captain ... took two parrots, very large and very different from those seen before. He found much cotton, spun and ready for spinning; and articles of food; and he brought away a little of everything; especially he brought away four or five bones of the arms and legs of men. When we saw this, we suspected that the islands were those islands of the Caribe, which are inhabited by people who eat human flesh ...

Before Columbus had begun his investigations, the local inhabitants had already fled in terror, leaving behind everything they owned. It was a response that had taken them a little over a year to learn.

During his first voyage in 1492, Columbus referred to

all of the native people as 'Indios', but by a year later a distinction had been made between the peaceful Arawaks (also called Tainos) and another group known to the locals as the Caribes (or more commonly, Caribs). What Columbus would never know was that the indigenous inhabitants were actually a diverse assemblage that had been living on the islands for hundreds of years. Their ancestors had set out from coastal Venezuela, where the outflowing currents of the Orinoco river carried the migrants into the open sea and far beyond. At each island stop these settlers developed their own cultures and customs, so that by the time the Spaniards arrived, the entire Caribbean island chain had already been colonised, with settlements extending as far north as the Bahamas.

Columbus, though, cared little about local customs or history. Instead, he noted that the Arawaks were gentle and friendly, and he wasted little time in passing this information on to his royal backers in Spain, '[The Arawaks] are fitted to be ruled and to be set to work, to cultivate the land and do all else that may be necessary ...'

Although no one is quite sure who was doing the translating, soon after his initial arrival the Arawaks reportedly told Columbus that the Caribs inhabited certain of the southern islands, including those that would eventually be called St Vincent, Dominica, Guadeloupe and Trinidad. Columbus was informed that the Caribs were infamous not only for brutal raids against their peaceful neighbours – but also for their unsettling habit of eating their captives. But these were not the Caribs' only vices. Each year they would meet up with a tribe of warrior women. These fighting females were reportedly 'fierce to the last degree, strong as tigers, courageous in fight, brutal and merciless'.

With more than a fleeting resemblance to a fictional race of Amazons dreamed up by the ancient Greeks, these warrior women lived on their own island (Martinique) and killed any men they encountered ... except, that is, for the

Caribs, who got a yearly invite to drop by for feasting and debauchery. Possibly the invitations stemmed from the fact that the Caribs were renowned for their cooking ability – preparing their viands by smoking them slowly on a wooden platform. It was a setup the Spanish began referring to as a *barbacoa*. After manning the grill and servicing the gals, the Caribs returned home, taking with them any new-born males who had shown up nine months after the previous year's party. Female babies would, of course, remain behind to be raised as warriors.

In retrospect, it is difficult to determine where Arawak tall tales ended and Columbus's vivid and self-serving imagination kicked in. What is known is that European history and folklore were already rich with references to encounters with bizarre monsters and strange human races. Although most of the stories emerging from the New World were greeted with enthusiasm back in Seville, some of Columbus's patrons expressed scepticism after hearing that the Caribs also hunted with schools of fish. These had been trained to accept tethers and dispatched with instructions to latch on to sea turtles, which could then be reeled in for butchering.*

Easier to accept, perhaps, were Columbus's claims that some Caribs had dog-like faces, reminiscent of the *Cynocephali* described nearly 1,400 years earlier by Pliny the Elder, the Roman author and naturalist. Still other New World locals were said to possess a single, centrally located eye or a long tail, an appendage that necessitated the digging of holes by its owner in order to sit down. These creatures were considered to be anything but a joke since, as late as 1758, Linnaeus's opus *Systema Naturae* listed three species of man: *Homo sapiens* (wise man), *Homo troglodytes* (cave man) and *Homo caudatus* (tailed man).

But whether or not these strange savages had tails (and even if they were supported by trained fish and Amazonian girlfriends), plans were soon being formulated to pacify the Caribs, who were now being referred to as Canibs. According to scholars, the transition from Carib to Canib apparently resulted from a mispronunciation, although in light of stories describing locals as having canine faces, 'Canib' may also be a degenerate form of *canis*, the Latin for dog. Eventually canib became the root of 'cannibal', which replaced *anthropophagi*, the ancient Greek mouthful previously used to describe people eaters.

But whatever the locals were called, and whatever the origins of the term, the first part of Columbus's grand plan centred on relieving them of the abundant gold he

---

* In Northern Australia, East Africa, and the Indian Ocean, some cultures do employ a family of sucker-backed fish called remoras (Echeneidae) to hunt for sea turtles. Remoras are renowned for attaching themselves to larger fish as well as to turtles. The original behaviour is a form of commensalism – a relationship in which one species (the remora) obtains a benefit (in this case protection and food dropped by the host) while the other species gains nothing but isn't harmed.

was convinced they had in their possession. One reason for Columbus's certainty on this point was the commonly held belief that silver formed in cold climates while gold was created in warm or hot regions. And considering the heat and humidity of the New World tropics, this could only mean that there would be plenty of it around.

Unlike his first voyage, which consisted of three ships and 120 men, Columbus's second visit to the New World was more of a military occupation force. Accompanying him were seventeen ships and nearly 1,500 men, many of them heavily armed. Although he had begun to look at slave raiding as a means to finance his voyages, his prime directive was to find gold – and lots of it. To facilitate the collection of this massive treasure, he levied tribute on those living in regions like El Cibao, in what is now the northern part of the Dominican Republic. His orders stated that every male between fourteen and seventy years of age was to collect and hand over a substantial measure of gold to his representatives every three months. Those who failed at what quickly became an impossible task had their hands hacked off. Anyone who chose to flee was hunted down – the Spaniards encouraging their vicious war-dogs to tear apart any escapees they could run to ground.

In the end, very little of the precious metal was turned in. Presumably the island residents, under the very real threat of losing their limbs or being eaten alive by giant dogs, quickly ran through any gold they might have had on hand. Since it played only a minor role (or none at all) in their traditions, in all likelihood the locals just didn't know where to find it – especially in the quantities demanded by the Spanish invaders.

Deeply disappointed at the meagre results, Columbus penned a letter to his royal supporters in Spain in May 1499. In it he wondered 'why God Our Lord has concealed the gold from us'. There is no record of a response, but Columbus soon refocused his efforts toward the collection of a resource that was available in great supply – humans.

In 1503 this bloodthirsty new take on the exploration of the New World got a significant boost when the self-proclaimed Admiral of the Ocean Sea received a royal proclamation from Queen Isabella. In it she stated that those locals who did not practise cannibalism should be free from slavery and mistreatment. More significantly, though, she also instructed Columbus and his men about what they *could* do to them if they were determined to be cannibals:

> …if such cannibals continue to resist and do not wish
> to admit and receive to their lands the Captains and
> men who may be on such voyages by my orders nor

to hear them in order to be taught our Sacred Catholic Faith and to be in my service and obedience, they may be captured and taken to these my Kingdoms and Domains and to other parts and places and be sold.

This new position was supported by the Catholic Church several years later, when Pope Innocent IV decreed in 1510 not only that cannibalism was a sin, but also that Christians were perfectly justified in doling out punishment for cannibalism through force of arms.

What happened next was as predictable as it was terrible. On islands where no cannibalism had been reported previously, man-eating was suddenly determined to be a popular practice. Regions previously inhabited by peaceful Arawaks were, upon re-examination, found to be crawling with man-eating Caribs, and very soon the line between the two groups was obliterated. 'Resistance' and 'cannibalism' became synonymous, and anyone acting aggressively towards the Europeans was immediately labelled a cannibal.

In an effort to organise the cannibal pacification efforts, Rodrigo de Figueroa, the former Governor of Santo Domingo (now the Dominican Republic), was given the job of making judgements on the official classification of all the indigenous groups encountered by the Spanish during their takeover. Testimonials and other 'evidence' were used to place the cannibalism tag on island populations, and by a strange coincidence the designations seemed to change with the priorities of the Spanish for the islands in question. Trinidad, for example, was declared a cannibal island in 1511 but the ruling was changed in 1518. Rather than relating to concerns over the welfare of the local people, though, the reclassification came about because of reports of gold in Trinidad and the Spaniards' desire to maintain the local population for use in mining operations. It was more than coincidental, then, that once the Spanish mining efforts on Trinidad failed to produce any gold, word began filtering in that the locals were cannibals after all. Soon after, the order was given to colonise Trinidad and to depopulate it of its remaining man-eating inhabitants. As a result, the pre-Columbian indigenous population in Trinidad (estimated to be somewhere between 30,000 and 40,000 individuals) dropped to half that number within a century.

Even in places that hadn't initially been designated as cannibal islands, populations dropped precipitously as the locals were either hauled off to toil as slaves, murdered, or died from newly arrived diseases like measles, smallpox, and influenza (the latter may have been a form of swine flu carried by some pigs that Columbus had picked up on the Canary Islands during the early part of his second voyage). According to historian David Stannard, 'Wherever the marauding, diseased, and heavily armed Spanish forces went out on patrol, accompanied by ferocious armoured dogs that had been trained to kill and disembowel, they preyed on the local communities, already plague-enfeebled, forcing them to supply food and women and slaves, and whatever else the soldiers might desire.'

The diseases the Spaniards carried (the precise identities of which are still debated) spread with alarming speed through local communities, killing inhabitants in numbers that, according to one writer at the time, 'could not be counted'. Stannard believes that, by the end of the sixteenth century, the Spanish had been directly or indirectly responsible for the deaths of between 60 and 80 million indigenous people in the Caribbean, Mexico and Central America. Even if one were to discount the millions of deaths resulting from diseases, this would still make the Spanish conquest of the New World the greatest act of genocide in recorded history.

In the end, regardless of the true occurrence of cannibalism, it was tall tales, especially those with a bestial or man-eating angle, that effectively dehumanised the islanders. Not only did this serve to justify Spain's rapidly evolving slave-raiding agenda, it also established an attitude towards the locals that came to resemble pest control. Leaving behind neither pyramids nor stone glyphs, the indigenous cultures of the Caribbean have all but disappeared.

9

BONES OF CONTENTION: RITUAL CANNIBALISM

I do not think it is an exaggeration to say history is largely a history of inflation, usually inflations engineered by governments for the gain of governments.

F. A. von Hayek, *Denationalisation of Money: The Argument Refined*

REMEMBER DR CHANCA, whom we saw at the beginning of the previous chapter depicting the recovery of 'four or five bones' of human arms and legs in a hastily abandoned hut? In what might come as a surprise, given that if you read Chanca's work, his repeated use of the word 'we' gives the impression that he had experienced the horrors of the 'cannibal hut' first-hand, he never actually saw the scene he wrote about in 1493.

Though not an actual witness, Dr Chanca *was* a strong supporter of Columbus, and because of his professional status his written accounts carried tremendous weight. His letters make up much of what we know (or thought we knew) about the Admiral's second voyage to the New World, and the contemporary view of the Caribs as sub-human man-eaters fit only for enslavement. Incidentally, Chanca's account of the cannibal hut was sent back to

Spain accompanied by a letter from Columbus, requesting that the doctor's salary be increased substantially. Since Columbus was already using the cannibal angle to justify his attempts to 'pacify' the local inhabitants, it hardly seems simply coincidental that Dr Chanca would have penned an accompanying document contradicting his master's description of the Caribs as subhuman eaters of men.

At best, then, Dr Chanca's letter provides a brief, second-hand account of what may or may not have been the aftermath of cannibalism by the inhabitants of a single hut on the island of Guadeloupe. Meagre evidence? Certainly, but the story gained far greater significance as additional authors wrote about the incident. It would become a blueprint for cannibal tales throughout history, as descriptions of the practice were penned decades or even centuries after the actual event and without the input of additional witnesses.

But even if the events described by Chanca did take place, the bones Columbus and his men collected from the infamous hut were more likely part of a funerary ritual rather than proof of cannibalism. According to historians and anthropologists, rather than burying their departed ancestors, some Amerindians preserved and worshipped their bones. In 1828, author and historian Washington Irving pointed out that during Columbus's first voyage, when human bones were discovered in a dwelling on Hispaniola, they were taken to be relics of the dead, reverently preserved. On Columbus's second visit, however, when bones were found in a hut presumably inhabited by Caribs, the finding became incontrovertible evidence of cannibalism.

Regardless of politically motivated tall tales, the question remains whether there was any *real* cannibalism going on in the Caribbean when Columbus arrived. The debate continues. Anthropologist Neil Whitehead suggests that, while many reports are blatant examples of imperial propaganda, there are several reasons to think that the Caribs and other Amerindian groups *did* practise some forms of ritualised cannibalism. Whitehead's rationale is that in addition to the self-serving allegations of man-eating, other Spaniards reported cannibalism in social context – as a funerary rite or ritual related to the treatment of enemies slain during battle. For example, in the seventeenth century, Jacinto de Caravajal wrote, 'The ordinary food of the Caribs is cassava, fish or game ... they eat human flesh when they are at war and do so as a sign of victory, not as food ...'

According to anthropologists, ritualised cannibalism can be differentiated into two forms: exocannibalism and endocannibalism. Exocannibalism (from the Greek *exo* – 'from the outside') refers to the consumption of individuals from outside one's own community or social group while endocannibalism (from the Greek *endo* – 'from the inside') is defined as the ritual consumption of deceased members from inside one's own family, community or social group.

With regard to exocannibalism, a number of historical accounts claim that the Caribs consumed their enemies – those killed in battle, taken prisoner, or captured during raids. The belief was that this form of ritual cannibalism was a way to transfer desired traits, like strength or courage, from the deceased enemy to themselves.

Exocannibalism has been reported in a range of circumstances through the centuries, used as a way both to terrorise an enemy and to feed the hungry. In the 1960s anthropologist Pierre Clastres lived with the Ache of Paraguay and claimed that one of the four groups he studied ate their enemies. Similar claims have been made about the Tupinambá of eastern Brazil, most famously by Hans Stadin, a sixteenth-century German shipwrecked while serving as a seaman on a Portuguese ship. In his 1557 book *True Story and Description of a Country of Wild, Naked, Grim, Man-eating People in the New World, America,*

Stadin, who reportedly spent a year in captivity before escaping, described raids in which the Tupinambá killed and ate everyone they captured (except, apparently, him).

Nearly four hundred years later, in the Pacific Theatre during World War II, Allied prisoners of war described numerous instances in which their Japanese captors tortured and then ate their prisoners. In post-war tribunals, survivors testified that their captors acted systematically, selecting one individual each day and hacking off limbs and flesh while they were alive and conscious. American soldiers also became even more insistent about removing the bodies of their fallen comrades from the battlefield after it was discovered that the Japanese sometimes sliced off pieces of the dead with bayonets – a gory ritual some Americans began to practise as well.

Perhaps the most famous wartime twentieth-century incidence of exocannibalism was the 'Ogasawara Incident' in which Lieutenant General Yoshio Tachibana ordered his starving men on the island of Chichi Jima to execute a group of downed American fliers who had been captured after carrying out a bombing raid. Medical orderlies were then instructed to cut the livers from the bodies and the organs were cooked and served to the senior staff. Tachibana and several others were arrested after the war but since cannibalism was not listed as an official war crime, in the end they were actually convicted and hanged for preventing the honourable burial of the prisoners the officer and his men had eaten. Later was it revealed that an American submarine had recovered one of the nine downed fliers, thus saving him from a similar fate at the hands of the starving Japanese. The lucky man's name was Lieutenant George H. W. Bush.

There is no such element of terror involved in the practice of endocannibalism, although it too can be carried out in order to transfer the spirit of the dead or their strengths into the bodies of the living. Anthropologists have proposed that, much like Christian burial rituals or the administration of last rites, endocannibalism was undertaken by some groups in order to facilitate the separation of the deceased's soul from its body. The Melanesians (living in Fiji, the Solomon Islands, Vanuatu and Papua New Guinea) reportedly practised a form of mortuary cannibalism for this reason, consuming small titbits from the bodies of their deceased relatives, as we will see in the next chapter.

Anthropologist Beth Conklin studied the Wari' from the western Amazonian rainforest of Brazil. She reported that, until the 1960s, the Wari' consumed portions of human flesh as well as bone meal mixed with honey. Having conducted extensive interviews with Wari' elders, she concluded that the Wari' were keenly aware that prolonged grieving made it hard for mourners to get on with their lives. With the corpse being the single most powerful reminder of the deceased, the Wari' believed that consuming the body would eradicate it once and for all. Nonetheless, they were forced by missionaries and government officials to abandon their funerary rites and to bury their dead according to the Western tradition. According to Conklin, the Wari' found this ritual to be particularly repellent since they considered the ground to be 'cold, wet and polluting', and that 'to leave a loved one's body to rot in the dirt was disrespectful and degrading to the dead and heart-wrenching for those who mourned them'.

Getting back to the question of whether or not the Caribs were cannibals, I met Cristo Adonis, the spiritual leader of the Trinidadian Amerindians, during a trip to Trinidad. Rather than use the European colonial assigned names Carib and Arawak, Adonis refers to his ancestors as the Karina and Locono people. Today, only around 600 members survive, none of whom are full-blooded members of the tribes. Adonis told me that his people did in fact practise both endocannibalism, in the context of religious practices, and exocannibalism, as a way to gain power from their defeated enemies. His evidence for this claim derives solely from ethnohistorical accounts and stories passed down over hundreds of years, which are far from concrete proof, though he questioned 'why indigenous historians pass on stories about their ancestors practising cannibalism if the stories weren't based on real customs'.

Actually, I can think of some potential reasons for claiming one's ancestors were cannibals (e.g. to instil fear in their enemies), but Neil Whitehead also thinks that the Caribs were man-eaters. Whitehead offers accounts of Amerindians practising cannibalism, written by non-Spanish writers, arguing that since the English, French and Dutch were enemies of Spain, they would have wanted to develop alliances with the Amerindians. Since the non-Spaniards were presumably on friendlier terms with the locals, they would have been in better position to observe and report on the true behaviour of their native allies.

Arguing against Carib cannibalism, perhaps, is the fact that the documentation by non-Spaniards regarding the behaviour contains some seriously fanciful descriptions. For example, alongside his descriptions of anthropophagy, Sir Walter Raleigh wrote about some indigenous peoples having their heads located within their chests and their feet pointing backwards, the latter a characteristic that made them 'very difficult to track'.

As a result, readers – both casual and scholarly – were subjected to a 500-year indoctrination period during which they heard little if anything about the genocidal mistreatment of native populations. After all, who would sympathise with far-off, profoundly foreign indigenous populations or be able to appreciate the sociological significance of cannibalism (if the practice did occur)? Far more likely, they would come away believing that Columbus and the other European explorers had fought off hordes of cannibalistic subhumans, thus sparing many a grateful savage the horrors of the cooking pot. From the New World to

Africa, Australia and the Pacific islands, regardless of the true nature and extent of the practices, cannibalism was generally perceived to be a widespread phenomenon. It would be the role of the good Christians – explorers, and the missionaries who invariably followed them – to take control of the situation and thus put an end to this most horrific of human behaviours.

For the most part, this public mindset concerning ritual cannibalism remained until 1979, when Professor William Arens initiated what became a loud and serious debate over the validity of cannibalism as a social practice. In his book *The Man-Eating Myth*, Arens argued that, aside from some well-known starvation-induced instances, there was absolutely no proof that cannibalism, ritualised or otherwise, had ever been practised in any human culture. He also pointed out how cannibalism had become a handy symbol for any unacceptable behaviour practised by 'others' – a broad and malleable category of evildoers that included enemies, followers of non-Christian religions and any groups determined to retain their 'uncivilised' customs. Arens asserted that colonial groups had been guilty of making false accusations of cannibalism against native populations across the globe and throughout history, regardless of scant evidence. With Christopher Columbus acting as a poster boy, applying the cannibal tag justified the condemnation and, if necessary, the eradication of anyone accused of breaking this ultimate taboo – a practice whose validity (Arens was quick to point out) was always unsupported by anything resembling first-hand evidence.

The reaction to Arens's incendiary book was swift and mostly negative. Ultimately, though, I've found myself agreeing with much but certainly not all of his hypothesis, in part because of the brutal pounding colonial invaders doled out to indigenous groups over the centuries. On the other hand, my investigation into ritual cannibalism leads me to conclude that there is plenty of evidence to support the stance that some cultural groups practised cannibalism, and that they did so for a variety of reasons. As for the claims of Carib cannibalism specifically, the fact remains that beyond the second- and third-hand accounts, there isn't a shred of physical evidence, nor is there any indication that Columbus or his men ever actually witnessed man-eating themselves. The debate continues.

10

TAKE, EAT, THIS IS MY BODY: CANNIBALISM AND THE BIBLE

I had to eat a piece of Jesus once in a movie.

John Lurie, regarding *The Last Temptation of Christ* (personal communication)

THERE IS ANOTHER FORM of ritual cannibalism whose origins are as fascinating as they are close to home.

Descriptions of cannibalism in the Bible fall into two distinct categories. In the Old Testament, the behaviour was undertaken by the starving inhabitants of the besieged cities of Jerusalem and Samaria. There's no physical evidence that these events actually occurred (although, of course, that doesn't mean that they didn't), though more on the topic of survival cannibalism in Chapter 11.

The second type of cannibalism is found in the New Testament and relates to the literal or symbolic consumption of Jesus Christ's body and blood during the celebration of the Eucharist – the Christian commemoration of the Last Supper. Considering the paramount importance this ceremony has for all Christians, and in light of differing belief systems that exist throughout Christianity, it's no surprise that there are disagreements concerning the interpretation of the ritual. One thing common among the vast majority of Christians, however, is ignorance that this particular form of symbolic cannibalism led to the torture and murder of thousands of innocent people.

The following are two of the most famous passages from the New Testament.

> Now as they were eating, Jesus took bread, and when he had said the blessing he broke it and gave it to the disciples. 'Take it and eat,' he said, 'this is my body.' Then he took a cup, and when he had given thanks he handed it to them saying, 'Drink from this, all of you, for this is my blood, the blood of the covenant, poured out for many for the forgiveness of sins.'
>
> Matthew 26:26–28

> Jesus replied to them: In all truth I tell you, if you do not eat the flesh of the Son of Man and drink his blood, you have no life in you. Anyone who does eat my flesh and drink my blood has eternal life, and I shall raise that person up on the last day. For my flesh is real food and my blood is real drink. Whoever eats my flesh and drinks my blood lives in me and I live in that person.
>
> John 6:53–56

One way to interpret these passages is that Jesus was using a metaphor to convey a concept to his followers. It was certainly something he had done before, since surely even the dimmest of Jesus's supporters hadn't taken him literally when he said, 'I am the gate' (John 10:9) or 'I am the true vine' (John 15:1). Strangely, though, the leaders of several major Christian religions (including Catholicism) do not support this symbolic interpretation. Here's how that disagreement came about.

After the first four Crusades, and the capture of Constantinople and large parts of the Byzantine Empire, Pope Innocent III summoned over 400 bishops and many lesser ecumenical leaders to attend the Fourth Lateran Council in 1215. Also invited were representative rulers from Europe and the Levant (an area now made up of Lebanon, Israel, Jordan, the Palestinian territories, Syria and Iraq). During the meeting, there was apparently little discussion between the Pope and the council attendees. Instead, the pontiff presented a list of seventy-one papal decrees, which served notice to all present that the Pope's powers, as well as those of the Roman Catholic Church, had just been expanded. Among proclamations forbidding the founding of new religious orders, strengthening papal primacy and regulating and restricting Jewish communities, was a decree that spelled out the concept of transubstantiation.

From that moment on, the faithful would be required to believe that the consecrated elements in the Eucharist, the bread and wine, were literally changed into the actual body and blood of Jesus Christ. 'His body and blood are truly contained in the sacrament of the altar under the forms of bread and wine, the bread and wine having been changed in substance, by God's power, into his body and blood …'

If the council attendees had any gripes about these new decrees they apparently kept them to themselves. During the sixteenth century, however, the interpretation of biblical passages like those describing the Last Supper became pivot points for the controversies that arose between the Catholics and Protestants. In that regard, Martin Luther, leader of the Protestant Reformation, seemed to have a more than little problem with the whole idea of transubstantiation, beginning with the fact that the term did not appear in any biblical scriptures. (Archbishop Hildebert of Tours had coined the term, from the Latin *transsubstantiatio*, around 1079.) In October 1520, though, Martin Luther referred to it as 'an absurd and unheard-of juggling with words', stating that 'the Church had the true faith for more than twelve hundred years, during which time the Holy Fathers never once mentioned this transubstantiation – certainly, a monstrous word for a monstrous idea'.

A decade later, the Incan King Atahualpa took issue with the concept of transubstantiation. In their entertaining book *Eat Thy Neighbour*, Daniel Diehl and Mark Donnelly recounted the story of what took place after the capture of Atahualpa by Conquistador Francisco Pizarro in 1533, when he was threatened with execution unless he converted to Christianity:

> Atahualpa said he bowed to no man and told the Spanish exactly what he thought of their religion. His people, he said, only sacrificed their enemies to their gods and certainly did not eat people. The Spanish, on the other hand, killed their own God, drank his blood and baked his body into little biscuits which they sacrificed to themselves. He found the entire practice unspeakable. The Spanish were outraged and had Atahualpa publicly executed on 15 August 1533.

Unfortunately, other accounts of this incident offer a somewhat less heroic end to Atahualpa's story. In an alternative version, the captured Incan king converted to Catholicism and was given the name Juan Santos Atahualpa. His fellow Catholics then celebrated Juan's baptism by having him strangled with a garrotte.

Regardless, Roman Catholic leaders not only adopted the concept of transubstantiation but during the Eastern Orthodox Synod of Jerusalem of 1672 they took a moment to snub the upstart Protestants:

> In the celebration of [the Eucharist] we believe the Lord Jesus Christ to be present. He is not present typically, nor figuratively, nor by superabundant grace, as

in the other Mysteries, nor by a bare presence ... as the followers of Luther most ignorantly and wretchedly suppose. But truly and really, so that after the consecration of the bread and of the wine, the bread is transmuted, transubstantiated, converted and transformed into the true body itself of the Lord ... and the wine is converted and transubstantiated into the true blood itself of the Lord ...

Even as recently as 1965, Pope Paul VI made it clear that as far as he and the Roman Catholic Church were concerned, with regard to transubstantiation, their stance had not changed in the 400 years since the Council of Trent, one of the Church's most important ecumenical councils. As a result, beginning some thirty years after Pope Innocent's decree concerning transubstantiation, faithful Catholics started rounding up and executing Jews for the crime of 'torturing the host'.

But firstly, how, you might ask, did the accusers know that their hosts were being desecrated? Apparently, unimpeachable witnesses came forward, claiming to have seen the communion bread bleeding. Secondly, why were the Jews being blamed for this phenomenon? The answer appears to be that while there wasn't a shred of actual proof, everyone agreed that the Jews hated Jesus, and so perhaps they were re-enacting the Messiah's crucifixion or using the host as part of their own nefarious rituals. Rumours had begun circulating that Jews were applying the blood that flowed from the host to their faces, to give their cheeks a rosy appearance. Others suggested that the villains were using the saviour's blood to rid themselves of the *foetor Judaicus* ('Jewish stink').

And so it came to pass that, in the complete absence of anything remotely resembling evidence, Jews were rounded up, coerced and tortured – after which many of them confessed to entirely imaginary crimes. But whether

Adapted from a fifteenth-century German woodcut depicting host desecration by the Jews of the Bavarian town of Passau, in 1477. The hosts are stolen and brought to a temple where they are pierced with a dagger during some unspecified Jewish ritual carried out in the presence of a Torah. Eventually, the hosts are rescued in a commando-like raid and the communion wafers are shown to be holy. The guilty Jews are arrested. Some are beheaded, others tortured with hot pincers. Next, the entire Jewish community has their feet put to the fire before being driven out of town (or to their death). In the end, the good Christians kneel and pray.

they confessed or not, those found guilty of defiling the sacrament were subjected to additional torture before being burned at the stake, beheaded, or otherwise grue-somely dispatched. Additionally, their families, as well as any neighbours brazen enough to have lived nearby, often accompanied them to their deaths. These practices contin-ued for nearly 400 years in Jewish communities all across Europe, with massacres taking place in Germany, France, Austria, Poland, Spain and Romania. At some point, the execution of Jews for crimes against baked goods ended, though this had more to do with the rise in popularity of a new group – witches – to persecute for similarly unsubstantiated crimes, than any moral qualms on the part of those carrying out the pogroms.

But what about the bleeding hosts themselves? Were medieval witnesses just making that stuff up as an excuse to get rid of a group they despised? Maybe these people had simply imagined the ruby-stained bread? There is, however, an intriguing alternative hypothesis. In 1994 Dr Johanna Cullen, at George Mason University in Virginia, came up with an explanation for bleeding hosts that was neither mystical nor mental. It was instead, microbiological. *Serratia marcescens* is a rod-shaped bacterium and common human pathogen frequently linked to both urinary-tract and catheter-associated infections. The ubiquitous microbe can also be found growing on food like stale bread that has been stored in warm, damp environments. For this story, the key characteristic of *S. marcescens* is that it produces and exudes a reddish-orange pigment called prodigiosin, a substance that can cause the bacterial colonies to resemble drops of blood. Clinically, prodigiosin has been shown to be an immunosuppressant with antimicrobial and anti-cancer properties, and it's likely that these germ-killing properties protect *Serratia* colonies from attack by bacteria, protozoa and fungi, in much the same way that the *Penicillium* mould produces an antibacterial agent that has been co-opted for use by humans. In the fifteenth century, though, *Serratia* colonies growing on the host may very well have been mistaken for blood.

The work of another researcher, Dr Luigi Garlaschelli, backed up Dr Cullen's findings. The renowned organic chemist and part-time debunker of reputed miracles like weeping and bleeding statues examined various food items that were said to have bled spontaneously. To determine whether the 'blood' was real or not, Garlaschelli tested the items for the presence of haemoglobin, the oxygen-carrying pigment that gives vertebrate blood its red colour. In the end, the tests revealed no haemoglobin but plenty of contamination by *S. marcescens*, and the Italian chemist further demonstrated the likely origin of the bleeding hosts by culturing the bacterium on slices of ordinary white bread.

Quite possibly, then, a common microbe contaminated the bleeding hosts of the Middle Ages, which is actually kind of amusing until you realise how many thousands of innocent people were murdered because of this tragic bit of ignorance and misinterpretation.

A final word on the relationship between transubstantiation and cannibalism concerns the Uruguayan survivors of the Old Christians Rugby Club, who employed what became known as the 'communion defence' to justify the incidences of cannibalism that took place after their 1972 plane crash in the Andes. Soon after the sixteen survivors returned to civilisation, positive public opinion over their plight took a knock after it was revealed that the men had remained alive for seventy-two days by consuming the bodies of the dead. Not long after their rescue, and with their hero status now on shaky footing, a press conference was held. Survivor Pablo Delgado, a law student, told reporters that Christ's Last Supper had inspired him and the other survivors. Delgado explained, since Jesus had shared his body with his disciples, it was okay that they had done the same with their deceased comrades. After hearing this explanation, even the sceptics were won over and soon afterwards the Archbishop of Montevideo made it official by absolving the young men. Years later, some of the Andes survivors admitted that relating their cannibalistic acts to the sacrament was actually more of a public-relations exercise than a religious experience. According to survivor Carlos Páez Rodríguez, 'We were hungry, we were cold and we needed to live – these were the most important factors in our decision.'

11

SIEGES, STRANDINGS AND STARVATION: SURVIVAL CANNIBALISM

It is a long road and those who follow it must meet certain risks; exhaustion and disease, alkali water, and Indian arrows will take a toll. But the greatest problem is a simple one, and the chief opponent is Time. If August sees them on the Humboldt and September at the Sierra – good! Even if they are a month delayed, all may yet go well. But let it come late October, or November, and the snow-storms block the heights, when wagons are light of provisions and the oxen lean, then will come a story.

George R. Stewart, *Ordeal by Hunger*

IT WAS LATE JUNE and by the time we arrived at Alder Creek, the air at snout level (which was currently about an inch off the ground) had risen to an uncomfortable 105 degrees Fahrenheit. Kayle, a five-year-old black-and-white border collie, raised her head, searching in vain for a breeze. There was a rustling in the brush nearby and something (probably a chipmunk) provided a welcome distraction to the task at hand. Kayle took a step toward the commotion.

Kayle was in training as an HHRD dog, an abbreviation for Historical Human Remains Detection. In short, Kayle was searching for bodies – old ones.

I hitched my backpack higher and followed, taking a moment to survey the meadow where Kayle slowly sniffed her way in the direction of a large pine tree. At an elevation of 5,800 feet, we were in the foothills of the Sierra Nevada mountain range, just across the Nevada border and into California. It had been a dry spring throughout the American West and the fist-sized clumps of grass that had sprouted from the rocky soil were already turning brown. We'd passed several creek beds and I remembered reading about the muddy conditions that had led to the construction of a low boardwalk for the tourists visiting the incongruously named Donner Camp and Picnic Area.

No need for a boardwalk today, I thought.

We headed further and further away from the trail and into a mountain meadow strewn with wildflowers: orange coloured Indian paintbrush, yellow cinquefoils, purple penstemon. I'd come to the Alder Creek historic site to learn about the Donner Party: probably the most infamous example of cannibalism in US history.

In the summer of 1846 eighty-seven pioneers, many of them children accompanying their parents, set out from Independence, Missouri, for the California coast, eventually taking perhaps the most ill-advised shortcut in the history of human travel. Dreamed up by Lansford Hastings, a promoter who had never taken the route himself, the Hastings Cutoff turned out to be 125 miles longer than the established route to the west coast. It was also a far more treacherous trek, forcing the travellers to blaze a trail through the Wasatch Mountains before sending them on a forty-mile hike across Utah's Great Salt Desert. Tempers flared as wagons broke down and livestock were lost, stolen, or died from exhaustion. People also died, some from natural causes such as tuberculosis, while others were shot or stabbed. As the heat of summer transitioned into the dread of fall, the travellers found themselves in a desperate race to cross the Sierra Nevada before winter conditions turned the high mountain passes into impenetrable barriers. Along the way, sixty-year-old businessman George Donner had been elected leader of the group, though he had no trail experience.

On 26 September 1846 the wagon train finally rejoined the traditional westward route. Hastings's shortcut had delayed the Donner Party an entire month with potentially catastrophic consequences. Disheartened, the pioneers followed the well-worn Emigrants' Trail along the Humboldt river, which by that time of year had been reduced to a series of stagnant pools. As they made their way along the Humboldt, raids by Paiute Indians further depleted their weary and emaciated livestock.

By October, any ideas of maintaining the wagon train as a cohesive unit had been abandoned. Instead, bickering, stress, exhaustion and desperation split the group along class, ethnic and family lines. Those who could not keep up fell further and further behind. Afraid to overburden their oxen or slow down his own family's progress, pioneer Louis Keseberg had informed one of the older men, a Mr Hardcoop (none of the survivors could remember his first name), that he would have to walk. Hardcoop was having an increasingly difficult time with his forced march and eventually he was left behind on the trail. Another elderly bachelor was murdered by two of the teamsters (men tasked with driving the draught animals) accompanying the group.

By the end of October it still appeared that most of the Donner Party had overcome terrible advice, challenging terrain, short rations, injuries and death. With the group now split in two and separated by a distance of nearly ten miles, those accompanying the lead wagons stood before the final mountain pass, three miles from the summit and a mere fifty miles from civilisation. They decided to rest until the following day. But on the night before they were to make their final push, and weeks before the first winter storms usually arrived, disaster struck.

It began to snow.

On the morning of 1 November, the fifty-nine members of the Donner Party in the lead group awoke to discover that five-foot snowdrifts had obliterated the trail ahead, transforming what promised to be a final dash through a breach in the mountains into an impossible task. It soon became apparent that there would be no crossing over the Sierras until the following spring. So the dejected pioneers were forced to turn back, leaving behind the boulder-strewn gap that would become known as the Donner Pass.

A DAY BEFORE OUR TREK across Alder Creek meadow, I had stood with Kristin Johnson and two of her colleagues, John Grebenkemper and Ken Dunn, at the very same spot where the long, cross-country journey of the Donner Party had come to a halt. Looking down from the mountain, I was suddenly impressed by how resourceful and tough the pioneers had been to have made it even this far.

Johnson, an enthusiastic historian and researcher, was living proof that many of the mysteries surrounding the Donner Party remained unsolved, including the one we would be working on at Alder Creek. It was a mystery that involved the leader of the Donner Party and the very person for whom the group had been named.

On 1 November 1846 the pace-setting travellers whose journey had been halted at the mountain pass decided to backtrack several miles to Truckee Lake (now Donner Lake), where they had passed an abandoned cabin that the members of a previous wagon train had constructed two years earlier. Now they would overwinter there. The pioneers quickly built two more cabins and crowded in as best they could.

With the benefit of hindsight, questions have arisen as to why the Donner Party did not simply backtrack another thirty miles, which would have enabled them to overwinter out of the Sierras altogether. A possible explanation was their utter lack of knowledge about exactly where they had chosen to camp. Unlike other wagon trains, they had hired no seasoned mountain-men to guide them.

The twenty-one members of the Donner Party who had lagged behind never even made it to Truckee Lake. Nor did they experience the crushing disappointment of the final mountain pass. A broken wagon axle had halted the group, which included George Donner, his brother Jacob, their families and several teamsters. They eventually made it to the Alder Creek valley, two miles west of the Emigrant Trail and eight miles from the Truckee Lake cabin, when the winter storm caught them completely in the open. According to survivor Virginia Reed, they 'hastily put up brush sheds, covering them with pine boughs'. Although the intention seems to have been to use Alder Creek as a quick rest-stop before a final push into California, the weather and their weakened conditions dictated that, like those stranded at Truckee Lake, there would be no further travel until the spring thaw.

By now, George Donner had been incapacitated by what began as a superficial wound to his hand received while repairing his wagon. As the days and weeks passed, the infection crept up his arm and he would spend the last four months of his life trapped in a draughty shelter built beneath a large pine. Here, the head of the Donner Party would become a helpless observer of the horrors that would soon overtake his family and those who worked for him.

Now the entire party, separated by eight miles and trapped in hurriedly constructed shacks, faced a winter of starvation and madness.

THE DAY AFTER STANDING ATOP Donner Pass, Kristin, John, Ken and I visited Alder Creek, hiking away from the well-worn trails. Kayle led us around an L-shaped stand of ponderosa pines and into a meadow covered with white flowers.

I watched the dog, as, with her nose to the ground, the

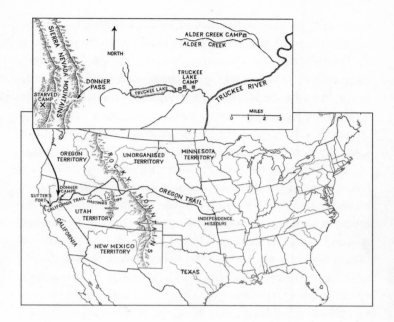

border collie made several passes over a bare-looking patch of earth, halting abruptly several times, only to double back over the same spot. Then she stopped, sat and quickly pointed her nose downward. As my companions and I watched, Kayle stood up, moved about a yard further and repeated the same motion.

John turned to me and explained that these were alerts. I had learned previously that when an HHRD dog detects the scent of decomposed human remains it responds with a trained action like this.

On 16 December 1846 a party of seventeen men, women and children stranded at the Truckee Lake camp fashioned snowshoes and attempted a break-out. Early on, two of them who had started the trip without the makeshift footwear decided to turn back. The group of fifteen, which also included a pair of Miwok Indians who had joined the company in Nevada, would become known as the Forlorn Hope, and they would be making their attempt through the heart of a storm-blasted winter in the country's snowiest region.* According to Kristin Johnson, sometime around 12 January the survivors stumbled into a small encampment of local Indians who gave them what food they could spare (mostly seeds and acorn bread).† They guided the wraith-like figures partway down the mountain but they did so warily. The pitiful travellers were not only frozen, but some of them had also begun to lose their grip on reality.

On 17 January 1847 Forlorn Hope member William Eddy reached the Johnson Ranch, located at the edge of a small farming community in the Sacramento valley. By the time he staggered up to one of the cabins, Eddy looked more like a skeleton than a man. The skin of his face was drawn tightly over his skull and his eyes were sunken deeply into their sockets. His appearance sent the cabin owner's daughter away from her own front door shrieking in terror. Several horrified locals reportedly retraced William Eddy's bloody footprints into the forest and discovered six more survivors – a man and five women. The Forlorn Hope had departed the Truckee Lake camp thirty-three days earlier with barely a week's worth of short rations. Eight of them eventually perished – all males – and, according to Kristin Johnson, 'there's no question' that seven of the dead were cannibalised.

Nearly 160 years later, science writer Sharman Apt Russell wrote about the results of a 1944–45 Minnesota University study on the effects of semi-starvation.

> Prolonged hunger carves the body into what researchers call the asthenic build [i.e. debilitated, lacking strength or vigour]. The face grows thin, with pronounced cheekbones, Atrophied facial muscles

---

* Alternatively known in the literature as the Snowshoe Group; I used the Forlorn Hope to avoid confusion.
† The Nisenan (sometimes referred to as the Maidu) were the indigenous people of the Sierra Nevada foothills.

account for the 'mask of famine', a seemingly unemo-
tional, apathetic stare ... the clavicle looks sharp as a
blade ... Ribs are prominent. The scapula(e) ... move
like wings. The vertebral column is a line of knobs ...
the legs like sticks.

Had modern physicians been present to monitor the
surviving members of the Forlorn Hope, in all likelihood
these unfortunates would have exhibited most of the physiological signs of starvation: low resting metabolic rates (the
amount of energy expended at rest each day), slow, shallow
breathing and lower body temperatures (which would have
been present even without the frigid conditions).* Another
bodily response to starvation is low blood pressure, a condition that can lead to fainting, especially upon standing
up. Like the lethargic movements that characterise starving
people, these physiological changes are the body's involuntary attempts at conserving energy.

Changes in the starved body occur at the biochemical level as well, and in the case of the Donner Party,
their hunger-racked bodies would have begun to consume
themselves. At first, carbohydrates stored in the liver and
muscles would have been broken down into energy-rich
sugars. Fat would have been metabolised next. Depending on the individual, these fat stores could have lasted
weeks or even months. Finally, proteins, the primary structural components of muscles and organs, would have
been broken down into their chemical components: amino
acids. In effect, during the latter stages of starvation, the
body's system of metabolic checks and balances hijacks
the energy it requires, obtaining it from the chemical bond
energy that had previously been used to hold together
complex protein molecules. This protein breakdown (in
places like the skin, bones and skeletal muscles) produces

---

* Fasting or starving people often exhibit increased sensitivity to cold.

the wasted-away appearance that characterises starvation victims.

Besides physiological and behavioural effects of starvation, researchers have identified changes that occur in groups experiencing food shortages or famines. In 1980 anthropologist Robert Dirks wrote that social groups facing starvation go through three distinct phases. During the first, the activity of the group increases, as do 'positive reciprocities'. This can be thought of as an initial alarm response during which group members become more gregarious as they confront and attempt to solve the problem. Although emotions may run high, communal activity increases for a short time. The second phase occurs as the physiological effects of starvation begin to exhibit themselves. During this time, energy is conserved and the group becomes partitioned, usually along family lines. Non-relatives and even friends are often excluded. Acts of altruism decline in frequency with a concurrent increase in stealing, aggression and random acts of violence.

The third or terminal phase of starvation is often characterised by a complete collapse of anything resembling social order. Efforts at cooperation also fall off, even within families. The rate of physical activity also decreases to near zero as the exhausted and starving individuals remain motionless for hours, basically doing nothing. Some victims of starvation do not fall into these broad patterns. These individuals are capable of heroic gestures. They are also capable of murder and cannibalism – and sometimes both.

In *The Cannibal Within*, Lewis Petrinovich argues that this type of cannibalism is an evolved human trait that functions to optimise the chances of survival (and thus, reproductive success). 'It is not advantageous to be a member of another species, of a different race, or even to be a stranger when people are driven by starvation. The best thing to be is a member of a family group, and not be too young or too old.'

ONLY THREE YEARS BEFORE the Minnesota University study, which came to be called the Minnesota Experiment, starvation was taking place on a massive scale in a major European city. For the inhabitants of Leningrad, the horror was far beyond the limits of a supervised research project.

Today known as St Petersburg, Leningrad was a major industrial city and the birthplace of the Russian Revolution. In June 1941 Adolf Hitler launched Operation Barbarossa – a massive, three-pronged assault against the Soviet Union. By September, the nearly three million Leningraders were completely surrounded by German and Finnish forces. With little advance preparation by the local authorities, food shortages and dwindling fuel supplies had become grave concerns. The city's zoo animals were killed and consumed, and soon after people began butchering and eating their pets. Most of the city's food reserves were housed in a series of closely spaced wooden structures that were destroyed after a single bombing raid by the Luftwaffe.

On 29 September 1941 Hitler wrote, 'All offers of surrender from Leningrad must be rejected. In this struggle for survival, we have no interest in keeping even a proportion of the city's population alive'. German commanders were forbidden from accepting any type of surrender from the city's inhabitants. 'Leningrad must die of starvation,' Hitler declared.

With essential supplies all but cut off, living conditions within the embattled city plummeted along with the temperatures, which routinely reached minus 30 degrees Fahrenheit, in what became a winter of record-breaking cold. Although daily artillery and aerial bombardments claimed citizens at random, far more Leningraders died of exposure, sickness and especially starvation. As a result, by December 1941 the unburied dead were accumulating by the tens of thousands.

As conditions worsened, social order began to unravel and violent criminals took to the streets. Leningrad's citizens were robbed or murdered for the food they carried home from the market or for the ration cards that allotted them as little as seventy-five grams of bread per day.*

According to historian David Glantz, 50,000 Leningraders starved to death in December 1941 and 120,000 died in January 1942. Archivist Nadezhda Cherepenina reported that, during the month of February 1942, 'the registry offices recorded 108,029 deaths (roughly 5 per cent of the total population) – the highest figure in the entire siege'.†

Pulitzer Prize-winning *New York Times* correspondent Harrison Salisbury wrote that once the harsh winter took hold, most of Leningrad's population was reduced to eating bark, carpenter's glue and the leather belt drives found in motors. But there were exceptions. 'These were the cannibals and their allies – fat, oily, steely eyed, calculating, the most terrible men and women of their day.'

As rumours of cannibalism swept the city, so too did reports of kidnappings. It was said that children were being seized off the streets 'because their flesh was so much more tender'. Women were apparently a popular second choice because of the extra fat they carried.

'In the worst period of the siege,' a survivor noted, 'Leningrad was in the power of the cannibals.'

Just as ominous, perhaps, was the sudden availability of suspicious-looking meat in Leningrad's central market. The traders were new as well, selling their grisly wares (which they claimed to be horse, dog or cat flesh) to those shoppers with enough money to buy them. According to numerous

---

* In a system designed to maximise industrial output, Leningrad's blue-collar workers received the greatest food allowance, followed by white-collar workers, and finally dependants (who received as little as the equivalent of a slice and a half of additive-adulterated bread per day). Rations were reduced a total of five times between September and November 1941.

† Most estimates put the eventual civilian death toll at somewhere between 800,000 and 1.5 million.

survivor accounts, meat patties made from ground-up human flesh were being sold as early as November 1941.

Also detailed were the gruesome finds made by those assigned to deal with the thousands of dead bodies that were stacking up at the city's largest cemeteries and elsewhere. After dynamiting the frozen ground, '[the men] noticed as they piled the corpses into mass graves that pieces were missing, usually the fat thighs or arms or shoulders'. The bodies of women with their breasts or buttocks cut off were found, as were severed legs with the meat cut away. In other instances, only the heads of the deceased were found. People were arrested for possessing body parts or the corpses of unrelated children.

But beyond the diaries and the accounts of Leningraders who lived through the siege, what other evidence for cannibalism has been uncovered? No physical evidence survives, no bones with cut marks suggestive of butchering or signs that they had been cooked.

As for the official line, a deliberate effort was made to eliminate any reference to this. 'You will look in vain in the published official histories for reports of the trade in human flesh,' Salisbury wrote in 1969, and this remained so until relatively recently. All mention of cannibalism had been purged from the public record – Stalin and other Communist Party leaders wanted to portray Leningrad's besieged citizens as heroes. Leningrad was the first of twelve Russian cities to be awarded the honorary title 'Hero City' for the resilience of its citizens during World War II. Rumours of cannibalism would have cast Leningraders in a far less glorious light.

In 2004 the official reports made immediately after the war by the NKVD (People's Commissariat for Internal Affairs) were released.* They revealed that approximately

---

* The NKVD was the Soviet secret police under Stalin from 1934 to 1943.

2,000 Leningraders had been arrested for cannibalism
during the siege (many of them executed on the spot). In
most instances these were normal people driven by impossible conditions to commit unspeakable acts. Cut off from
food and fuel and surrounded by the bodies of the dead,
preserved by the arctic temperatures, Leningrad's starving citizens faced the same difficult decisions encountered
by other disaster survivors: should they consume the dead
or die themselves? According to an array of independent
accounts as well as those from the NKVD, many of them
chose to live.

Back to the Sierra Nevada, where, on 26 December
1846, only ten days after leaving the Truckee Lake camp, the
members of the Forlorn Hope were lost deep in the frozen
mountains. Only a third of the way into their nightmarish trek, they reportedly decided that without resorting to
cannibalism they would all die. At first the hikers discussed
eating the bodies of anyone who died but soon they began
to debate more desperate measures: drawing straws with
the loser sacrificed so that the others might survive.

The procedure was known to seafarers as 'the custom
of the sea', a measure that provided (at least in theory)

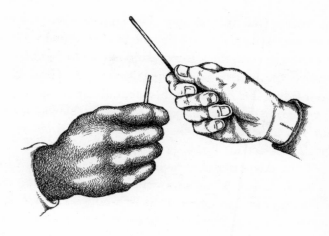

some rules for officers and their men should they find themselves cast adrift on the open ocean. Sailors drew straws, with the short-straw holder giving up his life so that the rest might eat. In some descriptions, the person drawing the next-shortest straw would act as the executioner. Although heroic in concept and theoretically fair in design, modified versions of 'the custom of the sea' were sometimes lacking in either quality.

In perhaps the most famous case, in 1765, a storm demasted the American sloop *Peggy*, leaving her adrift in the Atlantic Ocean. On board were the captain, his crew of nine and an African slave. They had been en route to New York from the Azores with a hold full of wine and brandy. After a month, they had nothing to eat but plenty to drink, a fact driven home when the spooked captain of a potential rescue vessel took one look at the *Peggy*'s raggedy-looking crew of drunks and promptly sailed away. The *Peggy*'s captain, perhaps fearing for his own life, remained in his cabin, armed with a pistol.

Soon after their thwarted rescue, the *Peggy*'s first mate appeared below deck, informing his captain that the men had already eaten the ship's cat, their uniform buttons, and a leather bilge pump. They had decided to draw lots, with the loser served up as dinner. The captain waved the mate away with a loaded pistol but the man returned moments later to report on the lottery results. By an incredible coincidence, the slave had drawn the short straw. Although the 'poor Ethiopian' begged for his life, the captain was unable to prevent the man's murder, later writing that as they prepared to cook the body, one sailor rushed in, tore away the slave's liver and ate it raw.

Three days later the line jumper was said to have gone insane and died. Then, in a demonstration that the crew of the *Peggy* had lost none of its well-honed survival skills, they tossed their mate's body overboard, fearful of the harmful effects of consuming a crazy man. Soon another round of straw-drawing took place, but this time the most popular and competent sailor drew the stubby stick (in this case an inked slip of paper). After hearing his final request that he be killed quickly, the man's drunken shipmates acted accordingly and gave him a twelve-hour reprieve, during which the doomed man reportedly went deaf and lost the remainder of his mind. Just in the nick of time, a rescue ship was spotted. This time, the crew feigned sobriety long enough to be rescued, though the reprieved man reportedly never recovered either his hearing or his sanity.

LOST IN THE SIERRA NEVADA with no food, the members of the Forlorn Hope had also decided to draw lots. Patrick Dolan, a thirty-five-year-old bachelor from Dublin, was the loser. At this point, no one had the heart, or possibly the strength, to carry out the killing. Someone suggested that two of the men fight it out with pistols 'until one or both was slain', but this proposal was also rejected. Two days later, and before they could reconsider their options, a snowstorm rendered such choices unnecessary. Three of the group members, including Patrick Dolan, died during the night.

The next morning, after one of the survivors was able

to light a fire, according to historian Jesse Quinn Thornton, 'his miserable companions cut the flesh from the arms and legs of Patrick Dolan, and roasted and ate it, averting their faces from each other and weeping'. Parts of the other corpses were eaten over the next few days, but it wasn't long before the survivors ran out of food again.

By now the party was exhibiting another symptom of starvation: they were bickering among themselves. A thirty-year-old carpenter, William Foster, reportedly suggested that they kill and eat three of the women (presumably not his own wife), but when this idea failed to take hold he proposed that they the shoot their Indian companions, Luis and Salvador, instead. The two men registered their votes by slipping away from the camp. Foster and the others eventually came upon them somewhere along the trail and there are several versions of what happened next.

In most accounts, Foster murdered the men, about whom little is known except that they had risked their lives on multiple occasions to save the stranded pioneers. In another version of the story, Salvador was already dead when the hikers discovered them and Luis died an hour later. However these men died, there is agreement on what happened next. According to John Sinclair, the *alcalde* (municipal magistrate) of Sacramento, who later presided over hearings related to the tragedy, 'Being nearly out of provisions, and knowing not how far they might be from the settlements, they took their flesh likewise.' Foster, who survived the whole ordeal, was never prosecuted, nor did he garner much blame for the incident. Most descriptions of the murders portray Foster's actions as being those of a decent man deranged by starvation.

Back in the mountain camps, more people were dying, and by the midpoint of the Forlorn Hope's dreadful trek, four men at the Alder Creek campsite, including George Donner's younger brother Jacob, had perished.

Beginning in early 1847, four rescue or relief parties

trekked into and out of the Sierras in fairly rapid succession. They met with varying degrees of success, tempered by cowardice, greed and inhumanity. The weather caused mayhem along the trail, sometimes proving fatal. During the ill-fated Second Relief, a blizzard forced rescuers to abandon two families of Donner Party survivors at what became known as 'starved camp'.* Alone on a mountain trail they thought would lead them to safety, the thirteen starved pioneers huddled in a frozen snow pit for eleven days. Three of them died and the survivors were forced to eat their own dead relatives, including children. They were eventually discovered by members of Third Relief, several of whom led them out of the Sierras and to safety.

One month earlier, in mid-February, First Relief, minus several men who had given up, crossed the high mountain pass where the Donner Party had been halted in November. They set up camp for the night, building their fire on a platform of logs that sat atop snow they estimated to be around thirty feet deep. The following day, seven men descended the eastern slope of the Sierras and set out across the icy expanse of Truckee Lake, arriving at the spot where the survivors of the Forlorn Hope had told them the cabins were located. First Relief member Daniel Rhoads told historian H. H. Bancroft what happened next.

> We looked all around but no living thing except ourselves was in sight and we thought that all must have perished. We raised a loud halloo and then we saw a woman emerge from a hole in the snow. As we approached her several others made their appearance in like manner, coming out of the snow. They were gaunt with famine and I never can forget the horrible, ghastly sight they presented. The first woman

---

* 'Starved camp' is thought to have been in Summit Valley, California, just west of Donner Pass.

spoke in a hollow voice very much agitated and said, 'Are you men from California or do you come from heaven?'

The First Relief rescuers were shocked by the condition of the survivors. Many of the skeletal figures could barely move as they spoke in raspy whispers, begging for bread. Some appeared to have gone mad. Others were unconscious as they lay on beds made of pine boughs. The stunned Californians handed out small portions of food to each of the survivors – biscuits and beef mostly – but that night a guard was posted to ensure that their provisions would remain safe from the starving pioneers.

Outside the cabin, the members of the rescue party saw smashed animal bones and tattered pieces of hide littering the area. Then there were the human bodies, twelve of them, scattered about the campsite, some covered by quilts, others with limbs jutting out of the snow. There were no signs of cannibalism.

The next day the weather broke clear, and three of the First Relievers headed for the Alder Creek camp. In a pair of tent-like shelters they found Tamzene Donner, George's wife, her newly widowed sister-in-law Elizabeth (who could barely walk), the twelve Donner children and several others, including George Donner. Feverish and infirm, his wounded hand had become a slow death sentence.

Taking stock of the situation, Reason Tucker, co-leader of First Relief, knew that they needed to get out of the Sierras before another storm trapped them all there. Tucker's other realisation was a difficult one, for he knew it would be physically impossible for many of the starving pioneers to hike out with them. Some were too young, others too far gone, and although he and his men had cached provisions along the trail, there would not be enough food for the entire group.

Sickly Elizabeth Donner decided that four of her

children would never make it through the deep snow and so they would remain with her at Alder Creek. Tamzene, on the other hand, was healthy enough to travel and she was urged to depart with her five daughters. She refused, insisting that she would never leave George alone to die. She decided to keep her three youngest children with her, presumably waiting for the next relief party, whose arrival they apparently believed to be imminent.

On 22 February six members of the Alder Creek camp hiked out with First Relief accompanied by seventeen others from Truckee Lake. That left thirty-one members of the Donner Party still trapped and starving.

A long week later, members of Second Relief arrived at the mountain camps, but by then conditions at both sites had taken a dramatic downturn. In late 1847 reporter J. H. Merryman published the following account, obtaining his information from a letter penned by Donner Party member James Reed. Exiled earlier in the journey for stabbing a man to death in a fight, Reed had ridden on to California. Now he had returned, leading Second Relief:

> [Reed's] party immediately commenced distributing their provisions among the sufferers, all of whom they found in the most deplorable condition. Among the cabins lay the fleshless bones and half eaten bodies of the victims of famine. There lay the limbs, the skulls, and the hair of the poor beings, who had died from want, and whose flesh had preserved the lives of their surviving comrades, who, shivering in their filthy rags, and surrounded by the remains of their unholy feast looked more like demons than human beings …

And in 1849, J. Q. Thornton (who also interviewed James Reed in late 1847) wrote the following about Reed's entry into one of the Truckee Lake cabins:

The mutilated body of a friend, having nearly all the flesh torn away, was seen at the door – the head and face remaining entire. Half consumed limbs were seen concealed in trunks. Bones were scattered about. Human hair of different colors was seen in tuffs [sic] about the fire-place.

Reed soon headed toward the Alder Creek camp, where Thornton's account continues:

They had consumed four bodies, and the children were sitting upon a log, with their faces stained with blood, devouring the half-roasted liver and heart of the father [Jacob Donner], unconscious of the approach of the men, of whom they took not the slightest notice even after they came up. Mrs. Jacob Donner was in a helpless condition, without anything whatever to eat except the body of her husband, and she declared that she would die before she would eat of this. Around the fire were hair, bones, skulls, and the fragments of half-consumed limbs.

Second Relief departed the camps on 1 March, but their blizzard-interrupted trek out of the mountains would become yet another misadventure.

When the small party of men that made up Third Relief arrived at the mountain camps nearly two weeks later, they found further scenes of horror at the cabins and more dead bodies at Alder Creek. With the last of her surviving children finally accompanying the rescuers, Tamzene Donner turned down one final opportunity to save herself, deciding instead to return to the side of her frail husband. When George Donner died in late March, she wrapped his body in a sheet, said her last goodbyes and headed back to the Truckee Lake camp. It would be Tamzene's final journey. Donner Party member Louis Keseberg, who had not come down from the mountain because of a debilitating wound to his foot, later testified that Mrs Donner had stumbled, half frozen, into his cabin one night. She had apparently fallen into a creek. Keseberg said that he wrapped her in blankets but found her dead the next morning. Sometime after the Fourth Relief (in reality a salvage team) showed up on 17 April, their leader, William Fallon, wrote in his diary, 'No traces of her person could be found.' There was no real mystery, though, since by his own admission Keseberg, whom they had found alive, had eaten Mrs Donner as well as many of those who had died in the mountain camps. In fact he had been eating nothing but human bodies for two months.

On 21 April 1847 Fourth Relief, accompanied by Louis Keseberg, left the Truckee Lake camp and four days later they reached Sutter's Fort (now Sacramento). The last living member of the Donner Party had come down from the mountains.

That summer, General Stephen Kearny and his men were returning east after a brief war with Mexico. They stopped at the abandoned Truckee Lake camp, finding 'human skeletons ... in every variety of mutilation. A more revolting and appalling spectacle I never witnessed', wrote one of Kearny's men.

The general ordered the men in his entourage to bury the dead, but instead they reportedly deposited the mostly mummified body parts in the centre of a cabin before torching it. At Alder Creek, Kearny and his men found the intact and sheet-wrapped body of George Donner. There is no consensus about whether they buried him or not.

ALTHOUGH THE TALE of the Donner Party has become one of the darkest chapters in the history of the American West, time has also transformed it into something else. The dead pioneers who stare at us blankly from cracked daguerreotypes are too often a source of amusement ('Donner Party, your table is ready') and the butt of macabre jokes. To a public that has, for the most part, become anaesthetised to the concepts of gore and gruesome death, the Donner Party is no longer the stuff of nightmares. Instead, any thoughts we might have about these pioneers usually relate to vague notions about cannibalism or perhaps the perils of taking ill-advised shortcuts.

In the spring of 2010 all that changed. The long-dead travellers were back in the news, and this time the story behind the renewed media interest was neither funny nor lurid. It was actually quite remarkable. During the previous decade, an archaeological team from the University of Montana and Appalachian State University unearthed the remains of a campsite at Alder Creek that would become known as the Meadow Hearth. It contained artefacts like cooking utensils, fragments of pottery and percussion caps – small, explosive-filled cylinders of copper or brass that allowed muzzleloaders to fire in any weather. Each of these items dated to the 1840s. There were also thousands of bone fragments and, given the Donner Party's reputation, interest soon centred on whether or not any of these bones were human in origin.

Six years later, the researchers had completed their analysis of the artefacts and were preparing a scientific paper that would detail their findings. Now, though, and before their paper could be published, a spate of articles and news blurbs announced that the scientists had uncovered physical evidence that led them seriously to question the very act for which the Donners had attained their infamy.

'Analysis finally clears Donner Party of rumored cannibalism', read one media report. Even *The New York Times* got into the act. 'No cannibalism among the Donner Party?' read the bet-hedging headline in a *Times*-associated blog. My personal favourite was a headline from a blog post at *The Rat*: 'Science crashes Donner Party.'

So was there any truth to the story of the Donner Party cannibalism?

Initially, the archaeological team working at the Meadow Hearth dig uncovered a thin layer of ash that they eventually determined to be the remains of an 1840s-era campsite. Their efforts also revealed concentrations of charred wood and deposits of burned and calcined bone fragments. The latter occur when bone is subjected to high temperatures resulting in the loss of organic material, like the protein collagen. What's left is a mineralised version of the original bone, and importantly, one that is more resistant to decomposition than it was in its original form. Calcined bone also provides anthropologists with strong evidence that the bones in question were cooked.

All told, the university researchers collected a total of 16,204 bone fragments from the Meadow Hearth excavation, a number that makes it far easier to understand why it took them six years to analyse their data. Unfortunately, not everyone was as patient as the scientists had been, and in 2010, an overeager public relations department at Appalachian State University rushed out a press release claiming: 'The legend of the Donner Party was primarily created by print journalists, who embellished the tales based on their own Victorian macabre sensibilities and their desire to sell more newspapers.'

They went on to add: 'The survivors fiercely denied allegations of cannibalism,' a statement contradicted by Donner Party survivors, rescuers and historians alike. Finally, and as if to further convince the world that Donner Party members were actually humans and not crazed cannibals, the ASU PR crew announced that pieces of writing slate and broken china found near the cooking hearth 'suggest an attempt to maintain a sense of a "normal life", a family intent on maintaining a routine of lessons, to preserve the dignified manners from another time and place, a refusal to accept the harsh reality of the moment, and a hope that the future was coming'.

The response was a predictable media storm. But in reality, the idea that the Meadow Hearth dig's findings proved that there was no cannibalism among the Donner Party was based on a misunderstanding of one of their findings. The PR release had claimed that the discovery of human bones among the varied calcined animal bones found at the site would have been statistically probable 'if humans were processed in the same way animals were processed'. And therein lies the problem, because as it turns out the Donner Party did not process human bones and animal bones in the same way. And here's why.

Of the thousands of bone fragments from the Meadow Hearth examined by researchers, 362 of them showed evidence of human processing. About one quarter of those had abrasions and scratch marks, which indicate that the bones had been smashed into bits. Other pieces of bone exhibited a condition known as 'pot polish', a smoothing of the edges that results from the bones being stirred in a pot. To anthropologists this was another strong indicator that the bone fragments had been cooked.

As starvation set in, the stranded members of the

Donner Party ate whatever they could find. According to historical accounts, they consumed rodents, leather belts and laces, tree bark and a gooey pulp scraped from boiled animal hides. By the end of January 1847 they began consuming their pet dogs. The analysis by Gwen Robbins and her co-workers indicated that bones from several types of mammals had been smashed, boiled and burned by someone at the Alder Creek camp. This would have been done in an effort to render the bones edible, while extracting every bit of nutrient possible. In all likelihood, these would have been the types of last-resort measures undertaken before the survivors resorted to cannibalism, which did not begin in the mountain camps until the last week of February 1847, sometime after the departure of First Relief on 22 February (and before the arrival of Second Relief a week later). The practice of consuming dead bodies continued until the survivors either died or were rescued, and for everyone except the soon-to-be christened Donner Party monster, Louis Keseberg, cannibalism would have lasted only a week or two at most, a vitally important point.

Given the large number of bodies present at the Truckee Lake and Alder Creek campsites, and the short amount of time during which cannibalism occurred, there would have been no need to process human bones in the same manner in which animal bones had been processed previously. Essentially, that's because once cannibalism began at the camps there would have been ample human flesh for the ever-dwindling number of survivors to eat, more than enough to make cooking and recooking the human bones completely unnecessary.

Because uncooked bones would not have been preserved in the acidic soil of the conifer-dense Sierras, there would be no human bones for archaeologists to uncover. Therefore, the absence of calcined human bones from the Meadow Hearth proves only that human and animal bodies were not processed in the same way. The evidence does not place the practice of cannibalism by members of the Alder Creek camp into doubt, nor does it have any bearing whatsoever on the cannibalism that took place at the Truckee Lake camp, within the Forlorn Hope, or at the Second Relief's 'starved camp'.*

IN ADDITION TO GEORGE DONNER, thirty-four members of the Donner Party died in the winter camps or trying to escape them – mostly from starvation and/or exposure. In 1990, anthropologist Donald Grayson conducted a demographic assessment of the Donner Party deaths and came up with some interesting information.

To be expected was the fact that children between one and five years of age, and older people (above the age of forty-nine), experienced high mortality rates (62.5 per cent and 100 per cent, respectively), primarily because both groups are more susceptible to hypothermia.

More surprising was that 53.1 per cent of males (a total of twenty-five) perished while only 29.4 per cent of females died (ten). Additionally, not only did more of the Donner men die, they also died sooner. Fourteen men died

---

* The tale of the Donner Party wasn't the only cannibalism story to emerge from the American West. In February 1874, gold prospector Alfred (or Alferd) Packer led a party of five men into Colorado's San Juan Mountains. When weather conditions deteriorated, preventing their return, he murdered and ate them. When the bodies were discovered the following spring, four of the five had been completely stripped of flesh. Although the skeletons showed evidence of butchery, each was relatively complete and the bones showed no signs of smashing or cooking. Similar to the cannibalism reported to have taken place at the Alder Creek camp, Packer had no need to process the skeletons further – in this case because he presumably had enough meat to survive until the spring. During Packer's sentencing, the judge was rumoured to have made the following statement, 'There were only seven Democrats in Hinsdale County, and you ate five of them, you depraved Republican son of a bitch!'

in between December 1846 and the end of January 1847, while females didn't begin dying until February.

Another intriguing detail is that all eleven Donner Party bachelors (over eighteen years of age) who became trapped in the Sierras died, while only four of the eight married men, travelling with their families, perished during the ordeal.

The explanation for all this is probably a combination of biology and behaviour. Biologically, nutritional researchers believe that three significant physiological differences between males and females come into play during starvation conditions: (1) females metabolise protein more slowly than males (i.e. they don't burn up their nutrients as quickly); (2) female daily caloric requirements are less (i.e. they don't need as much food); and (3) females have greater fat reserves than males, thus more stored energy that can be metabolised during starvation conditions. Also, much of this fat is subcutaneous, located just below the skin, where it functions as a layer of insulation, helping to maintain the body's core temperature during conditions of extreme cold.

The behavioural component of the gender survival differential relates to the fact that the Donner Party men did most of the hard physical labour on the journey, and that ultimately translated to serious health problems once their diets became compromised. Grayson later suggested a scenario that triggered the decline in the previously healthy males:

> [W]hen the Donner Party hacked a trail through the Wasatch range ... it was the men, not the women who bore the brunt of the labor ... There is no way to know exactly how much this grueling labor affected the strength of the Donner Party men, but they surely emerged from the Wasatch Range with their internal energy stores drained, stores they were unable to renew during the long and arduous trip across the Great Basin Desert that followed.

So what about the fact that married men out-survived bachelors by such a wide margin? The reason for this may have to do with differences in the mammalian physiological response to stress, related to blood levels of the hormone cortisol, a steroid hormone released by the adrenal gland. Cortisol is linked to stress and is part of the body's 'fight or flight' response to real or imagined threats. While it can have positive short-term effects, increased plasma levels of cortisol can also lead to decreased cognitive ability, depression of the immune system and impairment of the body's ability to heal.* In a 2010 study, researchers at the University of Chicago looked at hormone levels in test groups composed of married and unmarried college students who were placed in anxiety-filled situations. The bachelors had higher levels of cortisol than did married men subjected to the same levels of stress. Thus the experimenters concluded that 'single and unpaired individuals are more responsive to psychological stress than married individuals, a finding consistent with a growing body of evidence showing that marriage and social support can buffer against stress'.

If one adds these findings to the data from Robert Dirks's study in which one phase of starvation was for groups to become partitioned along family lines, what results is a strong indication as to why all of the mountain-stranded bachelors perished while fully half of their married counterparts survived.

WE'VE ALREADY LEARNED that cannibalism occurs across the entire animal kingdom, albeit more frequently in some groups than others. When the behaviour does happen, it happens for reasons that make perfect sense from an evolutionary standpoint: reducing competition, as a component

---

* The short-term, positive effects of cortisol release include a burst of energy (through an increase in blood sugar levels) and a lower sensitivity to pain (by reducing inflammation).

of sexual behaviour, or an aspect of parental care. Cannibalism in animals is also widely seen as a natural response to stresses like overcrowding and food shortages. The unfortunates involved in shipwrecks, strandings and sieges who have resorted to cannibalism were exhibiting biologically and behaviourally predictable responses to specific and unusual forms of stress. Extreme conditions provoke extreme responses.

Additionally, like the male spiders that give up their lives and bodies to their mates, ultimately increasing the survival potential of their offspring, so too did the bodies of Donner Party members like Jacob Donner serve similar functions for their families.

In cannibalism-related tragedies such as that which befell the Donner Party, survivors have been given something like a free pass for committing acts that would otherwise be considered unforgivable. But where did this taboo come from? Why is the very idea of human cannibalism so abhorrent that it has historically justified the torture, murder or enslavement of its alleged practitioners?

12

CULTURE IS KING: ORIGINS OF THE WESTERN CANNIBALISM TABOO

Baby, baby, naughty baby,
Hush you squalling thing, I say.
Peace this moment, peace or maybe,
Bonaparte will pass this way.
And he'll beat you, beat you, beat you,
And he'll beat you all to pap,
And he'll eat you, eat you, eat you,
Every morsel snap, snap, snap

The Oxford Dictionary of Nursery Rhymes

THE WORD 'TABOO' has a Polynesian origin, and the English explorer and navigator Captain James Cook reported that its use by the South Sea islanders related to the prohibition of an array of behaviours – from eating certain foods to coming into physical contact with tribal leaders. Unfortunately for Cook, the first official link between the terms 'taboo' and 'cannibalism' may have been based on his crew's initial though evidently mistaken fear that Cook himself had been cannibalised.

On 14 February 1779, after what turned out to be a

serious misunderstanding, Cook was clubbed to death by Hawaiian islanders, who then cooked and deboned his body before divvying it out to local chiefs as a way of incorporating him into their aristocracy. Since it was only right that Cook's own people got their share of the body, a charred section of it was returned to Lieutenant James King, who asked the Hawaiians if they had eaten the rest of it. According to King, 'They immediately shewed as much horror at the idea, as any European would have done; and asked, very naturally, if that was the custom among us.' So while the islanders had murdered, cooked and filleted the explorer, they *hadn't* eaten him, though the latter point is often misrepresented in accounts of the incident.

In 1975, historian Reay Tannahill wrote *Flesh and Blood*, the first scholarly study of cannibalism for the general public. Tannahill proposed that Judaeo-Christian customs related to the treatment of the dead contributed to the strongly held belief that eating people was wrong. Specifically, she referred to the 'belief that a man needed his body after death, so that his soul might be reunited with it on Judgement Day'. Since cannibalism involved dismemberment, it was no surprise that these practices induced in Christians and Jews alike 'an unprecedented and almost pathological horror'.

Decades later, others, including journalist and author Maggie Kilgore, addressed questions related to the prevalence of cannibalism taboos. They suggested that in addition to wanting the bodies of the dead to stick around intact until Judgement Day, our picky rituals concerning what foods could or couldn't be eaten (the most famous of which is probably the Jewish ban on eating pork) were just as important when it came to explaining our revulsion at the thought of consuming other humans.

To Kilgore, the term 'you are what you eat' is a reflection of the importance of food as a 'symbolic system used to define personal, national and even sexual differences'. By this logic, she maintains, outsiders and foreigners are often defined in terms of how and, especially, what they eat, and denounced on the grounds that they either have disgusting table manners or eat disgusting things. For example, the derogatory term 'frogs' for French people is based on their consumption of frogs' legs – something the British (who coined the term) would presumably never do. Likewise, calling someone a cannibal becomes a means of using dietary practices (whether real or imagined) to define a particular culture as savage or primitive.

Of course, this leads to the question of whether cannibalism might be more common or more readily accepted in cultures that don't hold similar beliefs about the afterlife or whose adherents follow diets with fewer religious restrictions. First, though, let's investigate how the Western cannibalism taboo became so widespread.

IN ALL LIKELIHOOD, the first mention of something akin to cannibalism in Western literature occurs in Homer's epic poem *The Odyssey*, which dates from approximately the eighth century BCE. On an island stopover, the adventurer Odysseus and his men enter the cave of Polyphemus, a Cyclops. Luckily, the giant is out tending his flock, so the Greeks make themselves at home, lighting a fire, eating some of his cheese and trying to decide what else they can steal. The party ends abruptly when Polyphemus returns home and blocks their exit with an enormous stone. Odysseus tries to bluff his way out, bragging about the city he recently sacked. He also tells Polyphemus to be extremely careful, since he and his pals are under the protection of the gods. The Cyclops, however, is somewhat less than impressed. According to Odysseus:

> Lurching up, he lunged out with his hands towards my
> men and snatching two at once, rapping them on the
> ground he knocked them dead like pups – their brains

gushed out all over, soaked the floor – and ripping them limb from limb to fix his meal he bolted them down like a mountain-lion, left no scrap, devoured entrails, flesh and bones, marrow and all!

After washing down the gruesome meal with milk, the giant falls asleep. The next day, Polyphemus consumes two more of the Greeks for breakfast and another pair for supper, and although Odysseus feels that the jury is still out on his intimidation ploy, his men suggest that he come up with an alternative plan. Soon after, our hero talks the Cyclops into drinking some wine he and his men had brought, claiming they'd intended to present it to him as a gift – before he started eating everybody, that is. After downing three bowlfuls, Polyphemus falls down drunk, 'as wine came spurting, flooding up from his gullet with chunks of human flesh …'

Skirting bits of their partially digested crewmates, the vengeance-minded Greeks reveal an oar-sized piece of wood they had previously sharpened and buried under the sheep dung littering the cave floor. After heating the tip, Odysseus and four mates use it as a battering ram, slamming the point home and poking out the snoozing Cyclops' eye. The following morning, after the blinded Cyclops rolls away the stone to let out his flock, Odysseus and his men make their escape – hanging beneath the bodies of the giant's sheep.

In *Theogony*, Homer's fellow poet Hesiod recounts the tale of Cronos, the Father of the Gods, who learns from his parents (Heaven and Earth) that his own son will one day overthrow him. To prevent this, Cronos eats his first four children, but the youngest, Zeus, is spared when the children's mother hands her husband a rock wrapped in swaddling clothes instead of baby Zeus.

According to classicist Mary Knight, the tale of Cronos suggests an early religious connection with the taboo on eating people, since Zeus would not do to his offspring what his father tried to do to him. She commented, 'The story may thus support cannibalism as a part of the ancient Greek view of a "primitive" past vs. the "civilised" present. Greeks came to see themselves as different, calling all non-Greeks "savages" – people who may have continued eating people.'

Although Polyphemus and Cronos were mythical characters (and not quite humans exactly), this may not have been the case with some of the man-eaters described by another Ancient Greek, Herodotus (c.484–425 BCE). In his *Histories*, he wrote that the Persian King Darius asked some Greeks what it would take for them to eat their dead fathers. 'No price in the world,' they cried. Next, Darius summoned several Callatians, who lived in India and 'who eat their dead fathers'. Darius asked them what price would make them burn their dead fathers upon a pyre, the preferred funerary method of the Greeks. 'Don't mention such horrors!' they shouted.

Herodotus (writing as Darius) then demonstrated a degree of understanding that would have made modern anthropologists proud. 'These are matters of settled custom,' he wrote, before paraphrasing the lyric poet Pindar, 'And custom is King of all.' In other words, society defines what is right and what is wrong. It's worth noting, though, that Herodotus himself strongly disapproved of the practice – and so may have had a hand in spreading the idea that it was a pretty repugnant act, thus helping to propagate a mindset that cannibalism was unacceptable. As such, his combination of history and myth offers important clues about the spread of the cannibal taboo.

Herodotus was also the first writer to document the practice of drawing lots during crises, with the person holding the short straw killed and eaten by his starving comrades. According to the historian, during King Cambyses' expedition to Ethiopia, his men ran out of provisions, and after slaughtering and consuming their pack animals they were reduced to eating grass. Herodotus describes how when they came to the desert, 'some of them did something dreadful'. They cast lots, resulting in one out of ten men being killed and eaten. After learning of this, Cambyses reportedly abandoned the campaign.

The Father of History also wrote extensively about the Scythians, horse-riding barbarian nomads living in the area north of the Black Sea. Among their many strange customs, the Scythians enjoyed smoking marijuana and eating their enemies. Additionally, like Ed Gein, the model for the fictional characters Norman Bates and *The Silence of the Lambs'* Buffalo Bill, Scythian warriors also found some unique uses for human skin and body parts, using severed hands for arrow quivers and carrying around human skins stretched upon frames.

In what may be Herodotus' most influential tale of cannibalism, he recounted the story of Astyages, the last king of the Median Empire. One night, the king awakens from a particularly bad nightmare in which his daughter Mandane '[made] water so greatly that she filled all his city', eventually flooding all of Asia. Several years later, as Mandane is carrying her first child, the king has another bad dream. In this one, an enormous vine grows out of 'his daughter's privy parts' until all of Asia falls under its mighty shade. The Magi are asked to interpret and they attempt to put their king at ease by telling him that Mandane will give birth to a son and that the boy will one day destroy Astyages' empire. Astyages sends his favourite general, Harpagus, to find Mandane and kill her child. Harpagus, however, refuses to spill innocent blood and instead hands the baby to a herdsman and his wife – the latter has just given birth to a stillborn son. The quick-thinking general departs with the body of the dead child, which he delivers to the king.

Ten years later, Mandane's son and his sheep-herding foster-father are granted an audience with King Astyages, who, while talking to the boy, recognises the family resemblance. After some quick calculations, the king realises what his general has done. Astyages sends the boy off with servants, then questions the herdsman, who quickly confesses. Harpagus is summoned and, seeing the herdsman, he attempts to weasel out of the predicament, admitting that he couldn't bring himself to kill the boy. He then tells the king that he did what anyone in his situation would have done – he ordered the herdsman to murder the child.

King Astyages then tells Harpagus: 'No problem, I felt bad about asking you to kill my grandson anyway,' or words to that effect. The general lets out a huge sigh of relief but, before he can relax, the King follows up with an invitation to come to dinner with his son to celebrate. Relieved, Harpagus returns home and instructs his son to head over to the banquet immediately.

According to Herodotus, this is what happened next:

> When Harpagus' son came to Astyages, the king cut his throat and chopped him limb from limb, and some of him he roasted and some he stewed ... When it was dinner hour and the other guests had come, then for those other guests and for Astyages himself there were set tables full of mutton, but, before Harpagus, the flesh of his own son, all save for the head and extremities of the hands and feet; these were kept separate, covered up in a basket.

After the meal, the general is asked by Astyages whether he liked the feast, only then to be shown the open basket containing his son's uneaten body parts.

If this story sounds familiar, that's because it has appeared in several versions since the time of Herodotus. Most notably, William Shakespeare co-opted it for *The Tragedy of Titus Andronicus*. In the Bard's most violent play, Titus, a Roman general, engages in an increasingly gory running battle with his arch enemy, Tamora, the Queen of the Goths. Late in the play, and after his daughter has been raped and mutilated by Tamora's two sons, Titus exacts his revenge. He kills the siblings and has their bodies baked in a pie, which he serves at a banquet to the queen and her husband, Saturninus. After Titus reveals his secret ingredient, things go haywire when Titus kills Tamora, Saturninus kills Titus, and Titus's son kills Saturninus.*

It's also possible that Shakespeare may have derived inspiration from Seneca's first-century Roman tragedy *Thyestes*, in which the title character not only tricks his twin brother, Atreus, out of the throne of Mycenae but also takes his sister-in-law as a lover. Thyestes continues by chiding Atreus that he can have the throne back as soon as the sun moves backward in the sky. Zeus however, overhears the taunt and 'drives the day back against its dawning', and Thyestes is forced to surrender the throne. Atreus, though, isn't done with his sibling and after learning of his wife's infidelity he invites Thyestes to a reconciliatory banquet. As part of the preparations, Atreus murders Thyestes' two sons from the forbidden relationship and serves them to their unsuspecting father. At dinner's end, Atreus presents Thyestes with the hands and heads of his slain children on a platter, hence the term Thyestian Feast, defined as one at which human flesh is served.

In short, from the ancient Greeks to William Shakespeare, and in stories written across a span of 2,500 years, cannibalism was depicted as either the ultimate act of revenge or the gruesome work of gods, monsters and savages. By the seventeenth and eighteenth centuries, with the taboo firmly established, the threat of cannibalism

---

* An alternative source for Shakespeare's cannibal scene may have been the Roman poet Ovid (43–17 or 18 BCE), who also lifted Herodotus' story of Astyages for parts of his own lyric poem, *Metamorphoses*.

would reach a new audience and serve a new purpose – as a way to terrorise children into behaving.

Jakob and Wilhelm Grimm (born in 1785 and 1786, respectively) were German academics who collected oral folk tales during the early 1800s. They did so by interviewing peasants, servants, the middle classes and aristocrats, and they published hundreds of fairy tales between 1812 and 1818. In the parade of new editions that followed, the brothers changed, added and subtracted stories, depending on their reception. Like the ancient Greek and Roman myths, the original fairy tales depicted violence, desire, heartbreak and fear. They also portrayed the all-too-common hardships of their own time – famine and the abandonment of children by destitute parents. The language was often scatological and, as such, many of the revisions were carried out so as to make them a little more child-friendly.

As the Grimms sanitised these tales for a much younger readership, themes were also modified. But rather than moulding them into the bedtime stories familiar to modern readers, the brothers transformed them into cautionary tales, many of which ended badly for those children who chose not to obey their parents. On one level at least, fairy tales can be seen as literary relics from a time when terror was an accepted educational tool. Grimm's fairy tales were tools employed by parents to socialise children, to increase their moral standing and to frighten them into obeying the directives of their elders.

The Grimm brothers were preceded as writers by Charles Perrault (1628–1703), a French writer whose 1697 *Histoires ou contes du temps passé*, provided readers with what may have been the earliest written collection of fairy tales. His most famous book, subtitled *Les Contes de ma Mère l'Oie (Tales of Mother Goose)* contained eight stories, including 'Red Riding Hood', 'Sleeping Beauty' and 'Puss in Boots', and its public reception elevated the fairy tale into a new literary genre. Perrault's fairy tales often contained a heavy dose of cannibalism. For example, most children and adults will recall that the wicked queen in 'Snow White' wanted the title character killed. Less familiar, perhaps, is that in the original tale the queen orders a huntsman not only to murder Snow White but also to return with her liver and lungs as proof that the deed had been done. Taking pity on the innocent beauty, the hunter slays a boar instead and brings the queen the entrails. Then, in a scene Disney somehow omitted, the misled monarch cooks up the offal in a stew, which she eats, thinking she has seen the last of Snow White.

An equally disturbing revelation is found in the source material for the Perrault fairy tale 'Little Red Riding Hood'. In the original French peasant tale from the tenth century, as translated by Paul Larue and reported by scholar Jack Zipes, instead of gobbling down the old woman whole (so that she can later emerge Jonah-like from his bisected belly), the wolf murders the old woman and cuts her up – storing pieces of her in the cupboard, along with a bottle of her blood. When Red Riding Hood arrives, the creature directs her to the cabinet, saying, 'Take some of the meat which is inside and the bottle of wine on the shelf.' After unknowingly eating her own grandmother and drinking her blood, Red strips and the wolf tosses her clothes into the fire. She then gets into bed with the hirsute granny and soon after, escapes by convincing the creature that she needs to go outside for a wee.

In Perrault's 'Hop o' My Thumb', seven young brothers, led by Little Thumb, the smallest but smartest sibling, are abandoned in the forest by their destitute parents in a time of great famine. A kindly woman, who turns out to be the wife of a cruel ogre who eats little children, eventually takes in the lost kiddies. In the nick of time, she hides them under a bed as her giant husband returns, but soon he smells 'fresh meat' and drags the children out from their hiding place. Even as the kids fall to their knees, begging for mercy, the ogre is already 'devouring them in his mind'.

The story ends badly for the ogre who, thanks to Little Thumb, slits the throats of his own seven daughters by mistake. Adding to the ogre's misery, Little Thumb manages not only to steal his magic boots but also to con Mrs Ogre out of all of their money. One moral of this story is that you should not knife anyone in a darkened room where your kids are sleeping. Another appears to be that child-eating cannibals don't live happily ever after.

The Brothers Grimm revisited a similar plot in 'Hansel and Gretel', which also detailed the abandonment of the young and the threat of cannibalism. The story begins with a concise and vivid portrayal of famine ('great scarcity fell on the land') but in the Grimm's tale, rather than an ogre's wife, a kindly old woman takes in the lost brother and sister. The hag, however, quickly reveals both her true identity and her intentions after she locks Hansel in the stable. 'When he is fat I will eat him,' she cackles, and later, 'Let Hansel be fat or lean, tomorrow I will kill him and cook him.'

Other fairy-tale writers also employed cannibalism to dramatic effect, most notably Englishman Benjamin Tabart (1776–1833) in his 1807 story 'The History of Jack and the Beanstalk'. Tabart, like Perrault and the Brothers Grimm, based his tale on older oral tellings of the story. Although the tale existed in many versions, it is Tabart's that would become definitive.

In his rendition, Jack is 'indolent, careless, and extravagant' and his actions bring his mother to 'beggary and ruin'. Trading in the family's milk cow to a stranger for a handful of seeds seems like a typical move for this lame incarnation of Jack but, of course, things get interesting when his mother tosses the seeds away and an enormous beanstalk shoots up just outside their cottage. Climbing the ladder-like stem, Jack meets a curiously tall woman and asks her for some breakfast. 'It's breakfast you'll be if you don't move off from here,' she tells him. 'My man is an ogre and there's nothing he likes better than boiled boys on toast.' But Jack is starving and, ignoring the danger, he convinces the wife to bring him back to her place for a bite. Soon enough, though, the ground is rumbling and Jack barely has time to jump into the oven before the giant bursts in, reciting the famous lines:

Fee-fi-fo fum,
I smell the blood of an Englishman,
Be he alive, or be he dead
I'll have his bones to grind my bread.

Unimpressed, his wife tells him that he's probably dreaming, 'Or perhaps you smell scraps of the little boy you liked so much for yesterday's dinner.' Satisfied, the ogre has his breakfast before settling down for a nap. Jack, showing just how thankful he is to have been spared, promptly steals not only the couple's gold and a harp that plays itself but also a goose that lays golden eggs. Next, after somehow hauling all of this loot down, Jack shows off his logging skills by cutting down the beanstalk just in time to send the ogre plummeting to his death.

In Joseph Jacob's revised epilogue, a 'good fairy' shows up and informs everyone that the giant had actually stolen the gold from Jack's late father. With the theft and killing justified, 'Jack and his mother became very rich, and he married a great princess, and they lived happily ever after.'

In story after story, the Grimms, Perrault and other fabulists piled on scenes of cannibalism or, at the very least, its threat, reinforcing the idea, for readers of all ages, that cannibalism was the stuff of nightmares and naughty children.

BEYOND THE HISTORIANS, playwrights, poets and compilers of fairy tales, there were others who contributed to our culturally ingrained ideas about cannibalism. Three of the most influential were the writer Daniel Defoe, Scottish anthropologist Sir James George Frazer and the founder of psychoanalysis Sigmund Freud.

Born in London in 1660 as Daniel Foe, Daniel Defoe eventually changed his name in an effort to conceal his lower-class origins. It was a childhood during which he survived not only London's Great Plague in 1665 but also the Great Fire the following year. After abandoning a troubled career as a businessman, Defoe began writing books, pamphlets and poems – many of them with a political bent. *Robinson Crusoe*, published in 1791, was his most famous work and by the end of the nineteenth century it had become a worldwide phenomenon.

The plot of *Robinson Crusoe* follows the decades-long adventures of the shipwrecked title character as he struggles to survive on a tropical island, possibly based on Tobago in the Caribbean. After establishing a relatively comfortable life for himself, Crusoe knows that the most serious threat to his safety comes from the man-eating savages who frequent the island. These wretches, the reader is informed, battled each other in canoes with the victors killing and eating their prisoners Carib-style. This grim predilection for murder and the consumption of human flesh is spelled out in sensational detail when the castaway comes upon the remains of a cannibal feast on the beach.

> I was perfectly confounded and amazed; nor is it possible for me to express the horror of my mind at seeing the shore spread with skulls, hands, feet, and other bones of human bodies; and particularly I observed a place where there had been a fire made, and a circle dug in the earth ... where I supposed the savage wretches had sat down to their human feastings upon the bodies of their fellow-creatures.

After spewing his lunch (the suitable response of any civilised Englishman), Crusoe hurries back to his side of the island and his 'castle', where, for the next two years he fixates about 'the wretched, inhuman custom of their devouring and eating one another up'. Crusoe fantasises gruesome plans for revenge, including one in which he sets off explosives under the cannibal cooking pit and another in which he blows off their heads from a sniper's nest. While brooding over his own obsession, Crusoe begins to doubt whether the savages actually knew that they were committing horrendous crimes. In what might seem to the modern reader a rare instance of eighteenth-century clarity on the topic of Columbus and those who followed him, Crusoe wonders whether killing the cannibals would 'justify the conduct of the Spaniards in all their barbarities practised in America, where they destroyed millions of these people'.

Initially, the fictional castaway decides to steer clear of the savages but he winds up killing one of them while rescuing Friday – a cooking-pot escapee, who is himself a cannibal. Once the main party of man-eaters departs, Crusoe and Friday return to the scene of the cannibal feast: 'The place was covered with human bones, the ground dyed

with their blood, and great pieces of flesh left here and there, half eaten, mangled, and scorched ... All the tokens of the triumphant feast they had been making there, after a victory over their enemies.'

After piling up the body parts and setting them ablaze, Crusoe observes that Friday 'still had a hankering stomach after some of the flesh', and he lets the savage know in no uncertain terms that death awaits should he give in to his cravings. Friday quickly gets his own point across (presumably via gestures, given that the two men don't share a common language) that he 'would never eat man's flesh any more'.

Years later, Crusoe and Friday come upon another cannibal banquet, and this time the next course appears to be Bearded White Castaway. At this point, all of Crusoe's previously developed ideas about non-involvement in local customs are put to the test. After downing a few shots of rum, the castaway and his sidekick ('now a good Christian') wade in, and 'Let fly ... in the name of God,' slaughtering seventeen or eighteen of the twenty-one man-eaters, with guns, swords and a hatchet.

Robinson Crusoe had a major impact on readers all over the world. According to University of Sorbonne professor of literature Frank Lestringant, 'Defoe's work is an effective contribution to the black legend of the Cannibals. It represents the normal English attitude towards them throughout the ages of discovery and colonisation.' In short, cannibalism was an abomination and cannibals were to be avoided, since God would ultimately sort out their fate. But if that didn't work, anyone who practised man-eating could be enslaved or killed by any method no matter how cruel or gruesome it might appear.

In 1890, James Frazer produced *The Golden Bough: A Study in Magic and Religion*, a massive, globe-spanning, comparative work on mythology and religion. Much of this material was accompanied by a hefty dose of archaeological support and Frazer's enormously popular compendium of rites, practices and religions greatly influenced the emerging discipline of anthropology. Throughout his magnum opus, Frazer discussed the practice of cannibalism, and other barbarous customs. He also advised his readers not to be fooled into 'judging the savage by the standard of European civilisation'.

Frazer pointed to several African tribes whose religious rites included 'the custom of tearing in pieces the bodies of animals and of men and then devouring them raw ... Thus the flesh and blood of dead men are commonly eaten and drunk to inspire bravery, wisdom, or other qualities for which the men themselves were remarkable.' According to Frazer, this type of cannibalism also took place among the mountain tribes of south-eastern Africa, the Theddora and Ngarigo tribes of south-eastern Australia, the Kamilaroi of New South Wales, the Dyaks of Sarawak, the Tolaalki of Central Celebes, the Italones and Efugao of the Philippines, the Kai of German New Guinea, the Kimbunda of western Africa and the Zulus of southern Africa.

During the first half of the twentieth century, *The Golden Bough* influenced an array of major authors including Joseph Campbell, T. S. Eliot, Robert Graves, James Joyce, D. H. Lawrence, Ezra Pound and William Butler Yeats. Frazer's work also became an enormously popular resource for the budding anthropologists who were beginning to trek into some of the most remote regions on the planet. Although each subsequent generation found flaws in Frazer's work or had to modify certain aspects of it, there is little doubt that his stance on the prevalence of cannibalism among indigenous people coloured the mindset of many. As a result, when such groups were encountered they were assumed to be savages whose behavioural repertoire would likely encompass all manner of strange rites, including cannibalism. Contributing to this attitude was perhaps the most well known of these new anthropologists, Margaret

Mead. She was famously quoted about some of the Pacific islanders she was studying, 'The natives are superficially agreeable but they go in for cannibalism, headhunting, infanticide, incest, avoidance and joking relationships, and biting lice in half with their teeth.'

Anthropologists were not the only professionals talking about cannibalism and the primitive mind. For Freud, it denoted a pre-cultural stage of human development. In *Totem and Taboo*, Freud borrowed Darwin's concept of a patriarchal horde, where a single mature male ruled over a harem of females. Immature males ('the brothers'), who were forbidden to mate, also belonged to this primitive social group. Freud assumed that these fellows would be quite grumpy and, as such, he proposed that they were hot to initiate some revision of the prehistoric status quo. They did so by killing their father, thus putting an end to the patriarchal horde. 'Cannibal savages as they were, it goes without saying that they devoured their victim as well as killing him' – each of the sons acquiring a measure of their father's strength. In order to commemorate the event, the brothers organised a totem feast, which Freud described as 'mankind's earliest festival'. This, though, was no ordinary party, since it marked the beginning of social organisation, moral restrictions and religion. Once cannibalism and its partner incest were abandoned, the group in question would be firmly on the road to civilisation – echoing the sentiment of early explorers and missionaries as they encountered indigenous cultures.

Freud also went on to say that taboos (cannibalism included) represent forbidden actions for which there exist strong and unconscious predispositions – primitive urges buried deep within each of us. From a zoological perspective, these 'primitive urges' can be seen as further evidence that we humans are, to paraphrase Stephen J. Gould, a part of nature, not apart from nature.

We are also, however, a lineage that has diverged greatly

during our long evolution – and the more recently added or modified sections of our genetic code have seen us evolve away from the behaviour of spiders, mantises and fish (though less so from our fellow mammals). Of course, a significant part of that divergence is that humans are cultural creatures. As such, for some of us the very underpinnings of our Western culture, starting with our literature, dictate that unless we are placed into extreme circumstances, certain practices, like cannibalism, are forbidden. But what about cultures where those taboos were never established?

13

CHINA: BEYOND THE
WESTERN TABOO

I think there is nothing barbarous and savage in that nation,
from what I have been told, except that each man calls barbarism
whatever is not his own practice; for indeed it seems we have no
other test of truth and reason than the example and pattern of the
opinions and customs of the country we live in.

Michel de Montaigne, *Of Cannibals*

ONE WAY TO SUPPORT a hypothesis that the origin, spread
and persistence of the Western cannibalism taboo can be
traced along a line leading back to the ancient Greeks would
be to find a culture with an extensive historical record that
existed for millennia without the significant influences of
Homer, Herodotus and the Western writers who followed
them.

Among many of the cultures that definitely weren't
reading the Greek mythology (the Aztecs and Caribs come
to mind), there is little if any proof as to their definitive
stance on cannibalism. While there is a significant body
of evidence regarding the Aztec practice of human sacrifice, which was clearly depicted in both carved inscriptions
(glyphs) and bark-paper books known as codices, there is
no such consensus among historians that the Aztecs ever

practised cannibalism, especially on a large scale. And while a few Spaniards present in Mexico during the Aztec conquest provided written accounts of cannibalism, sceptics might question whether such sources are genuinely reliable witnesses. Since there is no conclusive evidence that the behaviour was practised by either the Aztecs or Caribs, we need to look elsewhere for a group not influenced by the Ancient Greeks.

So, are there are non-Western cultures where we can find a different, more accepting, attitude to cannibalism? Surprisingly, to find evidence of this you need go not to the Wari' of Brazil or the Fore of New Guinea, but to China, whose leaders have maintained what is apparently the world's longest unbroken historical record. How did the Chinese deal with cannibalism – historically and in modern times?

There is general agreement among recent scholars that China has a long history of cannibalism.* The evidence comes from an array of Chinese classics and dynastic chronicles, as well as an impressive compendium of eyewitness accounts, the latter providing some unsparingly gruesome details about many of the most recent incidents.

In *Cannibalism in China*, historian Key Ray Chong specified two forms of cannibalism: survival cannibalism, which might occur during a siege or famine, and learned cannibalism, which the author described as, 'an institutionalized practice of consuming certain, but not all, parts of the human body'. He describes learned cannibalism as being publicly and culturally sanctioned, making it synonymous with the term 'cultural cannibalism'.

As we have already seen, survival cannibalism was not unique among the Chinese, but the practice is worth discussing for several reasons – not the least of which was the

---

* These authors include Jasper Becker, Key Ray Chong, Yang Jisheng, Lewis Petrinovich and Zheng Yi.

frequency with which it occurred in China, coupled with a succession of governments whose responses varied from turning a blind eye to something close to official sanction. Perhaps the saddest and most surprising case (and the one with the greatest death toll) actually occurred in the mid-twentieth century, when starvation and cannibalism were only two aspects of a national calamity of unprecedented scope.

Chong's investigation provides three examples of siege-related cannibalism recorded in Chinese classical literature. The oldest instance took place during a war between the states of Ch'u and Sung in 594 BCE and occurred in the Sung capital city. It was also notable because it was apparently the first time that starving Chinese began exchanging one another's children, so that they could be consumed by non-relatives – a practice made permissible by an imperial edict in 205 BCE. The other examples took place in 279 BCE in the besieged cities of Ch'u and Chi-mo, and in 259 BCE in the city of Chao. In the latter instance, soldiers defending a castle reportedly cannibalised servants and concubines, followed by children, women and men 'of low status'.

In total, Chong's exhaustive research efforts yielded 153 and 177 occurrences of cannibalism linked to war and natural disaster, respectively. With no statistical difference in the numbers reported from the Han Dynasty (206 BCE–CE 220) to the Ch'ing Dynasty (1644–1912), incidences of cannibalism in which varying numbers of people were consumed seem to have been fairly consistent throughout China's long history. But rather than the decrease in reports of cannibalism one might expect to find in modern times, the opposite turns out to be true. The greatest number of deaths by cannibalism in China came as a direct result of Mao Zedong's 'Great Leap Forward' from 1958 to 1961.

This government programme produced the worst famine in recorded history – a continent-spanning disaster in which at least 30 million, mostly rural, Chinese died of starvation.

In an effort to transform China's primarily agrarian economy into a modern communist society based on industrialisation and collectivisation, Mao Zedong, Chairman of the People's Republic, ordered nearly three quarters of a billion farmers to move from private farms to massive agricultural collectives. More often than not, these communal farms were run by government officials who had no farming experience at all. To make matters worse, Mao had them institute an anti-scientific agricultural programme that had sprung from the brain of semi-literate Soviet peasant Trofim Lysenko in the late 1920s. Lysenkoism initially led to a deadly purge of Russian scientists and intellectuals. Eventually, it set the Soviet Union's agricultural system back at least fifty years and resulted in millions of deaths by starvation.

Lysenko rejected the idea of selective breeding techniques, especially those based on Mendelian genetics. Instead he proposed his own muddled version of Jean-Baptiste Lamarck's early-nineteenth-century theory that environmental factors produce needs or desires within an organism that lead to new adaptations. Lamarck's infamous giraffes, their necks stretching and lengthening in an effort to reach leaves in an ever-higher tree canopy, remain a common misconception of how variation in traits like colour or size could be generated in any given population. Lamarck, trained as a naturalist, believed that the giraffes willed these changes to occur – changes that would then be passed on to future generations.

In Lysenko's interpretation, the organisms exhibiting these needs and desires were crop plants like corn, wheat and vegetables. In that regard, he boasted that he could grow citrus trees in Siberia by cold-storing the seeds the previous year. These sorts of preposterous claims went on for decades, with those who questioned Lysenko's ideas either eliminated or afraid to make their voices heard.

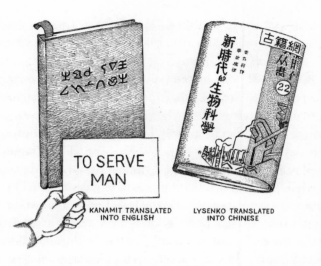

KANAMIT TRANSLATED
INTO ENGLISH

LYSENKO TRANSLATED
INTO CHINESE

Not to be outdone by the Russians, Mao decided to install an 'improved' version of Lysenko's agricultural programme in China. Instead of planting seeds apart from each other, for example, Mao instructed that they be 'close planted', since rather than competing for resources like water and nutrients, the tightly packed plants would, like the farmers Mao had packed into enormous communal farms, help each other to grow. The seedlings invariably died, although farmers were coerced into pretending that mature plants were so densely compacted that children could stand on them. Photographs depicting this 'miracle' were achieved by having the kids stand on a bench, hidden from view. Another of Mao's brainstorms led to war being declared on sparrows, with the subsequent success of farmers' efforts reflected by a concurrent increase in crop-munching insect populations.

Those who wrote about the catastrophe often did so at their own peril, but what they uncovered was truly shocking. For example, in *Mubei* (*Tombstone*), Yang Jisheng wrote that famine-starved 'people ate tree bark, weeds, bird droppings, and flesh that had been cut from dead bodies, sometimes of their own family members'. The author, who lost his father to starvation, also believes that 36 million deaths is a more accurate number, although some estimates run as high as 46 million.

Combined with forced collectivisation and a purge of expertise, the Great Leap Forward ended in catastrophe. Agricultural output (mostly grain) fell significantly, even though local officials grossly inflated their actual production numbers to curry favour with Mao. This imaginary surplus led to increases in government quotas, so that most of what was produced was immediately confiscated by the state and even exported. Meanwhile, the farmers and rural populations starved. Farm animals were eaten, then pets and finally the bodies of the dead, especially children. Foreign correspondent Jasper Becker, former bureau chief of the *South China Morning Post*, wrote: 'Travelling around the region over thirty years later, every peasant that I met aged over fifty said he personally knew of a case of cannibalism in his production team ... Women would usually go out at night and cut flesh off the bodies, which lay under a thin layer of soil, and this would then be eaten in secrecy.'

Critics of Mao's system were imprisoned or murdered and thousands of farmers were accused of hoarding grain and tortured to death. Fortunately, the Great Leap Forward, which was conceived as a five-year plan, was abandoned three years in. But although Chinese rulers looked the other way as starving populations consumed their dead, the cannibalism that took place was more of a necessity than a choice. These instances of survival cannibalism do not, therefore, definitively prove the absence of a cultural taboo against cannibalism in China.

Yet, under the banner of learned cannibalism, the Chinese appear to exhibit attitudes that differ significantly from those held in the West. For a start, Key Ray Chong provides a list of circumstances that might lead to an act of learned cannibalism. These were 'hate, love, loyalty, filial piety, desire for human flesh as a delicacy, punishment, war, belief in the medical benefits of cannibalism, profit, insanity, coercion, religion, and superstition'. Some of these, it seems, are uniquely Chinese.

As anyone who has ever visited China (or to a lesser extent any big-city Chinatown) can attest, the Chinese consume a diverse range of creatures and their body parts. Many of these, like scorpions and chicken testicles, fall outside the range of typical Western diets – but does this have any bearing on the possible leap to eating human flesh? Perhaps, since as Maggie Kilgore pointed out in 1998, some items like rats, snakes, shellfish and creatures with paws are proscribed (at least in theory) by religions that follow Judaeo-Christian law, then maybe it should not come as such a surprise that the Chinese, with no such list of forbidden foods, had fewer qualms about consuming other humans.

Chong devoted an entire chapter of his book on cannibalism to 'Methods of Cooking Human Flesh' with the subheading 'Baking, Roasting, Broiling, Smoke-drying, and Sun-drying'. And rather than an emergency ration consumed as a last resort, there are many reports of exotic human dishes prepared for royalty and upper-class citizens. T'ao Tsung-yi, a writer during the Yüan Dynasty (1271–1368), wrote that 'children's meat was the best food of all in taste', followed by women and then men. In *Shui Hu Chuan (Outlaws of the Marsh)*, a novel written in the twelfth century, there are numerous references to steamed dumplings stuffed with minced human flesh, as well as a rather nonchalant attitude among merchants and customers regarding the sale of human meat.

Even if epicurean cannibalism wasn't limited to the Chinese, the extent to which it was set down in detail certainly was. Amidst information on 'five regional cuisines' (Szechwan, Canton, Fukien, Shantung and Honon), the *San Kuo Yen Ki (Romance of the Three Kingdoms)*, written in 1494, contained 'many examples of steaming or boiling human meat'. Prisoners of war were preferred ingredients but when they ran out (figuratively or literally), General Chu Ts'an's soldiers seized women and children off the street, killed them then ate them. As recently as the nineteenth century, executioners reportedly ate the hearts and brains of the prisoners they executed, selling whatever cuts were left to the public.

Widespread epicurean cannibalism was still taking place in the late 1960s during the Cultural Revolution, although there was certainly an element of terror involved. Chinese dissident journalist Zheng Yi wrote the following in 2001:

> Once victims had been subjected to criticism, they were cut open alive, and all their body parts – heart, liver, gallbladder, kidneys, elbows, feet, tendons, intestines – were boiled barbecued, or stir-fried into a gourmet cuisine. On campuses, in hospitals, in the canteens of various governmental units at the brigade, township, district, and country levels, the smoke from cooking pots could be seen in the air. Feasts of human flesh, at which people celebrated by drinking and gambling, were a common sight.

Another form of cannibalism in China had nothing to do with persecution and punishment. Chong reported that, 'children would cut off parts of their body and make them into soup to please family members, particularly their parents'. This led him to study what he considered to be a truly unique aspect of learned cannibalism among the Chinese – its association with the Confucian philosophy of filial piety. In general terms, filial piety is a highly regarded virtue in which it is the duty of younger family members to demonstrate respect, obedience and care for their parents and elderly family members. In this case, however, it refers to an extreme act of self-sacrifice, with relatives providing parts of their own bodies for the consumption and benefit of their elders.

Although by no means a complete list, Chong used official historical records and came up with a total of 766 documented cases of such filial piety, spanning a period of over 2,000 years. The practice took place primarily between sons and fathers, sons and mothers, and daughters and mothers.* The most commonly consumed body part was the thigh, followed by the upper arm, both of which were prepared in a rice porridge called congee. Far less frequent, but recorded nonetheless, were instances where a young person volunteered a part of their liver, breast, finger or even eyeball.†

In each case, the practice was intended to provide nutrition to a starving loved one or as a treatment of last resort, to afford the sufferer some medical benefit – more on medicinal cannibalism in Chapter 14.

So, is there any link between the practice of filial cannibalism in humans and that exhibited in the animal kingdom by species like mouth-brooding cichlids? One similarity is that in both instances the parent gains a benefit at the expense of the offspring. In humans, though, culture dictates that the offspring consciously initiate the act of filial cannibalism.

In addition to the historical record of cannibalism contained within China's dynastic histories, the behaviour in its various incarnations is also abundantly documented in plays, poems and other works of fiction. For example, the fifteenth-century play *Shuang-zhong ji* (*Loyalty Redoubled*) tells of a general coming up with the idea of turning his concubine into soup to feed his besieged and starving troops. Happily, for the general at least, the concubine volunteers for this duty, thus sparing the general from having

---

* Rarely, this exchange took place between daughters-in-law and fathers-in-law, and between daughters-in-law and mothers-in-law.
† Although 'an official edict in 1261 banned cutting out the liver or plucking out the eyeballs'.

to murder an innocent woman. The concubine's devotion spurs the soldiers to fight on, which leads another servant (this one a boy) to volunteer his own body.

According to numerous sources, then, the practice of cannibalism in China was more or less accepted as a necessity during times of famine, as a right to be exercised during warfare and acts of vengeance, and as a way of honouring one's relatives. Similarly, there appear not to have been such widespread taboos regarding the behaviour as there are in the West.

But if I've given you the impression that cannibalism did not occur in the West, that would be an error. It was actually a common practice in Europe, where it was carried on in various forms into the twentieth century. It is also being practised today in the United States.

14

SKULL MOSS AND MUMMY POWDER: MEDICINAL CANNIBALISM

The ancients were very eager to embalm the bodies of their dead, but not with the intention that they should serve as food and drink for the living as is the case at the present time.

Ambroise Paré (1582)

THE CONSUMPTION OF PULVERISED human bones or organs in order to treat some malady falls under the general heading of 'medicinal cannibalism', which is, once you consider it, a form of ritual cannibalism. But however it's classified, the practice is as interesting as it is little known. It turns out that medicinal cannibalism was once widespread throughout Western culture, although reference to it has essentially disappeared from the historical record. The same, however, cannot be said for the Chinese, whose literature, medical texts and historical accounts span over 2,000 years and contain detailed descriptions of the preparation and use of body parts as curatives.

The first documented use of organs and human flesh to cure diseases in China took place during the Han Dynasty (CE 25–220), and medicinal cannibalism became increasingly popular beginning in the Tang Dynasty (618–907), when it became associated with filial piety. By the end of the Ch'ing Dynasty (1644–1912), Western missionary doctors were reporting that the Chinese medical treatments included the consumption of 'the gall bladder, bones, hair, toes and fingernails, heart and liver'. Thomas Chen, a pathology professor at the New Jersey Medical School, tells us that 'nail, hair, skin, milk, urine, urine sediments, gall, placenta and even flesh' were used in China for a variety of medicinal purposes.

But what about the reports of medicinal cannibalism in Europe (which took place into the twentieth century)? Considering how outraged the Spanish were upon learning about the man-eating behaviour of the indigenous people of the Caribbean, one might assume that cannibalism of any kind would have been frowned upon, but that was certainly not the case. As it turns out, many Renaissance Christians from Spain, England, France, Germany and elsewhere relied on medicinal cannibalism to treat a long list of problems. From kings to commoners, Europeans routinely consumed human blood, bones, skin, guts and body parts. They did it without guilt, though it often entailed a healthy dose of gore. They did it for hundreds of years. Then they made believe that it never happened.

Perhaps the most commonly consumed human product is blood – a substance that has, until fairly recently, been misunderstood. Until the twentieth century, most of what we knew (or thought we knew) about blood could be traced to the second-century Roman physician Claudius Galenus, known as Galen. Physician to the gladiators, Galen stressed the importance of four bodily humours: blood, black bile, yellow bile and phlegm. His theory was that the key to good health, both mental and physical, was to keep the body's humours in balance. Unfortunately, this doctrine would become the party line for medical practitioners for well over a thousand years, with Galen's followers routinely involved in serious bouts of bleeding, gorging and purging (the latter from both ends).

Since Galen believed that blood was the most important of the humours, bloodletting, usually initiated with a blade called a lancet, was prescribed to treat everything from fever and headaches to menstruation. Some of this blood, though, ended up back in the patient, where it was consumed to treat epilepsy. So popular was this practice that public executions routinely found epileptics standing close by, cup in hand, ready to quaff their share of the red stuff.

But drinking down blood while it was hot and fresh was not the only way to take one's medicine. It was also dried and made into powder or mixed into an elixir with other ingredients. Interestingly, consuming blood turned out to be far more than a medieval folk remedy, as evidenced by the fact that English physicians were still prescribing it as late as the mid-eighteenth century.

Although Galen's mistaken views would dominate the field of medicine for 1,500 years, the continued popularity of medicinal cannibalism can be primarily attributed to the rise of an alternative medical doctrine initiated by Philippus Aureolus Theophrastus Bombastus von Honheheim. Better known as Paracelsus (1493–1551), the Swiss physician is considered by some to be 'The Father of Chemical Pharmacology and Therapeutics', due to his pioneering use of substances like mercury, sulphur and opium. He has also been called the world's first toxicologist. Still, many of Paracelsus' beliefs were founded on bizarre magic like alchemy, often infused with astrological mumbo-jumbo. Long after his death, his followers touted a medical philosophy that stressed the healing powers of the human body, but not in the manner we're familiar with. Rather, Paracelsian physicians often prescribed medications made from human body parts, such as treating epileptics with a potion containing powdered human skull, a substance thought to do double duty as a cure for dysentery.

In *Mummies, Cannibals and Vampires: The History of Corpse Medicine from the Renaissance to the Victorians*, Richard Sugg writes that every imaginable body part was used, including 'human liver ... oil distilled from human brains, pulverised heart, bladder stones, warm blood, breast milk, and extract of gall.' Also popular in medicinal concoctions were bones, flesh, and fat, the latter applied to wounds or taken internally to treat rheumatism.

During the European Renaissance the popularity of medicinal cannibalism may have begun within the unwashed masses, but it was adopted as de rigueur by the enlightened, pious and well-heeled. The upper classes and even members of the British Royalty applied, drank or wore concoctions prepared from human body parts and they continued to do so until the end of the eighteenth century. According to Sugg, 'One thing we are rarely taught at school yet is evidenced in literary and historic texts of the time is this: James I refused corpse medicine; Charles II made his own corpse medicine; and Charles I was made into corpse medicine.'

Additional high-profile advocates of medicinal cannibalism included King Francis I of France, Berengario da Carpi (Italian anatomist), John Donne (poet and priest), Francis Bacon (pioneer of the scientific method), John Banister (surgeon to Elizabeth I), John Hall (physician and Shakespeare's son-in-law) and Robert Boyle (natural philosopher, chemist and inventor).

WITH AN EVER-INCREASING DEMAND for human body parts, the popularity of public executions rose dramatically in the seventeenth century. The already gruesome events became even gorier as the choicest cuts were harvested from prisoners, often while they were still alive.

Human skulls not ground into powder were often left out in the air, where they served as the substrate for 'skull moss' – a curative applied topically to stem bleeding and to treat disorders of the head. Researcher Paolo Modinesi

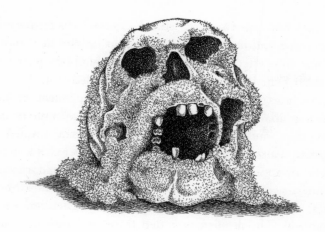

believes that the term actually refers to a taxonomic assemblage of mosses and lichens. Renowned for their ability to thrive on bare rock, these organisms had little difficulty growing on the calcium-rich crania. Ideally, the moss from the skulls of hanged men was preferred but, according to naturalist and philosopher Robert James (1703–1776), Paracelsus believed that moss grown on the bodies of the unburied dead was quite acceptable. One set of directions called for the moss collected from a meadow in April to be dried and ground into a powder. This was sprinkled with a strong, sweet wine to form a paste, which was spread over 'the cranium of a carcass that had been broken on the wheel'. Gardeners were advised to place their skulls in the sun and warned to take them indoors when it rained.

The lichen *Usnea humana* was also the main ingredient in a preparation called *Unguentum armarium*: 'weapon ointment'. This preparation, which also contained human blood and fat, was employed in a bizarre medical treatment known as hoplochrisma (*oplon* = weapon, *chrisma* = salve). Those administering this procedure might bandage a wound but would otherwise leave it untreated. They would use the ointment itself on either the weapon that had caused the injury (if available) or a wooden facsimile of it. A bandage would be added. Given the fact that hoplochrisma had no side effects, it might be classified as one of the most effective treatments available at the time, even if the benefits were simply a placebo effect.

Perhaps the most famous example of European medicinal cannibalism was the curious custom of pulverising Egyptian mummies to produce a substance known as mumia. This was either consumed (often as a drink ingredient) or applied topically as a salve or in a cloth compress. Mumia was used in the treatment of ailments ranging from epilepsy and bruising to haemorrhaging and upset stomachs. The problem was that there were only a limited number of genuine mummies being sent to Europe, leading to shortages and legions of disgruntled customers. In response, a thriving cottage industry popped up to supply ersatz mumia. Reportedly, by the end of the seventeenth century the quality of bootleg mummy was so bad that buyers were advised to 'choose what is of a shining black, not full of bones and dirt, and of a good smell'.

There were, however, some high-quality 'artificial mummies' to be had (or at least a recipe for their production), as anthropologist Karen Gordon-Grube uncovered in the official *London Pharmacopoeias* of the seventeenth century:

> [The Paracelsist Oswald] Croll recommended that mummy be made of the cadaver of a redheaded man, age 24, who had been hanged. The corpse was to lie in cold water in the air for 24 hours, after which the flesh was cut in pieces and sprinkled with a powder of myrrh and aloes. This was soaked in spirit of wine and turpentine for 24 hours, hung up for 12 hours, again soaked in the spirit mixture for 24 hours, and finally hung up to dry.

In an interesting turn of fate, the popularity of grinding

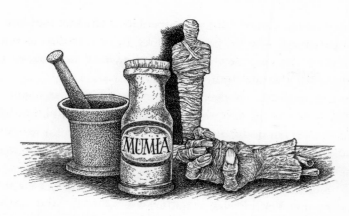

up mummies for medicinal purposes may have started because of a mistranslation. Apparently, Arabs often used the petroleum-based substance we call tar or bitumen as an adhesive and to staunch wounds. Their word for this material was *mumia*, but it also became their word for the mummified human remains they discovered after taking over Egypt in the sixth century CE. They mistakenly believed the mummies to have been prepared with bitumen during the preservation process. Centuries later, Europeans heard about the medical benefits of *mumia*. Unfortunately, they wound up hoarding *mumia* – the dried-up corpses, rather than *mumia* – the tarry stuff. Either the locals never figured out the mix-up (which seems highly unlikely) or they simply never bothered to tell the Europeans about it. As a consequence, mummy powder was available at the Merck Pharmacy in Darmstadt, Germany, until 1908. Listed as *Mumia vera aegyptica*, it sold for 17.50 marks/kg.

Essentially, then, as European adventurers, missionaries and colonists were condemning the indigenous people they encountered for practising cannibalism, their own rulers and countrymen in Europe were consuming human body parts to a degree and at a rate that would have made Hannibal Lecter proud. Until suddenly, they stopped.

Richard Sugg, the foremost expert on the topic, believes that the practice of medicinal cannibalism was abandoned because of, 'the rise of Enlightenment attitudes to science, superstition, and the general backwardness of the past; a desire to create a newly respectable medical profession; a changing attitude towards hygiene, the body and disgust; and the radically changed nature of the human body itself'. The latter Suggs described as 'a more mechanised model of the human body: an entity now drained (at least for the educated) of its animistic, essentially cosmic vitality'. In short, its spirit and soul were gone.

But not in every case ... In 2002, stories began circulating that Keith Richards had mixed his dad's ashes with some cocaine and snorted them shortly after Bert Richards's death that year. Not so, replied Keef:

> ...after having Dad's ashes in a black box for six years, because I really couldn't bring myself to scatter him to the winds, I finally planted a sturdy English oak to spread him around. And as I took the lid off the box, a fine spray of his ashes blew out onto the table. I couldn't just brush him off, so I wiped my finger over it and snorted the residue. Ashes to ashes, father to son.

15

TOO MUCH TO SWALLOW: PLACENTOPHAGY

'It gave me the wildest rush.'

The Placenta Cookbook, *New York* magazine

THUMBING THROUGH AN ISSUE of *New York* magazine three years ago, I stopped at what appeared to be a recipe feature by the alliteratively named Atossa Araxia Abrahamian. Across a two-page spread was a photo of what looked to be a veiny roast beef, bobbing in a black enamelled stew pot. Floating alongside the softball-sized steak was a sliced jalapeño, a walnut-sized chunk of ginger and a halved lemon. I read the title of the article – 'The Placenta Cookbook' – realising that the main ingredient in this particular dish wasn't beef at all.

Throughout the article there were quotes from several women, each of whom was enthusiastic about having consumed her own placenta. 'Perfect ... beautiful ... precious', gushed one woman who had tried it. I also learned that, while some mothers preferred their placenta raw, others favoured placenta smoothies, placenta jerky and even a particularly apt version of a Bloody Mary. For those turned off by the idea of turning their placentas into a meal, or even handling the organ themselves, there were professional placenta-preparers who could be hired to procure the placenta from the hospital or accept its delivery by mail. They would then transform it into a bottle of encapsulated nutritional supplements, thus placing the whole placentophagy experience on a par with popping a vitamin pill. On that note, the article included an illustrated handy section for readers wondering how these 'happy pills' were made, leading from 'Step 1: Drain blood and blot dry …' to 'Step 5: Grind in blender and pour placenta powder into pill capsules'.

From a biological viewpoint, the first question is, obviously, what is the function of a placenta? As a zoologist I was interested in determining what other mammals ate their own placentas and why they did it. There were claims from some midwives and alternative health care advocates that placenta consumption brought therapeutic benefits. What were these supposed benefits and, more importantly, was there any proof that they existed? I was also interested in determining whether additional human body parts had been (or were being) ingested for medicinal reasons. Finally, there was the inevitable question: What did placenta taste like?*

Advocates of placentophagy are likely to find it more than coincidental that the word placenta is derived from the Greek *plakous*, or flat cake. The Latin term *placenta uterine*, or uterine cake, was coined by the Italian anatomist Realdo Colombo. Tempering any culinary enthusiasm is the likelihood that the sixteenth-century scientist was referring to the flattened or slab-like nature of the roughly discus-shaped organ and not its potential as a base for chocolate frosting and candles.

---

* A 2013 study conducted by researchers at University of Nevada, Las Vegas, of women who had 'ingested their placentas after the birth of at least one child' found that they were most likely to be white, married and middle-class.

The placenta is the organ that gives more than nine out of ten mammals (or roughly 4,000 species) their classification as placental mammals. Also known as eutherians, the oldest placental mammals date from around 160 million years ago. Mouse-like, they generally kept out of sight while the dinosaurs ran the show. But using their relatively larger brains and enhanced thermoregulatory abilities, they carved out slender niches of their own. Then, approximately 65 million years ago, as the planet underwent cataclysmic environmental changes, mammals hunkered down and survived. Once the dust settled, mammals exploded in diversity, spreading rapidly across a planet suddenly filled with evolutionary opportunity.

Within approximately 10 million years of the dinosaurs' demise, mammals diversified into the existing mammalian orders – rodents, bats, carnivores, primates, etc. Some took to the air while others returned to the water – each group evolving and passing on its own suite of adaptations, like wings or fins, to supplement basal mammalian characteristics like hair and bigger brains. Many of these species went extinct themselves. Others thrived, eventually outcompeting many of the non-mammalian vertebrates that had also survived the great die-off. And except in isolated regions like Australia and South America, the eutherians even outcompeted the older, non-placental mammals – the marsupials and the egg-laying monotremes.*

The organ that gives placental mammals their name is

---

* Currently, there are five species of monotremes (four echidnas and the platypus) and 334 species of marsupials. The latter are commonly referred to as 'pouched mammals', although a pouch, or marsupium, is not a requirement for entry to the marsupial club. What all marsupials *do* share is a short gestation period, after which the foetus-like newborn takes a precarious trip from the vaginal opening to a teat (usually found within the marsupium). Upon finding one, the tiny creature latches on for dear life, and continues what is essentially the remainder of its foetal development for additional weeks or even months.

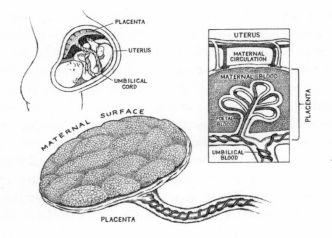

transient in nature, undergoing its entire, rapid development only after conception. The tissue is derived from the foetus, as opposed to the mother, and in humans it has an average diameter of about nine inches. Thickest at its centre (up to an inch), it thins out towards the edges and weighs in at just over a pound. The placenta functions as an interface between the mother and the developing foetus, connecting it to the mother's uterine wall but acting as a buffer as well. The organ itself is richly vascularised, which gives it its dark reddish-blue to crimson colour and relates to its life-support function: carrying oxygen and nutrients from the mother to the foetus via the umbilical artery. Structurally, most of the placenta is composed of cells called trophoblasts, which have a dual role. Some form small cavities that fill with maternal blood, thus facilitating the exchange of nutrients, waste and gases between the foetal and maternal systems. Other trophoblasts specialise in hormone production. Waste products and carbon dioxide travel from the foetus back to the placenta via the umbilical vein.

The placenta has additional functions, which include the production and release of several hormones, including oestrogen (which maintains the uterine lining during pregnancy) and progesterone (which stimulates uterine growth as well as the growth and development of the mammary glands). It also prevents the transfer of some, but not all, harmful substances – blood-borne pathogens for example – from the mother to the developing foetus. Finally, the placenta secretes several substances that effectively cloak the developing foetus from the mother's immune system – similar to the way immunosuppressant drugs prevent the body from rejecting a transplant.

Given its essential role in foetal development, the human placenta experiences after delivery what must surely amount to a precipitous fall from grace. Expelled by the uterine contractions associated with childbirth, this complex and amazing structure becomes a biohazardous 'afterbirth' faster than you can scream, 'PUSH!'

In the vast majority of mammals, though, the newly delivered placenta serves one last purpose.

IN 1930, PRIMATOLOGIST Otto Tinklepaugh took a break from his groundbreaking study on chimpanzee vaginal plugs to co-author an article on the birth process in captive rhesus monkeys. He noted that the monkeys, and just about every other terrestrial mammal except humans and camelids, consumed their own placentas after giving birth. More recently, the behaviour in the animal kingdom has been studied in rodents, lagomorphs, carnivores, primates and most hoofed mammals.

Mark Kristal, the world's foremost authority on placentophagology (and until recently the only one), began research into the subject over four decades ago. His work supports the hypothesis that, since placenta eating has been observed in such a variety of mammals, it probably evolved independently and in response to one or several survival challenges.

Kristal and his colleagues initially posited that eating the placenta kept the birthing area sanitary while eliminating smells that might attract predators. The fact that chimps giving birth in the trees hung around to eat their placentas, instead of simply moving off (or flinging them down on some cheetahs), suggested that a new hypothesis was needed. Answering the call, dietary researchers suggested that it replenished nutritional losses associated with late-stage pregnancy and delivery. Endocrinologists hypothesised that mothers might be acquiring and replenishing hormones present in the afterbirth. Other researchers suggested that placentophagy satiated a mother's hunger after the delivery, or demonstrated the new mothers' tendency to develop 'voracious carnivorousness' after giving birth.

Kristal was sceptical, and set out to investigate placentophagy in non-humans using lab rats. Their results supported none of the previous hypotheses, though Kristal did suggest that the previously proposed functions might provide secondary benefits, if they existed at all.

'The main thing that we found during our studies turned out to be an opiate enhancing property,' Kristal said. He explained that placenta consumption by new rat mothers appeared to increase the effectiveness of natural pain-relieving substances (opioid peptides) produced by the body. He added that these enhanced analgesic effects lasted throughout the litter's delivery period – an important point since rats generally give birth to between seven and ten kittens at a time.*

Kristal also told me that the results of a second set of experiments linked afterbirth consumption in rats to a form of reward for parental care. Briefly, the central nervous system, pituitary gland, digestive tract and other organs secrete pain-blocking peptides like endorphins, enkephalins

---

* Yes, rat babies are known as kittens (which should make dog lovers smile). The largest kitty litter I was able to uncover is twenty-six – presumably a tough number for the fourteen baby rats that didn't immediately latch on to their own nipple.

and dynorphins, which have been used to explain terms like 'runner's high' and 'second wind', as well as the phenomenon in which gravely wounded individuals report feeling little or no pain. Kristal's experiments indicated that those mothers who consumed their afterbirth received enhanced benefits from these natural painkillers, essentially getting an anaesthetic reward for initiating maternal behaviour like cleaning their pups.

I asked Kristal how long humans had been practising placentophagy and how widespread the process was.

'I haven't discovered any human cultures where it's done regularly,' he told me. 'When placenta eating is mentioned, it's usually in the form of a taboo. You have cultures saying things like "Animals do it and we're not animals, so we shouldn't do it."'

In 2010, researchers at the University of Nevada, Las Vegas, searched an ethnographic database of 179 preindustrial societies for any evidence of placenta consumption. Searching the terms 'placenta' and 'afterbirth', they found 109 references related to the special treatment and/or disposal of placentas. The most common practice, seen in 15 per cent of accounts, was disposal without burial (examples include throwing it into a lake), followed by burial (9 per cent). The latter narrowly beat out my personal favourite 'hanging or placing the placenta in a tree' (8 per cent). What the UNLV researchers did not find was a single instance of a cultural tradition associated with the consumption of placentas by mothers, or by anyone else for that matter.

Considering the ubiquitous nature of placentophagy in mammals, including chimps, our closest relatives, I was surprised they were unable to find any culture at all where placentas were regularly eaten. I mentioned to Kristal that I'd run across an example of placentophagy in the *Great Pharmacopoeia* of 1596, wherein Li Shih-chen recommended that those suffering from *ch'i* exhaustion (whose embarrassing symptoms included 'coldness of the sexual organs with involuntary ejaculation of semen') partake in a mixture of human milk and placental tissue.

'It is an ingredient in herbal medicine,' Kristal said. 'In fact, there are a lot of placentophagia/midwife/doula* websites where two things come up repeatedly. One – the benefits that I found in my research, which we never extrapolated to humans, and two – the [mistaken] idea that it's been done for centuries in China.'

He explained that in reality this was only rarely the case, and we don't know if it works. In terms of Chinese medicine, there are literally thousands of preparations, the efficacy of which has never been tested empirically.

On a more recent note, I had also come across a report that in rural Poland in the mid-twentieth century, peasants 'dry [placenta] and use it in powdered form as medicine, or the dried cord may be saved and given to the child when he goes to school for the first time, to make him a good scholar'. I ran this by a Polish colleague, who did a bit of investigation himself. The answer came back '*nie*', with my friend telling me it was probably safe to assume that the iPad had overtaken the uCord as an educational tool.

'So why is placenta-eating becoming more popular in the US?' I asked Kristal.

He cited two trends, one from the sixties and seventies and one current. The first had a lot to do with a kind of back-to-nature, hippie-commune philosophy. However, he lays the responsibility for the new fad on the midwives and doulas who spread the word about the positive female health benefits.

The evidence, when you try to track it down, is more

---

* A doula (from the Ancient Greek for 'female servant') is a non-medical person who assists the mother before, during and after childbirth. After reportedly engaging in turf-battles with medical personnel, some hospitals banned doulas while others encouraged them – presumably in an effort to reduce the number of birthing-room-related fistfights.

anecdotal than scientific. To learn why people were currently eating their own placentas, I contacted Claire
Rembis, the owner/founder of Your Placenta, a one-stop
centre for all of your placental needs. Working from her
home in Plano, Texas, Rembis not only offers the standard placenta encapsulation services but will also prepare
placenta skin salves, placenta-infused oils and placenta
tinctures, which she describes as 'organic alcohol' in which
a mother's placenta has been soaked for six or seven weeks.
Additionally, there's placenta artwork, in which a client's
placenta can be used to make an impression print (balloons
and flowers seem popular, with the umbilical cord standing
in quite nicely for the balloon string or flower stem). During
the impression-making process, vegetable- and fruit-based
paints are dabbed on to the placenta, which is then pressed
between a clean surface (like baby's changing pad) and a
piece of heavy art-stock paper. Immediately after its modelling gig, the placenta is rinsed off and undergoes further
preparation in order to assume its rightful place within
a gel capsule. For those mothers who want to keep their
placenta closer to their hearts, Claire also makes necklaces
– tiny, stoppered bottles, full of 'placenta beads' (a secret
formula) and available with or without gemstones.

Soon after an introductory email, Claire invited me
down to Dallas. I thanked her but declined, explaining that
I hoped a phone interview would suffice.

'Well, if you're ever in Texas, I'd be happy to prepare
one for you,' she responded.

Wait a minute, I thought as I read her email. *Was she
inviting me down to Texas to eat placenta?*

I followed up.

She was.

'I've got some of my daughter's placenta in the freezer
right now,' Claire said.

With an offer like that on the table, how could I refuse?

I PULLED UP to the Rembis house a little after 6 p.m. with a bagful of camera gear and a bottle of Amarone. (Surprisingly, the clerk at a local liquor store had no idea what wine would go well with placenta.) Claire's husband, William, had previously narrowed my menu choices down to placenta fajitas with hatch pepper and cilantro rice or placenta *osso bucco* with sides. I opted for the Italian.

Seconds after chef William ushered me into their ranch home in a quiet suburban neighbourhood, I was hit by a wall of their ten children.

I decided to interview Claire on her front lawn and she politely told her kids to remain inside, the older ones charged with keeping the little ones occupied.

I asked her what had got her interested in consuming placenta.

She explained that she had heard about the experiences of other mothers from the homebirth midwives she had begun working with when having her seventh child. Her midwife, who had been practising since the seventies, explained to her that the placenta was one of things she used to help with problems like post-birth haemorrhaging. (Since midwives can't prescribe medicines like a doctor, they can only use natural remedies to help moms when they have issues at home.) So she decided to try it for herself.

I asked Claire what specific health benefits she thought she was getting from consuming placenta. She responded by first telling me that she'd initiated her own research study to investigate just such questions. So far, Claire had interviewed over 200 mothers but chose to speak about only those benefits that she herself had experienced. She also said that, because she hadn't started consuming her placentas until her seventh pregnancy, she had established a baseline against which to compare her own experiences. Claire explained that after each of her first six births she'd gone through 'the baby blues', which she attributed to the hormonal drop caused by the loss of her placenta.

'The first thing I noticed after taking placenta products [capsules] was the energy. I felt very energetic. The most significant thing, though, was not feeling like I was on an emotional yoyo – one minute crying, the next minute happy. Any mom knows exactly what I'm talking about, and it was the thing I dreaded most about having children. Consuming my placenta made me feel a little bit more normal – like I did when I was pregnant but before giving birth.'

Claire went on to tell me that what really convinced her that there were benefits was the fact that she'd get 'emotional and out of sorts, and weepy and cranky, when it was time for another pill'. When she took one, she said, those emotions levelled out.

'With my eighth child I was severely anaemic, both while pregnant and post-partum.' She recounted that her haemoglobin counts were low and that rather than taking the iron pills typically prescribed by doctors, she took her placenta pills instead. She also pointed out that she prepared her pills from raw placenta, 'so that you're not losing so many of the nutrients' from the cooking process. 'By two weeks post-partum my haemoglobin was just below ten [grams per decilitre].' Normal values for an adult woman are twelve to sixteen.

Next, I asked Claire if there was any evidence for the positive benefits she'd spoken about. She immediately brought up Mark Kristal's papers. 'Granted,' she said, 'his research is mostly with mice [rats, actually]. There is, you know, no professional, scientific research in humans right now. Not truly scientific research.* What I'm doing

---

*In a 1954 study, Czech researchers claimed that placenta consumption increased lactation in post-partum women having lactational difficulty (compared to a control group fed beef). According to Mark Kristal, though, 'this study does not conform to modern-day ideas about scientific methods or statistical analyses'. He noted that 'the experiment was methodologically flawed' and that the hormones responsible for increased lactation would have been denatured in the preparation they described.

[gathering information on placentophagy] isn't scientific. I'm interviewing and getting feedback from moms.'

In Claire's view this list was certainly an acceptable alternative to the evidence a more formal scientific study might provide.

When we came to discuss the potential toxicity of the placenta, I told her that I had read about studies in which placental tissue from infected mothers also contained hepatitis-, herpes- and AIDS-infected cells, and she agreed that under certain circumstances, consuming the placenta was *not* a good idea. She told me that to avoid coming into contact with pathogens her contract had a clause stating that clients were unaware of having any blood-borne diseases.

I posed the same question to Claire as I had to Mark Kristal. Why did she think there was currently so much interest in placentophagy?

'People try it and it works for them. Then they tell their friends. It's just spreading like a virus.'

In short order, William and his son Andrew returned with the supplies and so we headed inside and into the kitchen. Team Placenta quickly split their organ-related duties – he dicing veggies near the stove, she disinfecting the sink-side counter before covering the surfaces and adjacent floor with the aforementioned baby changing pads. Once the place had been sanitised and covered in absorbent blue, Claire carried over a medium-sized Tupperware container. Prying off the lid, she revealed a roughly Frisbee-shaped organ that was perhaps seven inches across and half an inch thick. (It was smaller than I was expecting.)

'You won't be eating this one,' Claire told me, since it belonged to a client. She gestured to a bed of ice in the sink that held up a small baggie containing what looked to be several strips of calves' liver. 'That's mine,' she said.

'And I'll be cooking it up for you,' William chimed in happily. Now clad in an embroidered chef's apron, he was chopping away at carrots and tomatoes. 'All organic,' he assured me (and thank goodness for that).

Wearing disposable gloves, Claire placed her client's placenta on a pad, unfolded it a bit and allowed me to move in for a peek. The surface was irregularly shaped and reminded me more of scrambled eggs than of an organ (albeit liver-coloured scrambled eggs holding clots of bluish blood).

'This side faced the wall of the uterus,' Claire told me as she de-clotted the irregular surface. She spent several more minutes examining the placenta carefully (seemingly looking for defects) before gently flipping it over like a large bloody pancake. This side was smooth, dark blue and glistening. A fan of large blood vessels ran from the periphery, converging on a twelve-inch section of umbilical cord and winding around it like the stripes on a barber's pole.

I turned my attention to William, who was sweating vegetables in a sauté pan. He added a little beef stock, allowing the flavours of the tomatoes, garlic and onions to mingle as the veg softened. A minute or two later he retrieved the baggie containing his wife's placenta from its ice bath and emptied the bloody slivers onto a paper plate and into the pan. Within seconds the kitchen was filled with an aroma that reminded me of beef.

The thin strips coiled up during the cooking process, now looking a bit like larger versions of the bacon chunks in a can of pork and beans, but without the fat. William added about a quarter cup of the Amarone – the steam rising as the placenta simmered.

It smelled delicious.

Two or three minutes later, William plated my placenta *osso bucco* and passed me the dish. Without hesitation, I took a forkful – making sure to skewer two of the four bite-sized pieces. Placing Claire Rembis's placenta into my mouth, I started chewing.

BEFORE EXPERIENCING PLACENTOPHAGY first-hand I had done some research into what human flesh might taste like. I was somewhat puzzled at the scarcity of credible reports, although a number of notable cannibal crazies had been perfectly happy to discuss the topic.

The term 'long pig' has become the most popular reference point to describe the supposed pork-like taste of human flesh. The oldest reference I could find comes from a letter written by Revd John Watsford in 1847 describing the ritual cannibalism practised by the inhabitants of the Marquesas, a group of approximately fifteen Polynesian islands located around 850 miles north-east of Tahiti. But while the letter does represent the translation of a Polynesian term for the use of human flesh as food, there is no real mention of how it tasted.

> The Somosomo people were fed with human flesh during their stay at Bau [a tiny Fijian islet], they being on a visit at that time; and some of the Chiefs of other towns, when bringing their food, carried a cooked human being on one shoulder, and a pig on the other; but they always preferred the 'long pig', as they call a man when baked.

More reliable support for the pork hypothesis came from the infamous cannibal Armin Meiwes, who is currently serving a life term for killing and devouring Bernd Brandes. The latter, a forty-two-year-old computer technician, answered Meiwes's cannibalism chat room post in 2001. It was the perfect match, with Meiwes obsessed with cannibalism and Brandes fixated on being eaten. Shortly after entering Meiwes's dilapidated house in Rotenburg, the recently acquainted pair decided to sever Brandes's penis, which they reportedly tried to eat raw. Finding it too tough and chewy, they resolved to cook the wiener but ended up burning it – Meiwes eventually feeding it to his dog.

Brandes, nearly unconsciousness from a combination of blood loss and the pills and alcohol he'd swallowed, eventually died – helped along by the knife-wielding Meiwes. The internet's first cannibal killer then dismembered his counterpart. He stored the body parts in a freezer and consumed them over the course of several months.

'I sautéed the steak of Bernd, with salt, pepper, garlic and nutmeg,' Meiwes told interviewer Günter Stampf. Reportedly, Meiwes ate more than forty pounds of Mr Brandes during the months following the killing. 'The flesh tastes like pork, a little more bitter,' he said, noting that most people wouldn't have been able to tell the difference. 'It tastes quite good.'

The pork comparison, however, was not shared by all.

Issei Sagawa, an unrepentant Japanese cannibal who murdered and ate a female Dutch student in 1981 (and got away with it because of powerful family connections), compared his victim's flesh to raw tuna.*

In the 1920s, *New York Times* reporter William Seabrook set out to eat a chunk of human rump roast with some Guero tribesmen in West Africa. Upon returning home he began writing a book about his adventures. Depending on what source you believe, either Seabrook discovered that the tribesmen had tricked him into eating a piece of ape, or they had simply refused to share their meal with him. With the validity of his book in jeopardy, Seabrook set out to procure some real human flesh – this he claimed to have

---

* On the topic of Meiwes and Sagawa (albeit briefly), some readers may be wondering why I've essentially steered clear of the criminal cannibalism typified by this pair and their ilk. One reason is that the topic has been covered in sensational (and often gory) detail in a number of previous books. More importantly, though, several of these psychopaths are still alive (or recently deceased) and out of respect for the families and loved ones of their victims, I have chosen not to provide these murderers with anything that could even vaguely be interpreted as acclaim.

gotten from an orderly in a Paris hospital who had access to recently deceased patients. Seabrook says that he cooked the meat over a spit – seasoning it with salt and pepper and accompanying it with side of rice and a bottle of wine. It did not taste like pork, he said, 'It was good, fully developed veal, not young, but not yet beef.'

IN PLANO, TEXAS, the Rembis family stood by waiting for my reaction, I took my time, chewing Claire's placenta slowly. The first thing that came to mind wasn't the taste – it was the texture. Firm but tender, it was easy to chew. The consistency was like veal.

The taste, though, had none of its delicate, subtly beefy flavour. It was definitely dark meat, organ meat, but it wasn't exactly like anything I'd ever eaten before, though it faintly reminded me of the chicken gizzards I used to fry up as a student. It had a strong but not overpowering flavour 'It's very good,' I told the assembled Rembis clan and they responded with a chorus of moans, groans and giggles.

So is there any real benefit to this practice? If one were to gauge the benefits by the number of societies that practise placentophagy, the answer would be a resounding 'No'.

Maggie Blott, a spokeswoman for the Royal College of Obstetricians and Gynaecologists, believes that there's no medical justification for humans to consume their own placenta. 'Animals eat their placenta to get nutrition,' she told a BBC journalist, 'but when people are already well-nourished, there is no benefit, there is no reason to do it.'

But what about the alternative scenario – that consuming placentas could possibly have detrimental effects?

According to Kristal, 'The sharp distinction between the prevalence of placentophagy in non-human, non-aquatic mammals, and the total absence of it in human cultures, suggest that different mechanisms are involved. That either placentophagia became somehow disadvantageous to humans because of illness or sickness or negative side effects, or something more important has come along to replace it.'

Ultimately, though, the possibility of negative effects and the lack of evidence for beneficial effects doesn't faze people like Claire and William Rembis and, similarly, it didn't prevent Oregon representative Alissa Keny-Guyer from sponsoring bill HB 2612, which was passed unanimously by the state Senate in 2013. The new law allows Oregon mothers who have just given birth to bring home a second, though slightly less joyous, bundle when they leave the hospital.

Except in rare cases, it appears that medicinal cannibalism is no more or less than a harmless placebo. But, if that's true, then beyond our culturally imposed taboo, maybe there exists another reason why we don't indulge in cannibalism on a more regular basis. Recalling that UNLV researchers found no mention of placentophagy in the 179 societies they examined, I wondered if perhaps these groups knew something that ritual cannibals, proponents of medicinal cannibalism and modern placentophiles have missed.

16

NO LAUGHING MATTER: CANNIBALISM AND KURU IN THE PACIFIC ISLANDS

Nothing it seems to me is more difficult than to explain to a cannibal why he should give up human flesh. He immediately asks, 'Why mustn't I eat it?' And I have never yet been able to find an answer to that question beyond the somewhat unsatisfactory one, 'Because you mustn't.' However, though logically unconvincing, this reply, when backed by the presence of the police and by vague threats about the Government, is generally effective in a much shorter time than one could reasonably anticipate.

J. H. P. Murray, *Papua; or British New Guinea*

IN THE SPRING OF 1985, veterinarians working in Sussex and Kent were puzzled when dairy farmers reported that a few of their cows were exhibiting some peculiar symptoms. The normally docile creatures were acting skittish and aggressive. They also exhibited abnormal posture, difficulty standing up and walking and a general lack of coordination. Most of the cows were put down and sent on to rendering plants – facilities that process dead, often diseased animals into products like grease, tallow and bonemeal. It wasn't until the following year that the

Ministry of Agriculture, Fisheries and Food launched an investigation.

According to research biochemist Colm Kelleher, microscope slides were prepared from the brains of stricken cows and they showed the tissue to be riddled with holes, like Swiss cheese. But the veterinary pathologists who examined the slides blamed the holes on faulty slide preparation. By November of the following year, however, researchers knew that the abnormal spaces had once been filled with neurons that had shrunk and died. They also thought that the sticky concentrations of brain protein might be a contributing factor to the neuron deaths. The holes and plaques were characteristic of a number of neurological diseases, with sheep scrapie and Creutzfeldt-Jakob disease (CJD) being the best-known of these. These and other similar diseases were classified as transmissible spongiform encephalopathies (TSEs) because of the spongy appearance of infected brain tissue. The new disease soon had a name: Bovine Spongiform Encephalopathy (BSE), or 'Mad Cow Disease' to the press.

HEALTHY
BRAIN
TISSUE

CREUTZFELDT-JACOB
DISEASE
(MAD COW)

SCRAPIE

KURU

By 1987 there were approximately 420 confirmed cases of BSE, which had spread to cattle herds across England and Wales, and while scientists looked for answers, nervous government officials repeatedly reassured the public that it was safe to eat British beef. And why not, they rationalised; hadn't scrapie been killing sheep for centuries with no harm to the humans who consumed them? Why, then, should a bovine version of the disease be any different?

Other researchers, though, were not so sure, and a few of them began comparing BSE to a disease that *had* killed humans – thousands of them. To these professionals, this particular affliction was still known by its indigenous name: kuru, the trembling disease.

And kuru was spread by cannibalism.

IN THE EARLY 1950S, anthropologists and medical researchers began arriving at one of the wildest and most primitive regions on the planet, New Guinea, the world's second-largest island. Upon their arrival, the scientists saw no roads. Instead they were found themselves crossing parasite-ridden mangrove swamps and rainforests whose primary inhabitants seemed to be biting insects, terrestrial leeches and venomous snakes. But even after reaching their destination in the foreboding Eastern Highlands, conditions were no less dangerous, for the researchers had come to study New Guinea's infamous cannibals.

Numbering approximately 36,000 in the mid-twentieth century, the Fore (pronounced for-ay) spoke three distinct dialects and inhabited some 170 villages situated among New Guinea's lush mountain valleys. Desiring and having little or no contact with the outside world, the Fore practised the same slash-and-burn agriculture that had sustained them for thousands of years. Currently what made them especially interesting to researchers was not their lack of contact with the modern world, their farming techniques, or even the reports that they practised ritual cannibalism. It was the fact that something was killing them – horribly and at an alarmingly rapid rate.

Decades earlier, as colonialism extended its reach to the Pacific islands following the Great War, Australian patrol officers in New Guinea began encountering some of the most isolated of the island's inhabitants.* Like the missionaries who had arrived, preached, and often disappeared for their troubles, the Australian officials (whom the Fore called *kiaps*) encouraged the locals to curtail what they considered bad behaviour. Sorcery and tribal warfare, the Aussie officials said, were prohibited. The Fore were also kindly requested to stop eating each other, a practice that formed part of their funeral rituals to honour their dead. The indigenous people seemingly soon agreed to the requests, though today many anthropologists believe that some simply concealed their long-held rituals whenever the white people were around.

Meanwhile, the *kiaps* started to notice something akin to a plague taking place, one that took its primarily toll on the island's women and children. In addition to uncontrollable laughter, victims of the affliction experienced tremors, muscle jerks and coordination problems that gradually gave way to an inability to swallow and finally, complete loss of bodily control. The Fore responded to their stricken relatives with kindness – feeding, moving and cleaning them when they could no longer care for themselves. Invariably, though, their loved ones died – all of them – of starvation, thirst, or pneumonia, their bodies covered in sores. The mystery disease was killing approximately 1 per cent of the population each year.

Fore elders told the Australians that the sickness resulted from a form of sorcery: sorcerers would stealthily obtain an item connected to their intended victim, like faeces, hair, or

---

* The Territory of New Guinea was administered by Australia from 1920 until 1975.

discarded food. After wrapping the object in leaves, they would place it in a swampy area where it couldn't be found. As the sorcery bundle began to decompose so, too, the Fore said, would the victim. The elders also claimed that the condition could not be cured or even treated, and they tried to explain that preventing this sort of thing was the main reason they sometimes killed each other. The unfortunate ones accused of such sorcery, without evidence, were generally men or boys, usually several days after someone in their own village had died of kuru. They were then hacked, stoned or bludgeoned to death in a form of ritual murder known as *tukabu*.

To the Australians, the best way to stop the killing was to gain an understanding of the mystery ailment, and a number of hypotheses were developed. Initially, it was suggested that the deaths were stress-related and had resulted from the Fore making contact with the whites. Others, though, feared that whatever was killing the Fore had a more pathological nature.

By the time Ronald and Catherine Berndt arrived in the New Guinea highlands in 1951, they had already spent years in the field studying Australia's aboriginal communities. At first, the indigenous highlanders threw parties for the couple, reportedly believing them to be the spirits of their dead ancestors, returning to the fold to relearn the language they had apparently forgotten. Soon enough, though, the Fore lost interest in rehabilitating their pale relatives – but not in the strange goods they had brought along with them. Fascination soon turned to envy and not long after the Berndts settled in, they wrote that the locals were 'difficult people to deal with', requiring 'payments for stories: salt, tobacco, newspapers, wool strands, matches, razors, and so on'. The anthropologists also reported 'plenty of cannibalism'.

'Actually these people are "bestial" in many ways,' Ronald Berndt wrote. 'Dead human flesh, to these people is food, or potential food.' He also described cannibalism among the Fore as an outlet for sexual violence, employing the phrase 'orgiastic feast'.

A decade later, the not-yet-controversial anthropologist Bill Arens commented on Ronald Berndt's influential 1962 book on social interactions among the Fore. According to Arens, Berndt's *Excess and Restraint* displayed 'too much of the former and too little of the latter'. Arens was particularly galled by the description of a Fore husband copulating with a corpse as the man's wife simultaneously butchered the body for a meal. As these things go, she accidentally cut off her husband's penis with her knife. 'Now you have cut off my penis!' the man cried. 'What shall I do?' In response, according to Berndt, the woman 'popped it into her mouth, and ate it'.

Arens was not alone in his criticism of the Berndts, as others concluded that while the pair had made some important anthropological contributions, there were more than a few problems with their work, not least the many instances of outrageous behaviour Berndt detailed in his book – coupled with the growing suspicion that he had made much of it up.

Fortunately, following the Berndts' inauspicious studies, a new group of researchers arrived in the late fifties. Daniel Carleton Gajdusek (Guy-doo-shek), a Yonkers, New York, native, graduated from Harvard Medical School in 1946. Gajdusek had no real interest in practising medicine but instead chased his fascination with viral genetics and the anthropology of so-called 'primitive' communities across the world. He studied rabies and plague in the Middle East, hemorrhagic fever in Korea and encephalitis in the Soviet Union. Arriving in Melbourne in 1955, the brilliant but eccentric researcher frequently 'went bush', studying child development among the aboriginals and collecting blood serum for several Australian research labs.

Gajdusek flew to New Guinea in 1957 and, with nothing

but his own meagre funds to support this venture, he began working on a new problem. To a colleague in the United States, Gajdusek wrote:

> I am in one of the most remote, recently opened regions of New Guinea, in the center of tribal groups of cannibals, only contacted in the last ten years – still spearing each other as of a few days ago, and cooking and feeding the children the body of a kuru case, the disease I am studying – only a few weeks ago.

But Gajdusek had never seen any actual cannibalism and he had very little real knowledge about kuru. Beyond the stress hypothesis, there was some conjecture that the deadly condition might be the result of an environmental toxin. Others believed that kuru was a hereditary disorder. Consequently, Gajdusek got busy. He spent months collecting blood, faeces and urine from the locals. He ran tests on those stricken by the disease and, with the aid of translators, he conducted interviews with victims and their family members.

By mid-1957 Gajdusek was working with Vin Zigas, a medical doctor who had already been gathering information, as well as his own blood samples. That November their initial findings were published in the prestigious *New England Journal of Medicine*. Kuru, the authors claimed, was a degenerative disease of the central nervous system. They described the clinical course of the disease as well as its curious preference for striking three times as many women as men. The skewed sex ratios were difficult to pick up, however, since more men were being killed for having been kuru sorcerers. For the Fore, ritual murder had become the great equaliser. Significantly, Gajdusek also noted that kuru occurred equally in children of both sexes.

The researchers sent off blood and tissue samples for analysis but the results showed no evidence of viral infection, nor did they appear to indicate the presence of a toxin (they had suspected that the Fore were being poisoned by heavy metals in their diet). But a number of the tissue specimens did show something remarkable. After examining the brains of eight kuru victims, scientists at the National Institute of Health (NIH) in Bethesda, Maryland, reportedly found no evidence of inflammation or any immune response whatsoever. That meant the victim's body had not been fighting off a pathogenic organism like a virus, bacterium or fungus. In most cases, at the first signs of a viral, bacterial or fungal intruder, the body initiates a sustained, multi-pronged defence consisting of responses like swelling and inflammation, cell-mediated responses (like an attack by white blood cells), and the production of antibodies – proteinaceous particles that bind to surface proteins found on foreign cells and viruses.

What the investigators did find, however, was that large regions of the cerebellum (which sits like a small head of cauliflower behind the cerebral hemispheres) were full of holes.

Igor Klatzo, a NIH researcher, had seen a disease like this only once before. The closest condition he could think of was that described by Jakob and Creutzfeldt.

Another NIH scientist noticed a similarity between kuru and the transmissible spongiform encephalopathy (TSE) known as scrapie, an unusual infectious agent of sheep. Scrapie, which was present in European sheep by the beginning of the eighteenth century, was named for one of its symptoms, namely the compulsive scraping of the stricken animal's fleece against objects like fences or rocks. It had been previously been classified as a 'slow virus', an archaic term for a virus with a long incubation period, in which the first symptoms might not appear for months or even years after exposure. Klatzo and William Hadlow, who had made the kuru/scrapie connection, now suspected that the cause of kuru might also be a slow virus.

At this point, Ronald Berndt stepped in, writing his own article on kuru, reemphasising the importance of sorcery and resurrecting his original hypothesis of stress causation. Fear alone, Berndt claimed, was probably enough to initiate the irreversible symptoms of kuru.

Gajdusek, for his part, dismissed Berndt's assertions, believing instead that the high occurrence of kuru among young children argued against a psychological origin for the disease. He was leaning toward the explanation proposed by genetics professor Henry Bennett, who attempted to explain the discrepancy between male and female adults deaths.

Bennett proposed that a mutant kuru gene 'K' was dominant (K) in females but recessive (k) in males. Accordingly, only males who were KK (and who had inherited a dominant form of the gene from each parent) died of kuru, while males who were either normal (kk) or carriers (Kk) were unaffected by the disease. Alternatively, females who were either KK or Kk died of kuru, while only those females who were normal (kk) were unaffected.

In the end, the fact that kuru victims included equal numbers of male and female children, but few adult males, was deeply troubling to Gajdusek, and it raised serious questions about Bennett's genetic disease hypothesis, which was soon abandoned.

Meanwhile, the condition was garnering sensational reports in the press. *Time* magazine, for example, opened its 11 November 1957, article 'The Laughing Death' with the following:

In the eastern highlands of New Guinea, sudden bursts of maniacal laughter shrilled through the walls of many a circular, windowless grass hut, echoing through the surrounding jungle. Sometimes, instead of the roaring laughter, there might be a fit of giggling. When a tribesman looked into such a hut, he saw no cause for merriment. The laugher was lying ill, exhausted by his guffaws, his face now an expressionless mask. He had no idea that he had laughed, let alone why ... It was kuru, the laughing death, a creeping horror hitherto unknown to medicine.

For his part, Gajdusek hated the media coverage and he considered the term 'laughing death' to be a 'ludicrous misnomer'.

The worldwide media coverage did at least increase the public's awareness of the deadly problem facing the Fore. Because of this, universities began to funnel funds into kuru investigation and this money helped support a new influx of professional researchers into the region.

Two of the first to arrive were cultural anthropologists Robert and Shirley Glasse (now Lindenbaum), who came from Australia to New Guinea on a university grant in 1961. Studying kinship among the Fore, they returned to continue their research in 1962 and 1963. Their work in the New Guinea Highlands would ultimately allow them to make the definitive connection between kuru and cannibalism.

WHEN I ASKED Dr Lindenbaum how she had finally been convinced of the mode of kuru transmission, she explained that once the epidemic began in the New Guinea Highlands, she and her then-husband were instructed to gather genealogical data about people who had kuru. In doing so, they spoke to Fore elders who had seen the first cases of the disease in their villages.

'They could remember these cases and even the names of the people in the North Fore who came down with the disease some couple of decades earlier. There were these tremendously convincing first stories and we said, "What happened to those people?" And the Fore said, "Well, they were consumed." We *knew* they were cannibals.'

Dr Lindenbaum continued her tale.

'We knew cannibalism was customary in this area but

that the disease had only appeared in the last few decades. And so we thought, "Well, that's very interesting." When we began collecting ethnographic data about who ate whom, it became clear that it was adult women, not adult men, but children of both sexes. At that time the director of kuru research in New Guinea was a guy named Richard Hornabrook, a neurologist. And he said to us, "What is it that adult women and children do that adult men don't do?" and we said, "Cannibalism, of course." The epidemiological evidence matched the cultural/behaviour evidence, and that matched the historical origin evidence. It was such a neat package, you know?'

I nodded. 'So what did you do with that information?'

'We told everybody,' she said.

'And?'

'And nobody believed us.'

Nevertheless, Robert Glasse published their hypothesis that kuru was transmitted by consuming the body parts of relatives who had died from the disease. As support, he cited the fact that women commonly participated in ritual cannibal feasts but not men. He also wrote that children of both sexes had become infected because they accompanied their mothers to these ceremonies and participated in the consumption of contaminated tissue, including brains. In a later study, Glasse calculated that kuru appeared anywhere between four and twenty-four years after the ingestion of cooked human tissue containing an unidentified pathogenic agent, although we now know that the symptoms may not appear until five decades after exposure.

Nearly fifty years after Glasse published the couple's findings, anthropologist Jerome Whitfield and his colleagues used an extensive set of interviews as well as previously collected ethnohistorical data to provide a detailed description of Fore mortuary rites. Whitfield told me how his research group deployed the educated young Fore members of their team to conduct interviews in a sample group composed of elderly family members who had witnessed, taken part in, or were informed about traditional mortuary feasts.

The interviews revealed funerary practices that ranged from burial in a basket or on a platform to the practice of 'transumption', a term Whitfield and some of his colleagues adopted as an alternative to using 'cannibalism' to describe the ritual consumption of dead kin. As for how the funerary practices would be carried out: if possible, the dying person made his or her preference known. In other cases though, the deceased's family made the call. Generally, the Fore believed that it was better to be consumed by your loved ones than by maggots and that, by eating their dead, relatives could express their grief and love, receive blessings, and ensure the passage of the departed to Kwelanandamundi, the land of the dead. For these reasons transumption was the favoured funerary practice.

According to those interviewed by Whitfield's team, the corpse was placed on a bed of edible leaves in order to ensure that 'nothing was lost on the ground as this would have been disrespectful'. The body was cut up with a bamboo knife and the parts handled by several women whose specific roles were defined by their relationships to the deceased. Pieces of flesh were placed into piles to be divided up among the deceased's kin. Next, the women leading the ceremony enlisted the daughters and daughters-in-law of the deceased to cut the larger sections into smaller strips, which were stuffed into bamboo containers with ferns and cooked over a fire. Eventually, the deceased's torso was cut open, but during this portion of the ritual the older women formed a wall around the body to prevent younger women and children from seeing the removal of the intestines and genitals. These parts were presented to the widow, if there was one. Once the flesh was cooked, it was scooped out and placed onto communal plates made of leaves. The funerary meal was shared among the dead person's female kin and their children.

The deceased's head also became part of the ritual. Initially cooked over a fire to remove the hair before being defleshed with a knife, the skull was then cracked with a stone axe and the brain removed. Considered to be a delicacy, the semi-gelatinous tissue was mixed with ferns, cooked and consumed. Bones were dried by the fire, which made it easier to grind them into a powder that would be mixed with grass and heated in bamboo tubes. According to the accounts obtained by Whitfield's team, the Fore ate everything, including reproductive organs and faeces scraped from the intestines.

Shirley Lindenbaum told me that, initially at least, members of the Fore were receptive about answering questions related to kuru and cannibalism. Later though, as more missionaries and journalists came through and wanted to ask about it, they became very defensive.

So how did kuru spread from village to village and from one region of the Fore territory to another? According to Lindenbaum, kinship relations were the key. She explained that although Fore women moved from their natal homes to marry men from other groups, they still maintained their kinship affiliations with their former communities. When deaths occurred, women from adjacent and nearby hamlets who were related to the deceased travelled back to take part in the mortuary feasts. Similarly, individuals and families who moved into new communities maintained kinship ties with their former communities, especially on special occasions. Additionally, like other diseases throughout history, kuru travelled along well-defined trade/exchange routes, in this case those connecting the villages of the New Guinea Highlands.

Factors like these did much to explain how kuru had spread through the villages and additional research put a timeline on the dispersal. By tracing the path of the kuru reports, from the earliest to the latest, Lindenbaum and her husband calculated that the first cases of kuru occurred around the turn of the twentieth century in Uwami, a village in the Northwestern Highlands. By 1920 kuru had spread to the North Fore villages, and by 1930 into the region inhabited by the South Fore.

Jerome Whitfield, who conducted nearly 200 interviews in the kuru-affected region for his dissertation, believes that the practice of cannibalism in the New Guinea Highlands may have begun forty or fifty years earlier than the first cases of kuru – which would make it sometime in the mid-nineteenth century.

Eventually, these findings became strong evidence against a genetic origin for the disease – since had there been a genetic link, researchers would not have expected the first reports of kuru to begin so suddenly and only sixty years earlier. Additionally, had kuru been a genetic abnormality, in all likelihood it would have reached something known as epidemiological equilibrium, a condition in which the prevalence of a genetic disorder in a population becomes stable, rather than changing over time. In this case, the Glasses' data indicated that, from its first appearance at the turn of the century, kuru deaths had increased over the subsequent five decades, peaking between 1957 and 1961, with around a thousand victims in total. With the prohibition of cannibalism beginning in the late 1950s, the number of kuru deaths hit a steep decline in the sixties and seventies, with fewer than 300 deaths between 1972 and 1976.

The plague was over. Or so it seemed.

17

APOCALYPSE COW:
THE ORIGINS OF BSE

Unfortunately, the custom of consuming human flesh, like exotic
sexual practices, polygamy, and other alien habits, raises violent,
unintellectual passions in the Western scholars who study them.

Brian Fagan, *The Aztecs*

IN THE 1980S researchers in the United Kingdom, like those
in New Guinea, were also seeking to explain how a strange
form of spongiform encephalopathy was being transmitted,
and where it had come from. Also like their southern counterparts, they struck lucky after making a connection to
diet – in this case, after examining the diets of dairy cows.

In order to maximise milk production, farmers typically
supplemented livestock diets with protein – most often in
the form of soya bean products. However, in the 1940s meat
and dairy industries in the UK came up with an alternative,
rendering the waste products of livestock slaughter into
an innocent-sounding material they called 'meat and bone
meal'. Noting the cost-saving benefits, the US and other
nations followed suit. In addition to ingredients like bones,
brains, spinal cords, heads, hooves, udders and viscera, meat
and bone meal also called for the bodies of sick animals

(including poultry, pigs, sheep and so-called 'downer cattle'*) that had been deemed unfit for human consumption. This was then sent off to the knacker's yard. During the rendering process, the above-mentioned were ground, cooked and dried into a greyish, foul-scented powder which was sold as a source of dietary protein, calcium and vitamins for dairy cows, beef cows, pigs and poultry.

Although a comparison of livestock feeding practices with the ritualised consumption of relatives by the Fore seems to be a bit of a stretch, in reality there is an important similarity. In the case of the Fore, ritual cannibalism of kuru victims exposed practitioners to a deadly infective agent. And although nobody knew it at the time, beginning in the 1940s, livestock were exposed to similar pathogens after being forced to consume dietary supplements derived (at least partially) from sickened members of their own species.

But why had the bovine spongiform encephalopathy (or BSE) epidemic struck so suddenly four decades later? The livestock industry had been using meat and bone meal for forty years and nothing like this had ever happened before.

In searching for answers, the British government enlisted epidemiologist John Wilesmith, who examined the records of rendering plants across the UK. He soon determined that several modifications related to the rendering process had been instituted in the early 1980s. The first was that most of the plants had discontinued the separation of tallow (a creamy fat used to made candles and soap) from the material being converted into meat and bone meal. Previously, dangerous solvents had been used to extract tallow during the rendering process, but after a massive industrial explosion in 1974 safety measures were introduced regarding the handling of solvents in the workplace. Rather than

---

* A US Department of Agriculture term for cows that have become too sick to walk or die before being slaughtered.

deal with the expensive modifications mandated by the new rendering industry regulations, all but two of the plants chose to abandon the tallow-extraction process altogether. As a result, substances that had once been removed by the solvent extraction process now remained in the meat and bone meal. Presumably, these substances included the still-unidentified infective agent causing BSE.

Additionally, Wilesmith and his team learned from herdsmen that several recent changes had been made to livestock diets. The first was a significant increase (from 1 per cent to 12 per cent) in the amount of meat and bone meal added to dairy cow feed. Calves were also receiving the protein supplement at an earlier age. As in other spongiform encephalopathies, there appeared to be a direct correlation between the amount of contaminated material ingested and the likelihood of contracting BSE. Similarly, the incubation period for BSE was apparently shorter in younger animals. In theory, then, before industry-wide changes in diet were implemented, calves received less of the contaminated supplement and did not start ingesting it until later in their lives. As a consequence, infected animals would have been slaughtered before they had a chance to get sick.

The results of Wilesmith's epidemiological study were presented to ministry officials in May 1988. He told them that the BSE problem could be traced to the popular nutritional supplement that had been contaminated with sheep scrapie. This material had subsequently been fed to cows, making them ill in turn.

BACK IN THE USA in 1963, Gajdusek realised that his fellow researchers had been correct about the striking similarities between kuru-infected brains, brains from victims of Creutzfeldt-Jakob disease, and those from sheep with scrapie. The puzzle was just beginning to come together when yet another piece was discovered – and this one was several decades old.

In 1947 an outbreak of what would become known as transmissible mink encephalopathy (TME) in farm-raised mink led investigators to search for links between the ranches where infected animals had been identified. They discovered that it was a common practice for adjacently located ranches to share animal feed. In these instances, when mink from one ranch came down with TME, invariably so did those on the adjacent ranch. The feed itself was a vile mess composed of cereal, fish, meat-packing-plant by-products like sheep entrails and other internal organs, and flesh from downer cattle. By the time another outbreak of TME occurred in 1963, veterinary researchers suspected that something very strange had happened – the disease had been transmitted across species, in this case from sheep to mink.

By September 1963, similarities in kuru, scrapie and TME-infected brain tissue, coupled with the discovery that TME and scrapie could be transmitted within and between species, led Gajdusek and NIH researcher Joe Gibbs to an important experiment. At the Patuxtent, Maryland, lab they inoculated a trio of chimpanzees with liquefied brain tissue from kuru victims. If the chimps came down with the disease, it would prove once and for all that kuru was *not* a genetic abnormality or a stress-related psychosis, but an infectious or transmissible agent. As Gajdusek left the US for another field season in New Guinea, he worried about the long, symptom-free incubation period for scrapie, which sometimes extended up to five years post-exposure. What if his experimental animals didn't get sick for five years or more?

Gajdusek need not have worried. Less than two years after being inoculated, two of the chimps, Georgette and Daisy, began showing the telltale signs of kuru – at first a drooping lower lip in Georgette, and then changes in behaviour as both primates became more lethargic. Eventually the apes began to show even more clear symptoms of the disease: occasional unsteadiness and trembling followed by a gradual loss of balance.

On 28 October 1965 Georgette was euthanised by the heartbroken researchers. Her entire body was deconstructed, fixed and preserved and her brain was sectioned for microscopic analysis. The results were conclusive. Slides of Georgette's cerebellum were indistinguishable from those of human kuru victims.

Gajdusek and his colleagues had discovered a brand-new disease.

Meanwhile, Michael Alpers, who had been studying kuru since 1961 and who had taken time out from his own fieldwork to collaborate with Gajdusek and Gibbs on the NIH primate study, waded through six years of Gajdusek's epidemiological data on the Fore. After examining hundreds of Fore genealogies, Alpers and Gibbs came up with a remarkable observation: instances of kuru were beginning to decline in children, starting with the youngest age group. Their question was, why? Shortly after conferring with Glasse and Lindenbaum, Alpers came up with a hypothesis.

According to information gathered from interviews with the Fore, kuru victims were favoured at mortuary feasts because the physical inactivity that characterised the latter stages of the disease left the stricken individuals with a tasty layer of subcutaneous fat. Starting in the 1950s, though, government authorities in New Guinea began cracking down on the practice of ritual cannibalism and with mortuary feasts now forbidden by law, fewer people were eating infected tissue. As a result, incidences of the disease were decreasing. Additionally, since kuru had a shorter incubation period in children than it did in adults, the reduced occurrence of ritual cannibalism translated swiftly into a decreased incidence of kuru in the young.

In a February 1966 article in *Nature*, Gajdusek, Gibbs, and Alpers described the experimental transmission of a 'kuru-like syndrome' to their chimpanzees although the identity of the disease-causing agent was still unknown. Gajdusek, who still believed that they were dealing with a slow virus, was also reluctant to attribute the transmission of kuru to the consumption of infected flesh. Instead, he supported the view that, during the process of handling and cutting up the dead, the agent was transmitted via cuts or across the thin mucous membranes that line the human mouth, eyes and nose (a form of exposure known as inoculation).

By 1973, however, Gajdusek had come around to the idea that inoculation *and* consumption were both viable routes for kuru transmission.

> The mechanism of spread of kuru is undoubtedly contamination of the population during their ritual cannibalistic consumption of their dead relatives as a rite of respect and mourning. They did the autopsies bare-handed and did not wash thereafter; they wiped their hands on their bodies and in their hair, picked sores, scratched insect bites, wiped their infants' eyes, and cleaned their noses, and they ate with their hands ...

Other researchers such as Joe Gibbs stuck to the hypothesis that Fore mortuary practices, rather than the actual consumption of infected flesh, were the primary routes of kuru transmission. In a radio interview, the NIH researcher admitted that initial attempts to transmit kuru to chimps via a gastric tube (which modelled the consumption of infected flesh by humans) had failed, and that it was only after the animals were injected with liquefied brain material from kuru victims that they came down with the disease. As for how kuru was transmitted to the Fore, Gibbs explained that the Fore had multiple routes of inoculation, including their eyes and mouths, as well as skin lesions caused by leeches, mosquito bites and the razor-sharp blades of *puni* grass.

Today, in regions of West Africa, the Ebola virus is often spread because of ritual practices that involve handling of recently deceased victims. For example, some Muslims believe that family members should wash the bodies of the dead, a practice that also includes the elimination of certain bodily fluids. When performed under less than sanitary conditions, this ritual can place individuals in grave danger if they come into contact with infectious body fluids like blood, vomit and diarrhoea – all of which characterise advanced Ebola.

I asked Lindenbaum if she thought that Fore mothers had encouraged their children to handle the dead during mortuary ceremonies.

'Mothers handed food to their small children to eat,' she said. 'Since people eat with their hands, most children would touch the food given to them by their mothers and other female relatives. Children would not have been involved in the cutting of bodies, though one of my interpreters remembered sitting with others watching his mother being cut [up] and eaten. So, just as with adults, handling the food was one possible one route of infection, but as I recall, this depended on cuts and scrapes that allowed the infectious agent to enter the bloodstream – which the rest of us agree could not explain the dimensions of the epidemic [1,100 deaths between 1957 and 1968]. That would require a lot of cuts and scrapes, an unlikely scenario.'

In October 1976, fifty-three-year-old Daniel Carleton Gajdusek shared the Noble Prize for Medicine for his research on kuru. Although he was still attributing the disease to an unidentified 'slow virus', other scientists had their doubts. By now, with cases of kuru dwindling to a few per year and confined to a 'Stone Aged society' few outsiders had ever seen, research on the disease was winding down. Interest in kuru appeared to have run its course, and with it funding for research. Fortunately for the researchers (but unfortunately for a lot of shepherds), scrapie, a disease that mimicked kuru's destruction of the central nervous system, was beginning to attract more significant attention.

Considering the importance of the European sheep industry it was no surprise that by the early 1970s many researchers, including Gajdusek, were pressing to understand the mechanism behind scrapie. At the forefront of the mystery was the observation that whatever the scrapie-causing agent was, it could not be killed or inactivated by disinfectants like formalin or carbolic acid. Additionally, extracts from scrapie-infected brains lost none of their lethality after being heated, frozen or dried. In another set of experiments, South African radiation biologist Tikvah Alper and her colleagues bombarded the mystery agent with an electron beam from a linear accelerator. Although the beam was strong enough to disrupt the molecular structure of any known pathogenic cell or virus, there was no change in the infectivity of the scrapie extract. The researchers also tried mega-doses of ultraviolet light, a proven disruptor of viral DNA and RNA – all to no avail. The extracts retained their lethality. Alper's research team soon reached a couple of conclusions about scrapie: (1) it was far smaller than any known virus, and (2) it could replicate without nucleic acids – the chemical rungs of the helical ladder that became Watson and Crick's model for DNA. This last finding appeared to contradict one of the central tenets of biology – the fact that all organisms require nucleic acids to reproduce.

After reading Alper's work, English mathematician J. S. Griffith came up with an unusual hypothesis. Perhaps, he suggested, the agent that caused scrapie wasn't a virus at all but a self-replicating protein. Griffith proposed that this mutant protein could function as a template for the production of additional mutants, each in turn taking on its own role as a template.

Researchers from competing labs scoffed at Griffith's idea and Tikvah Alper was ridiculed as a female version of virologist/biochemist Wendell Stanley, who had won a Nobel Prize in 1946 for determining that the infectious agent in tobacco mosaic virus was actually a self-propagating protein – a fact that was disproved only *after* he won the award.

But Stanley Prusiner, a young biochemist from the University of California at San Francisco, read the papers by Alper, Griffith and others, saw an opportunity and jumped into the fray. In the early 1970s Prusiner moved to Montana, where his work with scrapie expert William Hadlow confirmed Alper's findings about the absence of nucleic acids. Prusiner and Hadlow's results also indicated that when exposed to substances like enzymes that could destroy or denature proteins the disease-transmitting ability of the scrapie extract was eliminated.

Prusiner tried to tell Gajdusek and the other NIH researchers about what he had found but he was rebuffed. Among the kuru researchers, who were now mostly working on other projects, only Michael Alpers was supportive, inviting the American to the Goroka Institute in New Guinea, where Prusiner studied a group of nine kuru sufferers.

In 1982 Prusiner published his lab findings on scrapie in the journal *Science*. He coined the name prion (pronounced 'pree-on') to describe an aberrant form of protein, which he claimed was responsible for the suite of neurodegenerative disorders known as transmissible spongiform encephalopathies (TSEs). Prusiner claimed that, unlike viruses, prions were not biological entities, but they could be infectious – transmitted orally or through contact with infected material. They could also be inherited or spontaneous in origin.

When asked about why the body's immune system didn't appear to mount a defence against them, Prusiner explained that, unlike viruses or bacteria, prions weren't foreign invaders, they were an altered form of one of the body's own proteins. Because of this, the body never

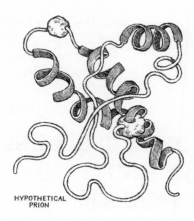

HYPOTHETICAL
PRION

recognised them as a threat. As a result, prions would spread through the body of a TSE victim unchecked.

Prusiner hedged his bets by stating that current knowledge did not exclude the potential existence of a small core of nucleic acid within the prions – which might explain how they replicated. Nevertheless, he co-opted Griffith's protein-as-template model, with his misfolded prion proteins (which were too small to see with even the most powerful microscopes) building up into the amyloid plaques that characterised fatal TSEs like kuru, Creutzfeldt-Jakob disease, TME and scrapie.

For his work on prions, Prusiner won the Nobel Prize for Medicine in 1997, an achievement that provoked a cannibalism-related controversy of a very different form. Some have argued that he should have shared the award with other researchers, pointing to the fact that several people had been bumped out or worse by the American. In his book *Deadly Feasts*, Pulitzer Prize-winning writer Richard Rhodes wrote that Prusiner 'invaded and colonized the work of others in his apparent pursuit of a Nobel Prize'. According to Rhodes, Prusiner's list of enemies grew even longer after accusations that he had used the peer review process to stonewall publication of another researcher's results while submitting his own paper on a similar topic.

18

TRUTH OR CONSEQUENCES:
BSE, CJD AND
HUMAN HEALTH

I have taken advice from the leading scientific and medical experts
in this field. I have checked with them again today. They have
consistently advised me in the past that there is no scientific
justification for not eating British beef and this continues to be
their advice. I therefore have no hesitation in saying that beef can
be eaten safely by everyone, both adults and children, including
patients in hospital.

Sir Donald Acheson, Chief Medical Officer, UK's Department of Health

THE KURU/BSE STORY now jumps to 1988.

Despite epidemiologist John Wilesmith's warning on
how BSE was being spread, because they still believed that
they were dealing with a disease that hadn't been transmitted to humans, the UK government dragged its feet.
Many officials were concerned with preventing a panic that
might impact negatively on the meat-processing and beef
industries. The government also knew that closing rendering plants would have placed the burden of eliminating
unwanted livestock parts squarely on the shoulders of the
beef industry, a significant new expense that would have

resulted in higher meat costs and a concurrent decrease in the competitiveness of British beef on the world market. So, rather than demanding immediate and industry-wide changes, the politicians quietly called for the formation of a 'blue ribbon' panel. It was to be led by the eminent Oxford zoologist Richard Southwood, and the Southwood Working Party met for the first time on 21 June 1988 and again in November and December of that year. The problem was that neither Southwood nor his three-member team had any experience dealing with spongiform encephalopathies.

Earlier in June, government officials had met with members of the UK Renderers Association. On the strength of the data provided by Wilesmith, the ministry informed the renderers that they would be suspending the sale of ruminant-based protein (i.e. meat and bone meal) as a dietary supplement for cows and sheep. Although the ban went into place the following month, that would become the extent of the good news. Farmers were also asked to voluntarily stop feeding meat and bone meal to their cows. Unfortunately, many of them had already spent thousands of pounds on what had suddenly become an illegal nutritional supplement. But since the government hadn't offered to buy the protein supplement back from them, and since there were no efforts to enforce the government's request, there was little incentive for the farmers to stop using it. The results were predictable.

After acknowledging the fact that removing infected cattle from the system was an important step in curtailing BSE, the ministry did decide to compensate cattle owners who turned in their visibly sick animals. But instead of offering to purchase the diseased cattle at market value they low-balled the herd owners, offering them only 50 per cent of market value for their animals. By comparison, the government was already handing out 75 per cent of market value for cows infected with tuberculosis.

Ultimately, it's impossible to know just how many sick cows were rushed to the slaughterhouse, but the numbers are thought to have been significant.

Until this time, there hadn't been much publicity about what was going on and the British government made an effort to keep it that way. Their veil of secrecy might have remained in place far longer if several publications hadn't broken the BSE story in April 1988. The industry standard, *Farming News*, ran a front-page headline that read 'Spongiform Fear Grows', while the *Sunday Telegraph* set the stage for the term 'Mad Cow Disease' with a story entitled 'Raging Madness Attacks Cattle'. An earlier paper in *Nature* also demonstrated that scrapie had been experimentally transmitted from sheep to monkeys, supporting Wilesmith's hypothesis that cows had got sick from eating scrapie-infected sheep rendered into meat and bone meal, though scientists now believe that it is more likely that BSE originated from a spontaneous mutation in cows and did not result from sheep scrapie jumping to a new species.

The Southwood Committee published its official report in February 1989. Their most important finding supported the government's claim that they were dealing with scrapie, and so they reported that, 'the risk of transmission of BSE to humans appears remote'. They also concluded that there was no evidence the disease was related to Creutzfeldt-Jakob disease (CJD), the rare but deadly form of human spongiform encephalopathy.

The authors of the Southwood report also painted a rosy picture for anyone concerned about the spread of BSE, predicting that it would begin to decline in the early 1990s and die out spontaneously sometime after 1996. No further effort was required. Beef was safe.

No one has ever seen a prion protein (PrP), but according to Yale neuropathologist Dr Laura Manuelidis the reason has nothing to do with size, it's because they probably don't exist.

Manuelidis has been researching neurodegenerative diseases for over thirty years, and she and her colleagues have performed a wide range of studies on TSEs such as Creutzfeldt-Jakob disease, kuru and BSE. Their results support a very different though far from new conclusion – that viruses are the cause. Since the name prion implies infectivity (the ability of a pathogen to establish infection), in Manuelidis's book, clumps (or plaques) of misfolded proteins exist but since they aren't infective, prions do not exist. According to Manuelidis, then, what is being called a prion requires a new name.

She explained that proteinaceous plaques aren't confined to neurological disorders like kuru but are also seen in peripherally located viral diseases. 'Conventional viruses also induce protein aggregates and amyloid fibres that are prion-like. The plaques are an end-stage product that doesn't occur early in these infections.' I later learned that the abnormal protein masses were also characteristic of diseases like rheumatoid arthritis and diabetes – and in none of these instances were the clumps or the proteins that comprised them transmissible.

But if these plaques aren't pathogens and they're not infective, what exactly are they?

According to Manuelidis, they're a runaway defence mechanism against the infecting agent, which she believes is viral in origin.

'When these misfolded proteins do show up, infectivity drops through the floor,' she told me. In other words, once the body's defences kick into gear (which ultimately leads to the production of amyloid plaques) the pathogen is less able to infect another host. The spread of the virus is curtailed.

ON 16 MAY 1990, John Gummer, the UK's Minister of Agriculture, infamously responded to the public concerns over potentially contaminated beef in the UK by feeding a

hamburger to his four-year-old daughter on the BBC television show *Newsnight*.

In 1993, two British dairy farmers died of CJD, a disease that was supposed to strike one out of every million people. The government stated that it was a coincidence. In May of the same year, fifteen-year-old British schoolgirl Victoria Rimmer began having trouble keeping her balance and within weeks she was falling constantly. Admitted to hospital, Rimmer underwent a battery of tests – all of which came back negative. Finally, a brain biopsy was obtained and the doctor who examined the results was stunned. Her brain was riddled with holes and amyloid plaques identical to those seen in the brains of kuru victims. With hesitancy, the physician informed Victoria's grandmother, Beryl Rimmer, that the girl had spongiform encephalopathy – mad cow disease. What took place next was even more incredible. An investigator from the government's CJD-surveillance unit in Edinburgh visited Mrs Rimmer, warning her not to speak out about her granddaughter's condition, and to think of the consequences to the Common Market.

Victoria Rimmer died in November 1997. After an inquest into her death, coroner John Hughes concluded that she died of natural causes.

In 1994, a sixteen-year-old schoolgirl and an eighteen-year-old boy were diagnosed with CJD, which had hardly ever been reported in people under thirty years of age. By the following year seven people were already dead or dying.

On 8 March 1996 the hammer fell on the government's stance in the form of a memo written by Dr Eileen Rubery, a policy maker and long-time government advisor. Rubery confirmed what others had feared for eleven years – the emergence of a new form of spongiform encephalopathy, this one transmitted to humans via the consumption of contaminated beef. She also used the dreaded 'e' word – epidemic. The new disease was initially referred to as sporadic CJD or atypical CJD, but scientists eventually settled on variant Creutzfeldt-Jakob disease (vCJD).

By October 2013 the number of definite and probable deaths from vCJD in the United Kingdom stood at 177. Some researchers see the epidemic as over, pointing to the fact that after peaking in 2000, when twenty-eight people in the UK died of vCJD, deaths from the disease have fallen off dramatically to three deaths in 2009, three in 2010 and one in 2013. Others believe that these 177 deaths are only the tip of the iceberg. They rationalise that because thousands of Fore died as adults, sometimes fifty years after being exposed to kuru via ritual cannibalism, many who consumed contaminated British beef in the 1970s and 80s will not have been affected yet, and might not start showing symptoms for decades after exposure.

In a 2013 study published online by the *British Medical Journal*, researchers tested 32,000 'anonymous appendix samples from people of all ages who had their appendix removed between 2000 and 2012'. Sixteen of the samples, which came from forty-one hospitals across England, tested positive for the abnormal prion protein. This translates into one carrier for every 2,000 people in the United Kingdom, or 493 people per million inhabitants, in a population of 63.5 million.

On a more positive note, scientists like Simon Mead and John Collinge, both of whom are experts in the field of kuru research, think there's another reason why everyone exposed to prion-contaminated meat may not come down with a lethal neurodegenerative disease. As evidence they point to a common human gene (the prion protein gene or PRNP) with a worldwide distribution. The researchers and their colleagues discovered a mutated form of this gene in descendants of the Fore who survived the famous kuru outbreak. Initially, they hypothesised that this variant might have provided protection from kuru to the individuals who possessed it. These kuru-resistant survivors would have passed down their genes (and their resistance) to their descendants. In 2015 Collinge and his research team published a follow-up study in *Nature* in which they presented experimental evidence that when the genetic variant of PRNP was transferred to mice, it provided complete resistance to both kuru and classical CJD.

So, in a best-case scenario, at least some of the individuals consuming prion-contaminated meat in the 1980s were already resistant to the disease.* If this is true then gloom-and-doomers may be waiting for an epidemic that never arrives. From a therapeutic viewpoint, if these genetic variants can somehow be transmitted to humans, we may one day be able to confer resistance to the pathogens that cause spongiform encephalopathies – whether they turn out to be prions or viruses.

On the other hand if Laura Manuelidis is correct and spongiform encephalopathies are the results of viruses, it would be wise to remember one of their key characteristics: viruses mutate.

---

* According to Noel Gill, lead investigator of the 'appendix' study, further research is now under way to determine whether prion proteins also occurred in samples from the 1970s and earlier – before the appearance of BSE in the UK. Such a finding could reduce the significance of the 2013 study, since it would suggest that prion proteins in a population do not necessarily translate to a major outbreak of spongiform encephalopathy.

EPILOGUE

ONE STEP BEYOND

Hunger hath no conscience.

Anon

IN SOME WAYS, then, cannibalism seems to make perfect evolutionary sense. If a population of spiders has an abundance of males from which a female can choose, then cannibalising a few of them may serve to increase Charlotte's overall fitness by increasing the odds that she can raise a new batch of young. On the other hand, in a population where males aren't plentiful or where the sexes cross paths infrequently, cannibalising males would likely have a negative impact on a female's overall fitness by decreasing her mating opportunities. As a zoologist, I find this kind of dichotomy pleasing, since it's logical and appears to be a more or less predictable occurrence. In nature, as far as cannibalism is concerned, there are no grey areas, no guilt and no deception. There is only a fascinating variety of innocent, though often gory, responses to an almost equally variable set of environmental conditions – too many kids, not enough space, too many males, not enough food.

The real complexity and the uncertainty emerge only on our own branch of the evolutionary tree. It was here that I found cannibalism painted in equal shades of red and grey.

Sigmund Freud believed that, in humans, atavistic urges like cannibalism and incest are hidden below a veneer of culturally imposed taboos, and that the suppression of such forbidden behaviours signalled the birth of modern human society. Yet, compared to other groups such as insects and fishes, cannibalism occurs less frequently in mammals and even less frequently in our closest relatives, the primates – where most examples appear to be either stress-related or due to a lack of alternative forms of nutrition.

Though we humans do share some of our genetic makeup with fish, reptiles, and birds, we've evolved along a path where cultural or societal rules influence our behaviour to an extent unseen in nature. Freud believed that these rules and the associated taboos prevent us from harking back to our guilt-free and often violent animal past. Similarly, my studies have led me to conclude that the rules we've imposed in the West regarding cannibalism serve as constraints to practices that might otherwise be deemed acceptable if we were looking at protein-starved Mormon crickets instead of indigenous Brazilians consuming their unburied dead.

There is a considerable body of evidence that cultures that were never exposed to these taboos (like *Homo antecessor*) or encountered them only relatively recently (the Chinese and the Fore of New Guinea) had little issue with undertaking a range of cannibalism-related behaviours as they developed their own sets of rules and rituals. Indeed, some of these cultural mores extolled the virtues of cannibalism as an honour bestowed upon a deceased relative or a slain foe, or as a respectful way to treat a gravely ill parent. But even in societies where cannibalism might once have been a perfectly acceptable practice, given the pervasive influence of Western culture across the world today it's unlikely that ritual cannibalism currently exists, even on a small scale.

It's also likely that Freud would have called upon

long-hidden impulses to explain our titillation with all things violent, gruesome or forbidden. But although it's unclear to me the extent to which atavistic urges are involved, there is no doubt that we are, and have always been, fascinated by cannibalism. We need look no further than the popularity of novels like Cormac McCarthy's *The Road* (with its depiction of post-apocalyptic cannibalism), or even our obsession with vampires and zombies. A long list of popular films might begin with *The Night of the Living Dead* and its cinematic progeny, and according to *Variety*, 17.29 million viewers helped turn *The Walking Dead*'s season five premiere into the most watched cable TV show of all time. Perhaps the violent scenarios we watch and read about on a daily basis are a form of drug – one that creates excitement in lives that might otherwise be mundane and unfulfilled. According to Andrew Silke, head of criminology at the University of East London, 'Viewing anything that involves violence or death will kick-start a lot of psychological processes, such as stress and excitement. Your brain's neocortex becomes psychologically aroused, but not in a dangerous way since you're in the safe environment of your own home.' Whatever the underlying reason, our language is filled with cannibal references: a woman who uses men for sex is a man-eater, while back in the twenties and thirties a cannibal was 'an older homosexual tramp who travelled with a young boy'. To 'eat someone' is a popular term for performing oral sex.

Most real-life cannibalism-related crimes are thought to stem from psychological aberrations. Forensic pathologist George Palermo believes that cannibal killers 'are people who have a tremendous desire to destroy – a tremendous amount of hostility that they need to release. They have something stored up inside them in order to reach the point of where they want to destroy the human body and eat human flesh and they feel a need to release that violence.' Of course, such incidents are immediately condemned, although once again they often lead to fame for the cannibal and millions of dollars in revenue for those who care to recreate their stories in books or on film.

If one goes by the examples in the media ('Woman Dies After Cannibal Eats Her Face'; 'Nude Face-eating Cannibal? Must Be Miami') it would certainly seem that there are more cannibal killers out there than ever before. Even if the same percentage of cannibal killers exists now as have in the past (even the recent past), the population explosion across the planet would make it likely that their numbers are growing. Then there's the fact that overpopulation and overcrowding are key catalysts for cannibalistic behaviour in nature. Of course, some would consider it a stretch to extrapolate human behaviour from the examples of spiders, fish or hamsters. But for a zoologist, those comparisons are far less problematic.

I believe there's a scientific basis for outbreaks of widespread cannibalism, and the trigger could be something that has initiated it again and again throughout history.

The process of desertification is taking place right now, in the United States, in places like Texas and even California, where researchers Daniel Griffin and Kevin Anchukaitis used soil moisture to measure drought. They determined the 2012–2014 period to be the most arid on record in 1,200 years, with 2014 coming in as the driest single year. Around the globe, across vast expanses of China, Syria and central Africa, regions that only recently experienced dry seasons are becoming deserts. The populations of Kenya, Somalia and Ethiopia, three of the poorest countries in the world, are suffering through the worst drought conditions in sixty years.

In 1973 Hollywood imagined just such an environmental disaster scenario in *Soylent Green*, starring Charlton Heston. His character, Frank Thorn, is a policeman in the hyper-crowded city of New York, circa 2022. Real food is now an extremely rare extravagance and most of the

population subsists on nutrition wafers – including every-body's new favourite: Soylent Green. With the aid of his old friend Sol (Edward G. Robinson, in his last role), Thorn is working to solve the murder of a rich Soylent Corporation executive.

During his examination of the crime scene, Thorn removes some 'evidence' from the executive's apartment. This includes real food, a bottle of bourbon and a classi-fied oceanographic survey, dated 2016. Sol and his cronies (a group of like-minded researchers referred to as 'Books') learn that the oceans are dead and therefore unable to produce the algal protein from which Soylent Green is reputedly made. They speculate on the real ingredients and the news is not good. Heartbroken, Sol shuffles off to a government euthanasia centre, downs a lethal cocktail and dies, but not before he whispers his secret into Thorn's ear. Outside the building, the cop sneaks into the back of a truck supposedly transporting the bodies of the euthanised to a crematorium, but instead it heads straight to the

Soylent manufacturing facility where Sol's dying words are confirmed.

'They're making our food out of people!' Thorn tells a fellow cop (after the requisite gun battle). 'Next thing they'll be breeding us like cattle.' Seriously wounded, Thorn is carried away on a stretcher, screaming what would become the American Film Institute's seventy-seventh most famous quote in movie history.

'Soylent Green is people!'

Though the special effects are dated and the action is reduced to the standard 'cop chases the bad guys', *Soylent Green* remains a scary 1970s take on a world ravaged by climate change, pollution and overpopulation.

But while we should be alert to the possibility that climate change, and the likely environmental catastrophes associated with it, will almost certainly bring with them a rise in survival cannibalism, we should also look back on the role that other manifestations of cannibalism have played in our species' history. Far from being the nightmarish aberration we tell ourselves it is – in films, novels and tabloid sensationalism – cannibalism has woven itself into our myths and legends, formed the basis of miracle cures ancient and modern, helped discipline naughty children (and entertain good ones), popped up in the Bible, fascinated anthropologists, zoologists and biologists and – sadly – played a significant role in colonialism, conquest and war. Though it might not always be immediately obvious, none of us is untouched by this most ancient and enduring aspect of life.

ACKNOWLEDGEMENTS

I'd like to thank my agent, Gillian MacKenzie, for her hard work, great advice and perseverance in getting my book off the ground. Thanks also to Kirsten Wolff and Allison Devereux of the Gillian MacKenzie Agency for their assistance, especially during the bumpy stretches.

I also offer my sincere thanks to Cecily Gayford, my incredibly talented editor at Profile Books. Thanks also go out to Fran Barrie, Andrew Franklin, Trevor Horwood, Kirty Topiwala and everyone else at Profile and Wellcome Collection.

I was very lucky to have worked with or received assistance from a long list of experts who were extremely generous with their time. Thanks and gratitude go out to: Cristo Adonis, Stephen Amstrup, William Arens, Ronald Chase, Ken Dunn, Rainer Foelix, Laurel Fox, John Grebenkemper (and his dog Kayle), Kristin Johnson (Donner Party expert extraordinaire), Walter Koenig, Mark Kristal, Nick Levis, Shirley Lindenbaum, John Lurie, Laura Manuelidis, Ryan Martin, Mark Norell, David and Karin Pfennig, Clair and William Rembis (and the eleven 'Rembi'), Raymond Rogers, Antonio Serrato, Stephen Simpson, Ian Tattersall, Simon Underdown, Marvalee Wake, Jerome Whitfield and Mark Wilkinson.

A special shout-out to Amy Gash (Algonquin Books), editor of *Cannibalism: A Perfectly Natural History*, the American version of *Eat Me*, as well as everyone at Algonquin Books.

I owe a huge debt of gratitude to my friends and colleagues in the bat research community and at my favourite place in the world, the American Museum of Natural History. They include Ricky Adams, Wieslaw Bogdanowicz, Frank Bonaccorso, Mark Brigham, Patricia Brunauer (RIP), Deanna Byrnes, Catherine Doyle-Capitman, Kristi

Collom, Betsy Dumont, Neil Duncan, Nicole Edmison, Arthur Greenhall (RIP), 'Uncle' Roy Horst, Tigga Kingston, Mary Knight (who told me to blame it on the Greeks), Karl Koopman (RIP), Tom Kunz, Gary Kwiecinski, Ross MacPhee, Eva Meade and Rob Mies (Organisation for Bat Conservation), Shahroukh Mistry, Maceo Mitchell, Mike Novacek, Ruth O'Leary, Stuart Parsons, Scott Pedersen, Nancy Simmons (it's good to know the Queen), Elizabeth Sweeny Taylor, Ian Tattersall, Merlin Tuttle, Rob Voss, John Walhert and Eileen Westwig.

I've been fortunate to have had several incredible mentors, none more important than John W. Hermanson (Cornell University, Field of Zoology). John took a chance on me in 1990 by taking me on as his first PhD student. Among other things, he taught me to think like a scientist as well as the value of figuring things out for myself. 'Here's to you, Chief.'

A very special thanks to my great friend, confidant, and co-conspirator, Leslie Nesbitt Sittlow, with whom I spent many hours discussing the pros and cons of cannibalism (among other things).

My dear friends Darrin Lunde and Patricia J. Wynne were instrumental in helping me develop this project from a vague idea into a finished work. A millions thanks also to Patricia for all of the amazing figures. I can't wait for our next project.

A special thank you goes out to my teachers, readers and supporters at the Southampton College Summer Writers Conference, especially Bob Reeves, Bharati Mukherjee and Clark Blaise.

At Southampton College (RIP) and LIU Post, thanks and gratitude to Ted Brummel, Scott Carlin, Matt Draud, Gina Famulare, Paul Forestell, Art Goldberg, Katherine Hill-Miller, Jeff Kane, Kathy Mendola, Howard Reisman, Jen Snekser and Steve Tettlebach. Thanks also to my LIU graduate students: Maria Armour, Aja Marcato, Megan Mladinich and Chelsea Miller.

Sincere thanks go out to the Adamo family, John E. A. Bertram, John Bodnar, Chris Chapin, Alice Cooper, J. R. Finch, Suzanne Finnamore Luckenbach (who predicted it all), John Glusman, Kim Grant, The Peconic Land Trust, Gary Johnson, Kathy Kennedy, Bob Lorzing, my former agent – the legendary and wonderful Elaine Markson, Carrie McKenna, Farouk Muradali (my friend and mentor in Trinidad), Erin Nicosia (American Cheese), the Pedersen family and various offshoots, Gerard, Oda and Dominique Ramsawak (for their friendship and all things Trinidadian), Isabella Rossellini, Jerry Ruotolo (my great friend and favourite photographer), Laura Schlecker, Richard Sinclair, Edwin J. Spicka (my mentor at the State University of New York at Geneseo) and Katherine Turman (*Nights with Alice Cooper*). Special thanks also go out to Mrs Dorothy Wachter, who listened patiently and provided encouragement, nearly forty years ago, when I told her I wanted to write books. I think she would have had a great laugh at the topic of this one.

Finally, my eternal thanks and love go out to my family for their patience, love, encouragement and unwavering support, especially Janet Schutt, Billy Schutt, Chuck and Eileen Schutt, Bobby and Dee Schutt, Rob, Shannon and Kelly Schutt, my cousins, nieces and nephews, my grandparents (Angelo and Millie DiDonato), all my Aunt Roses, and of course, my late parents, Bill and Marie Schutt.

NOTES

Prologue

p. ix   *in 2003, the American Film Institute* ... This information appears on AFI's website, www.afi.com/100years/handv. aspx.

p. ix   *Stefano's screenplay for* Psycho ... Robert Bloch, *Psycho* (New York: Random House, 1958).

p. x   *'She isn't missing,' Gein told them* ... House of Horror Stuns the Nation, *Life*, 43(23) (2 December 1957): 24–32. Quote from p. 28.

p. xi   *and a two-page spread in* Time ... Portrait of a Killer, *Time*, 70(23) (2 December 1957): 32–33.

p. xi   *'I had a compulsion to do it ...'* Moira Martingale, *Cannibal Killers* (New York: Carroll & Graf, 1993), p. 81.

p. xiii   *'Polar bears are now eating their own young ...'* Marsha Walton, Polar bears resort to cannibalism as Arctic ice shrinks, CNN, 5 December 2008, http://edition.cnn. com/2008/TECH/09/23/arctic.ice/index.html?iref=24hours

1   **Animal the Cannibal: Nature's Way?**

p. 6   *'cannibalism was also a consistent part ...'* Laurel Fox, personal communication.

p. 6   *By the time Fox's review paper ...* L. Fox, Cannibalism in natural populations, *Annual Review of Ecology and Systematics*, 6 (1975): 87–106.

p. 7   *some that were long considered to be herbivores ...* ibid., p. 88.

p. 7   *In 1980 ecologist and scorpion expert ...* G. Polis, The
        evolution and dynamics of intraspecific predation, *Annual
        Review of Ecology and Systematics*, 12 (1981): 225–251.

p. 8   *In 1992 zoologists Mark Elgar and Bernard Crespi ...*
        M. A. Elgar and B. J. Crespi (eds), *Cannibalism: Ecology
        and Evolution Among Diverse Taxa* (New York: Oxford
        University Press, 1992).

p. 8   *'the killing and consumption of ...'* ibid., p. 2.

p. 12   *David Pfennig and his colleagues proposed ...* D. W.
        Pfennig, The adaptive significance of an environmentally
        cued developmental switch in an anuran tadpole, *Oecologia*,
        85 (1990): 101–107.

p. 12   *Pfennig hypothesised that iodine-containing ...* D. W.
        Pfennig, Proximate and functional causes of polyphenism in
        an anuran tadpole, *Functional Ecology*, 6 (1992): 167–174.

p. 13   *Pfennig and his co-workers have previously ...* D. W.
        Pfennig, P. W. Sherman and J. P. Collins, Kin recognition
        and cannibalism in polyphenic salamanders, *Behavioral
        Ecology*, 5 (1994): 225–232.

p. 15   *In species like the flour beetle ...* F. K. Ho and P. Dawson,
        Egg cannibalism by *Tribolium* larvae, *Ecology*, 47 (1966):
        318–322.

p. 16   *questions related to kin recognition ...* D. W. Pfennig,
        Kinship and cannibalism, *BioScience*, 47(10) (1997):
        667–675.

p. 18   *This idea originated with the German/American geneticist
        Richard Goldschmidt ...* Richard Goldschmidt, *The
        Material Basis of Evolution* (New Haven, CT: Yale
        University Press, 1940).

2   **It's All Relative: Filial and Sibling Cannibalism**

p. 21   *a phenomenon exemplified by the rock snail ...* T. M.
        Spight, On a snail's chances of becoming a year old, *Oikos*,
        26 (1975): 9–14.

p. 21   *In the black lace-weaver spider ...* K. W. Kim and C.
        Roland, Trophic egg laying in the spider, *Amaurobius
        ferox*; mother-offspring interactions and functional value,
        Behavioral Processes, 50(1) (2000): 31–42.

p. 21   *The ravenous larva of the elephant mosquito* ... P. S.
        Corbett and A. Griffiths, Observations of the aquatic stages
        of two species of *Toxorhynchites* (Diptera: Culicidae) in
        Uganda, *Proceedings of the Royal Entomological Society of
        London A*, 38 (1963): 125–135.

p. 22   *Certain snail species* ... B. Baur, Effects of early feeding
        experience and age on the cannibalistic propensity of
        the land snail *Arianta arbustorum*, *Canadian Journal of
        Zoology*, 65 (1987): 3068–70.

pp. 22–3   *specifically in mammals, filial cannibalism* ... R. Elwood,
        Pup-cannibalism in rodents: causes and consequences, in
        Elgar and Crespi (eds), *Cannibalism: Ecology and Evolution
        Among Diverse Taxa*, pp. 299–322.

p. 23   *for fish, by far the largest* ... G. FitzGerald and F. Whoriskey,
        Empirical studies of cannibalism in fish, in Elgar and Crespi
        (eds), *Cannibalism: Ecology and Evolution Among Diverse
        Taxa*, p. 251.

p. 24   *Even in the ninety or so* ... ibid., pp. 244–245.

p. 26   *When researchers set out to determine* ... Noboru
        Okuda and Yasunobu Yanagisawa, Filial cannibalism
        by mouthbrooding males of the cardinal fish, *Apogon
        doederleini*, in relation to their physical condition,
        Environmental Biology of Fishes, 45 (1996): 397–404.

p. 26   *goes to sand tiger sharks* ... R. G. Gilmore, J. W. Dodrill
        and P. A. Linley, Reproduction and embryonic development
        of the sand tiger shark, *Odontapsis taurus* (Rafinesque),
        Fishery Bulletin, 8(2) (1983): 201–225.

p. 26   *These embryos (averaging nineteen in number)* ... Polis, The
        evolution and dynamics of intraspecific predation: 241.

p. 27   *Springer, the first to study the phenomenon* ... Stewart
        Springer, Oviphagous embryos of the sand shark,
        Carcharias taurus, *Copeia* (1948): 153–157.

p. 28   *Cannibalism of the young also occurs* ... Polis and Myers,
        A survey of intraspecific predation among reptiles and
        amphibians: 99.

p. 28   *significant juvenile mortality in the American alligator*
        ... M. Delany, A. Woodward, R. Kiltie and C. Moore,
        Mortality of American alligators attributed to cannibalism,
        Herpetologica, 67(2) (2011): 174–185.

p. 28   *Among birds, such behaviour is comparatively* ... D. Mock, Infanticide, siblicide, and avian nestling mortality, in Glenn Hausfater and Sarah Blaffer Hrdy (eds), *Infanticide* (Hawthorne, NY: Aldine, 1984), p. 6.

p. 28   *Cornell ornithologist Walter Koenig* ... Walter Koenig, personal communication.

p. 29   *In one study of a colony of 900 herring gulls* ...˙ J. Parsons, Cannibalism in herring gulls, *British Birds*, 64 (1971): 528–537.

p. 29   *Sibling cannibalism is best known* ... M. T. Stanback and W. D. Koenig, Cannibalism in birds, in Elgar and Crespi (eds), *Cannibalism: Ecology and Evolution Among Diverse Taxa*, pp. 285–286.

p. 30   *filial cannibalism in birds* ... ibid., pp. 285–287.

3   **Size Matters: Sexual Cannibalism**

p. 32   *Back then, several authors claimed* ... Two examples are: L. O. Howard, The excessive voracity of the female mantis, *Science*, 8 (1886): 326; J. H. Fabre, *Souvenirs Entomologiques*, vol. 5 (Paris: De Lagrave, 1897).

p. 33   *One hypothesis reasoned that* ... K. D. Roeder, An experimental analysis of the sexual behavior of the praying mantis (*Mantis religiosa*), *Biological Bulletin*, 69 (1935): 203–220.

p. 33   *Researchers* ... *now believe that, rather than acting as a stimulus* ... E. Liske and W. J. Davis, Courtship and mating behavior of the Chinese praying mantis, *Tenodera sinensis*, *Animal Behavior*, 35 (1987): 1524–1537.

p. 34   *After several papers in the thirties and forties* ... Two examples are: W. B. Herms, S. F. Baily and B. McIvor, The black widow spider, *California Agricultural Experimental Station Bulletin*, 59 (1935): 1–29; R. N. Smithers, Contribution to our knowledge of the genus Latrodectus in South Africa, *Annals of the South African Museum*, 36 (1944): 263–312.

p. 35   *They determined not only that most male spiders* ... R. F. Foelix, *Biology of Spiders* (Cambridge, MA: Harvard University Press, 1982).

p. 35 *sexual cannibalism has been reported in sixteen* ... M.
Elgar, Sexual cannibalism in spiders and other invertebrates,
in Elgar and Crespi (eds), *Cannibalism: Ecology and
Evolution Among Diverse Taxa*, pp. 129–143.

p. 37 *The next phase of redback courtship begins* ... L. M.
Forster, The stereotypical behavior of sexual cannibalism in
Latrodectus hasselti (Araneae: Theridiidae), the Australian
redback spider, *Australian Journal of Zoology*, 40 (1992):
1–11.

p. 38 *Mark Elgar and zoologist David Nash worked with this
species* ... M. Elgar and D. Nash, Sexual cannibalism in the
garden spider, *Araneus diadematus*, *Animal Behavior*, 36
(1988): 1511–1571.

p. 39 *To determine why, arachnologist Anita Aisenberg* ...
A. Aisenberg, F. Costa and M. Gonzalez, Male sexual
cannibalism in a sand-dwelling wolf spider with sex role
reversal, *Biological Journal of the Linnean Society*, 103(1)
(2011): 68–75.

p. 39 *Cannibalism by males also occurs in water spiders* ... D.
Schütz and M. Taborsky, Mate choice and sexual conflicts
in the size dimorphic water spider *Argyroneta aquatica*
(Araneae, Argyronetidae), *Journal of Arachnology*, 33
(2005): 767–775.

p. 41 *Even more shocking are banana slugs* ... H. Reise and J.
Hutchinson, Penis-biting slugs: wild claims and confusions,
Trends in Ecology & Evolution, 17(4) (2002): 163.

pp. 42–3 *Chase and his colleagues showed* ... R. Chase and K.
Blanchard, The snail's love-dart delivers mucus to increase
paternity, *Proceeding of the Royal Society B*, 273 (2006):
1471–1475.

p. 43 *A 2013 study by Japanese researchers* ... K. Kimura, K.
Shibuya and S. Chiba, The mucus of a land snail love-
dart suppresses subsequent matings in darted individuals,
Animal Behavior, 85 (2013): 631–635.

4   **Under Pressure: Stress-Related Cannibalism**

p. 44 *According to biologist and Mormon cricket expert* ...
S. J. Simpson, G. Sword, P. Lorch and I. Couzin, Cannibal
crickets on a forced march for protein and salt, *Proceedings*

of the National Academy of Sciences, 103(11) (2006): 4152–4156.

p. 45 *Simpson and his co-workers conducted food-preference tests* ... ibid.

p. 46 *Initially, cannibalism on poultry farms* ... R. Trudelle-Schwarz, Cannibalism: Chicken Little meets Hannibal Lector [*sic*]? *Behave: Stories of Applied Animal Behavior*, www.webpages.uidaho.edu/range556/appl_behave/projects/chicken_cannibalism.html

p. 46 *researchers now believe that it's actually misdirected foraging* ... B. Huber-Eicher and B. Wechsler, The effect of quality and availability of foraging materials on feather pecking in laying hen chicks, *Animal Behaviour*, 55 (1998): 861–873.

p. 47 *The results of a study on golden hamsters* ... R. Gattermann, R. Johnston, N. Yigit, P. Fritzsche, S. Larimer, S. Özkurt, K. Neumann, Z. Song, E. Colak, J. Johnson and M. McPhee, Golden hamsters are nocturnal in captivity but diurnal in nature, *Biology Letters*, 4 (2008): 253–255.

p. 48 *As a result of this catalogue* ... Elwood, Pup-cannibalism in rodents: causes and consequences.

p. 49 *the hamster has the shortest gestation period* ... Encyclopedia of Life. http://eol.org/pages/1179513/details

p. 49 *When non-human primates are compared* ... M. Hiraiwa-Hasegawa, Cannibalism among non-human primates, in Elgar and Crespi (eds), *Cannibalism: Ecology and Evolution Among Diverse Taxa*, pp. 323–338.

p. 49 *Initially, reports of chimpanzee cannibalism* ... ibid., pp. 324–325.

p. 49 *'A female who loses her infant ...'* J. Goodall, Infant killing and cannibalism in free-living chimpanzees, *Folia primatologica*, 28 (1977): 271.

p. 50 *Other attacks by male chimps on infant-bearing females* ... ibid., p. 260.

p. 50 *Goodall believes that the attacks* ... ibid., p. 269.

p. 51 *A team led by comparative psychologist* ... S. Anitei, Female chimps practice heavily infanticide and cannibalism. Softpedia, 15 May 2007. http://news.softpedia.com/

news/Female-Chimps-Practice-Heavily-Infanticide-and-
Cannibalism-54687.shtml

5   **Carnivore Cannibals: From Dinosaurs to Polar Bears**
p. 52   Personally, I suspect ... N. R. Longrich, J. R. Horner,
Gregory M. Erickson and Philip J. Currie, Cannibalism in
Tyrannosaurus rex, PLoS ONE 5(10): e13419.

p. 52   *'Polar bears are turning to cannibalism ...'* B. Johnson, Polar
bears are turning to cannibalism as Arctic ice disappears,
ThinkProgress, 8 December 2011. http://thinkprogress.
org/climate/2011/12/08/385037/polar-bears-are-turning-to-
cannibalism-as-arctic-ice-disappears/

p. 52   *'Is global warming driving polar bears ...'* N. Wolchover, Is
global warming driving polar bears to cannibalism?, Live
Science, 15 December 2011. www.livescience.com/17500-
global-warming-driving-polar-bears-cannibalism.html

p. 52   *'Polar bear cannibalism linked to ...'* O. Grigoras, Polar
bear cannibalism linked to climate change, Softpedia, 9
December 2011. http://news.softpedia.com/news/Polar-Bear-
Cannibalism-Linked-to-Climate-Change-239585.shtml

p. 53   *Cannibalism has been recorded in at least fourteen ...* Polis,
The evolution and dynamics of intraspecific predation: 231.

p. 53   *Heterocannibalism – in this case, eating cubs ...* B. Bertram,
Social factors influencing reproduction in wild lions,
Journal of Zoology, 177 (1975): 463–482.

p. 54   *polar bears will readily eat other polar bears ...* M.
Taylor, T. Larsen and R. Schweinsburg, Observations of
intraspecific aggression and cannibalism in polar bears
(*Ursus maritimus*), *Arctic*, 38(4) (1985): 303.

p. 54   *In the mid-noughties ...* S. C. Amstrup, I. Stirling, T.
Smith, C. Perham and G. Thiemann, Recent observations
of intraspecific predation and cannibalism among polar
bears in the southern Beaufort Sea, *Polar Biology*, 29 (2006):
997–1002.

p. 55   *'The underlying causes for our cannibalism ...'*, *'chance
observations of previously unobserved ...'*, *'the first
population segment to show ...'* ibid., p. 1001.

p. 55   *the first published report surfacing in 1897* ... F. Nansen, *Farthest North*. London: Macmillan, 1897), vol. 2, pp. 254–256.

p. 56   *Edwin Colbert made the dramatic announcement* ... Edwin H. Colbert, The Triassic dinosaur *Coelophysis*, Museum of Northern Arizona Bulletin 57 (1989).

p. 56   *Led by palaeontologists Sterling Nesbitt* ... S. Nesbitt, A. Turner, G. Erickson and M. Norell, Prey choice and cannibalistic behavior in the theropod *Coelophysis*, *Biological Letters*, 2 (2006): 611–614.

p. 57   *the only compelling evidence* ... R. Rogers, D. Krause and K. Curry Rogers, Cannibalism in the Madagascan dinosaur, *Majungatholus atropus*, *Nature*, 422 (2003): 515–518.

6   Skin Deep: The Weird World of Caecilian Cannibalism

p. 61   *All caecilians do share one characteristic* ... M. Wake, Fetal maintenance and its evolutionary significance in the Amphibia: Gymnophiona, *Journal of Herpetology*, 11(4) (1977): 384.

p. 62   *she referred to as 'secretory beds'* ... ibid., p. 380

p. 62   *Parker had previously labelled 'uterine milk'* ... ibid.

p. 62   *'a thick white creamy material ...'* ibid.

p. 62   *Wake proposed that foetal caecilians* ... ibid.

p. 63   *In 2006* ... A. Kupfer, H. Müller, M. Antoniazzi, C. Jared, H. Greven, R. Nussbaum and M. Wilkinson, Parental investment by skin feeding in a caecilian amphibian, *Nature*, 440 (2006): 926–929.

p. 64   *'The outer layer is what they eat,'* ... J. Owen, Flesh-eating baby 'worm' feasts on mom's skin, *National Geographic News*, 12 April 2006.

p. 64   *It also explained why mothers* ... Kupfer et al., Parental investment by skin feeding in a caecilian amphibian, p. 927.

p. 64   *Scientists now believe* ... ibid., p. 928.

7   Us and Them: Early Humans and Neanderthals

p. 68   *These anatomical differences led him to conclude* ... Roger Lewin and Robert Foley, *Principles of Human Evolution* (Blackwell: Oxford, 2004), p. 395.

p. 69   *Huxley announced that* Homo sapiens *had descended*
        ... T. H. Huxley, *Evidence as to Man's Place in Nature*
        (London: Williams & Norgate, 1864), p. 159.

p. 69   *The anthropologist also claimed* ... Ian Tattersall, *The Fossil
        Trail* (New York: Oxford University Press, 2009), p. 47.

p. 70   *In 'The Grisly Folk'* ... H. G. Wells, The Grisly Folk,
        Storyteller Magazine, April 1921. www.trussel.com/prehist/
        grisly.htm

p. 70   *'Every feature that Boule stressed ...'* N. Eldredge and I.
        Tattersall, *The Myths of Human Evolution* (New York:
        Columbia University Press, 1982), p. 76.

pp. 70–1 *what is known as the Regional Continuity hypothesis* ...
        M. H. Wolpoff, J. Hawks and R. Caspari, Multiregional,
        not multiple origins, *American Journal of Physical
        Anthropology*, 112 (2000): 129–136.

p. 72   *briefly argued in 1866* ... Ian Tattersall, *The Last
        Neanderthal: The Rise, Success, and Mysterious Extinction
        of Our Closest Human Relative* (New York: Macmillan,
        1995), p. 88.

p. 72   *researchers now believe that a hyena* ... T. White, N.
        Toth, P. Chase, G. Clark, N. Conrad, J. Cook, F. d'Errico,
        R. Donahue, R. Gargett, G. Giacobini, A. Pike-Tay
        and A. Turner, The Question of Ritual Cannibalism at
        Grotta Guattari [and Comments and Replies], *Current
        Anthropology*, 32 (2) (1991): 118–138.

p. 72   *multiple sites in northern Spain, south-eastern France
        and Croatia* ... T. White, Once were cannibals, *Scientific
        American*, August 2001, pp. 58–65.

p. 73   *'Bodies may be buried, burned, placed ...'* ibid., p. 61.

p. 73   *Archaeologists now consider this type* ... ibid., p. 62.

p. 73   *An excavation begun there in 1991* ... A. Defleur, T. White,
        P. Valensi, L. Slimak and E. Crégut-Bonnoure, Neanderthal
        cannibalism at Moula-Guercy, Ardèche, France, *Science*, 286
        (1999): 128–131.

p. 74   *In 2000, researchers working* ... R. Marlar, B. Leonard, B.
        Billman, P. Lambert and J. Marlar, Biochemical evidence of
        cannibalism at a prehistoric Puebloan site in south-western
        Colorado, *Nature*, 401 (2000): 74–78.

p. 75 *It is a finding that has been* ... K. Dongoske, D. Martin and T. Ferguson, Critique of the claim of cannibalism at Cowboy Wash, *American Antiquity*, 65(1) (2000): 179–190.

p. 76 *One instance in which the evidence* ... Y. Fernández-Jalvo, J. Diez, I. Cáceres and J. Rosell, Human cannibalism in the early Pleistocene of Europe (Gran Dolina), Sierra de Atapuerca, Burgos, Spain, *Journal of Human Evolution*, 37 (1999): 591–622.

p. 76 *The first fossils of this species* ... Tattersall, *The Fossil Trail*, p. 228.

p. 76 *Excavation of the pit* ... ibid., p. 229.

p. 76 *the site has yielded over 5,000 bone fragments* ... ibid.

p. 76 *including a large pelvis* ... ibid., p. 230.

p. 77 *tool-induced surface modification* ... Fernández-Jalvo et al., Human cannibalism in the early Pleistocene of Europe (Gran Dolina), Sierra de Atapuerca, Burgos, Spain, p. 599.

p. 77 *'the victims of other humans ...'* ibid., p. 620.

8 **Myths of the Other: Columbus, Caribs and Cannibalism**

p. 79 *The captain ... took two parrots* ... P. Hulme, Introduction: The cannibal scene, in Francis Barker, Peter Hulme and Margaret Iversen (eds), *Cannibalism and the Colonial World* (Cambridge: Cambridge University Press, 1998), p. 16.

p. 80 *'[The Arawaks] are fitted to be ruled ...'* U. Bitterli and R. Robertson, *Cultures in Conflict: Encounters Between European and Non-European Cultures, 1492–1800* (Stanford, CA: Stanford University Press, 1993), p. 75.

p. 80 *these warrior women lived on their own island* ... C. Sauer, *The Early Spanish Main* (Berkeley: University of California Press, 1966), p. 23.

p. 81 *preparing their viands by smoking them* ... R. Tannahill, *Flesh and Blood: A History of the Cannibal Complex* (London: Little, Brown, 1975; repr. 1996), p. 108.

p. 82 *some Caribs had dog-like faces* ... F. Lestringant, *Cannibals: The Discovery and Representation of the Cannibal from Columbus to Jules Verne*, trans. Rosemarie Morris (Berkeley: University of California Press, 1997), pp. 15–19.

p. 82   *the transition from Carib to Canib* ... D. Korn, M. Radice
and C. Hawes, *Cannibal – The History of the People-Eaters*
(London: Channel 4 Books, 2001), p. 11.

p. 84   '*...why God Our Lord ...*' Sauer, *The Early Spanish Main*,
p. 98.

p. 84   '*...if such cannibals continue to resist ...*' N. Whitehead,
Carib cannibalism: the historical evidence, *Journal de la
Société des Américanistes*, 70 (1984): 70.

p. 85   *Pope Innocent IV decreed in 1510* ... ibid., p. 72.

p. 85   *On islands where no cannibalism had been reported* ... W.
Arens, *The Man-Eating Myth* (Oxford: Oxford University
Press, 1979), p. 51.

p. 85   *Rodrigo de Figueroa, the former Governor* ... Whitehead,
Carib cannibalism, p. 71.

p. 86   *According to historian David Stannard* ... D. E. Stannard,
American Holocaust: Conquest of the New World (Oxford:
Oxford University Press, 1992), p. 69.

p. 86   *The diseases the Spaniards carried* ... ibid., p. 68.

p. 86   *Stannard believes that, by the end* ... ibid., p. 95.

9   **Bones of Contention: Ritual Cannibalism**

p. 88   *he never actually saw the scene* ... P. Hulme, Making sense
of the native Caribbean, *New West Indian Guide/Nieuwe
West-Indische Gids*, 67(3–4) (1993): 207.

p. 89   *It would become a blueprint* ... For example: F. MacNutt,
*De Orbe Novo; The Eight Decades of Peter Martyr
D'Anghera*, vol. 1 (New York and London: G. P. Putnam's
Sons, 1912), p. 72; J. Blaine, J. Buel, J. Ridpath and B.
Butterworth, *Columbus and Columbia: A Pictorial History
of the Man and the Nation* (Richmond, VA: B. F. Johnson
and Co., 1892), p. 172; J. Cummins, *Cannibals* (Guilford,
CT: The Lyons Press, 2001), p. x; Korn, Radice and Hawes,
Cannibal – The History of the People-Eaters, p. 11.

p. 89   *In 1828, author and historian Washington Irving* ... W.
Irving, *The Life and Voyages of Christopher Columbus*
[Orig. 1828], in *The Complete Works of Washington Irving*,
ed. John Harmon McElroy, vol. 11 (Boston, MA: Twayne,
1981), p. 192.

p. 89   *Anthropologist Neil Whitehead suggests* ... Whitehead, Carib cannibalism, pp. 69–88.

p. 90   *'The ordinary food of the Caribs ...'* ibid., p. 77.

p. 90   *ritualised cannibalism can be differentiated* ... L. R. Goldman, From Pot to Polemic: Uses and Abuses of Cannibalism, in Laurence R. Goldman (ed.), *The Anthropology of Cannibalism* (Westport, CT: Bergin & Garvey, 1999), p. 44.

p. 91   *in the Pacific Theatre during World War II* ... C. Hearn, *Sorties Into Hell: The Hidden War on Chichi Jima* (Westport, CT: Praeger, 2003).

p. 91   *The lucky man's name was Lt. George H. W. Bush* ... C. Laurence, George Bush's comrades eaten by their Japanese PoW guards, *The Telegraph*, 26 October 2003.

p. 92   *Anthropologist Beth Conklin studied the Wari'* ... B. A. Conklin, *Consuming Grief: Compassionate Cannibalism in an Amazonian Society* (Austin: University of Texas Press, 2001).

p. 92   *Wari' were keenly aware that prolonged grieving* ... ibid., p. xxi.

p. 92   *'cold, wet and polluting ...'* ibid., p. xviii.

p. 93   *Whitehead offers accounts* ... Whitehead, Carib cannibalism, pp. 78–80.

p. 93   *'very difficult to track'* ... W. Raleigh, *The Discovery of the Large, Rich and Beautiful Empire of Guiana*, ed. R. Schomburgk (London: Hakluyt Society, 1868), p. 85.

p. 94   *Arens argued that* ... Arens, *The Man-Eating Myth*.

p. 94   *The reaction to Arens's incendiary book* ... I. Brady, Review of *The Man-Eating Myth*, *American Anthropologist*, 84(3) (1982): 595–611; P. G. Riviere, Review of *The Man-Eating Myth*, *Man*, 15 (1) (1980): 203–205; J. W. Springer, Review of *The Man-Eating Myth*, *Anthropological Quarterly*, 53 (2) (1980): 148–150; William W. Arens, with a reply by M. Sahlins, Cannibalism: an exchange, *New York Review of Books*, 26(4) (22 March 1979): 46–47; G. Obeyesekere, *Cannibal Talk: The Man-Eating Myth and Human Sacrifice in the South Seas* (Berkeley: University of California Press, 2005), p. 2.

10   Take, Eat, This is My Body: Cannibalism and the Bible

p. 98   *'His body and blood are truly contained …'* Legion of
Mary, Tidewater, VA, 4th Lateran Council (1215), www.
legionofmarytidewater.com/faith/ECUM12.HTM

p. 98   *In October 1520, though …* Martin Luther, On
the Babylonian Captivity of the Church, pdf.
amazingdiscoveries.org/eBooks/BABYLONIAN_
CAPTIVITY_OF_THE_CHURCH.pdf

p. 99   *In their entertaining book …* D. Diehl and M. Donnelly, *Eat
Thy Neighbor: A History of Cannibalism* (Stroud: Sutton,
2006), p. 22.

p. 99   *'In the celebration of [the Eucharist] …'* J. H. Leith (ed.),
*Creeds of the Churches: A Reader in Christian Doctrine,
from the Bible to the Present* (Louisville, KY: Westminster
John Knox Press, 1982), pp. 502–503.

p. 100   *Even as recently as 1965 …* Mysterium Fidei. Encyclical of
Pope Paul VI on the Holy Eucharist, 3 September, 1965.
www.vatican.va/holy_father/paul_vi/encyclicals/documents/
hf_p-vi_enc_03091965_mysterium_en.html

p. 102   *In 1994 Dr Johanna Cullen …* J. Cullen, The Miracle of
Bolsena, *ASM News*, 60 (1994): 187–191.

p. 102   *The work of another researcher …* L. Garlaschelli, Starch
and hemoglobin: the miracle of Bolsena, *Chemistry and
Industry*, 80 (1998): 1201.

p. 103   *'We were hungry, we were cold …'* T. Taylor, *The Buried
Soul* (Boston, MA: Beacon Press, 2002), p. 74.

11   Sieges, Strandings and Starvation: Survival Cannibalism

p. 110   *'Prolonged hunger carves the body …'* S. A. Russell, *Hunger:
An Unnatural History* (New York: Basic Books, 2005),
p. 120.

p. 112   *In 1980 anthropologist Robert Dirks wrote …* R. Dirks,
Social responses during severe food shortages and famine,
Current Anthropology, 21(1) (1980): 21–44.

p. 112   *In* The Cannibal Within … L. Petrinovich, *The Cannibal
Within* (Piscataway, NJ: Transaction Books, 2000), p. 36.

p. 113   *which came to be called the Minnesota Experiment …*
L. Kalm and R. Semba, They starved so that others be

better fed: remembering Ancel Keys and the Minnesota
Experiment, *Journal of Nutrition*, 135 (2005): 1347–1352.

p. 113 *'All offers of surrender from Leningrad ...'* M. Jones,
Leningrad: State of Siege (New York: Basic Books, 2008),
Hitler quote from inside cover.

p. 113 *'Leningrad must die of starvation ...'* D. King, *Red Star
Over Russia: A Visual History of the Soviet Union from
the Revolution to the Death of Stalin* (New York: Harry N.
Abrams, 2009), p. 318.

p. 114 *In a system designed to maximise ...* M. Jones, *Leningrad:
State of Siege* (New York: Basic Books, 2008), pp. xxi–xxii.

p. 114 *Rations were reduced a total of five times ...* David M.
Glantz, *The Siege of Leningrad* (London: Cassell Military
Paperbacks, 2001), p. 83.

p. 114 *According to historian David Glantz ...* ibid., p. 89.

p. 114 *Archivist Nadezhda Cherepenina reported ...* Nadezhda
Cherepenina, Assessing the scale of famine and death in
the besieged city, in John Barber and Andrei Dzeniskevich
(eds), *Life and Death in Besieged Leningrad, 1941–44*
(Basingstoke: Macmillan, 2005), p. 44.

p. 114 *Pulitzer Prize-winning ...* Harrison Salisbury, *The 900 Days:
The Siege of Leningrad* (New York: Harper & Row, 1969),
pp. 478–479.

p. 114 *'because their flesh was so much more tender' ...* ibid.,
p. 479.

p. 114 *'In the worst period of the siege ...'* ibid., p. 478.

pp. 114–5 *According to numerous survivor accounts ...* Jones,
Leningrad, pp. 242–244.

p. 115 *'[the men] noticed as they piled ...'* H. Askenasy,
Cannibalism – From Sacrifice to Survival (New York:
Prometheus Books, 1994), p. 75.

p. 115 *'You will look in vain ...'* Salisbury, *The 900 Days*, p. 474.

p. 116 *'the official reports made right after the war ...'* Korn,
Radice and Hawes, *Cannibal – The History of the People-
Eaters*, pp. 83–86.

p. 118 *Although the 'poor Ethiopian' begged ...* E. Leslie, The
Ownership of the Plank: David Harrison on the Wreck of
the *Peggy*, in Joseph S. Cummins (ed.), *Cannibals: Shocking*

True Tales of the Last Taboo on Land and Sea (Guilford, CT: The Lyons Press, 2001), p. 50.

p. 118 *Someone suggested that two of the men ...* K. Johnson, J. Quinn Thornton (1810–1888), in Kristin Johnson (ed.), *'Unfortunate Emigrants': Narratives of the Donner Party* (Logan: Utah State University Press, 1996), p. 52.

p. 119 *'his miserable companions cut the flesh ...'* ibid., p. 53.

p. 119 *'Being nearly out of provisions ...'* Edwin Bryant, *What I Saw in California* (repr. Lincoln: University of Nebraska Press, 1985[1848]), part 3, chapter 20: The Donner Party, www.utahcrossroads.org/DonnerParty/Bryant3.htm

p. 119 *Foster, who survived the ordeal ...* K. Johnson, New Light on the Donner Family: The Murphy Family, www.utahcrossroads.org/DonnerParty/Murphy.htm#William%20McFadden%20Foster

p. 120 *'We looked all around but no living thing ...'* Esarey-Esrey & Rhoads-Esrey letters: records of a 19th century American migration, www.esarey.us/reunion/1873.htm

p. 122 *'[Reed's] party immediately commenced distributing ...'* J. Merryman, 'Adventures in California—Narrative of J. F. Reed—Life in the Wilderness—Sufferings of the Emigrants', *Illinois State Register*, 19 November 1847, p. 1, cc. 6–7, p. 2, c. 1; 26 November 1847, p. 1, c. 2. Also published as Narrative of the sufferings of a company of emigrants in the mountains of California, in the winter of '46 and '7 by J. F. Reed, late of Sangamon County, Illinois, *Illinois Journal*, 8 December 1847, p. 1, cc. 2–4.

p. 123 *'The mutilated body of a friend ...'* in Johnson, 'Unfortunate Emigrants', p. 90.

p. 123 *'They had consumed four bodies ...'* ibid., p. 91.

p. 124 *'No traces of her person could be found ...'* Dale Lowell Morton (ed.), *Overland in 1846: Diaries and Letters of the California–Oregon Trail*, vol. 1 (Lincoln: University of Nebraska Press, 1993), p. 362.

p. 124 *'human skeletons ... in every variety ...'* E. Rarick, *Desperate Passage* (New York: Oxford University Press, 2008), p. 229.

p. 125 *'Analysis finally clears Donner Party ...'* R. Preidt, Analysis finally clears Donner Party of rumored cannibalism.

MedicineNet, 19 April 2010. www.medicinenet.com/script/ main/art.asp?articlekey=115529

p. 125   *Even* The New York Times *got into the act* ... S. Dubner, No cannibalism among the Donner Party? Freakonomics, 16 April 2010. http://freakonomics.blogs.nytimes. com/2010/04/16/no-cannibalism-among-the-donner-party/

p. 125   *'Science crashes Donner Party ...'* Science crashes Donner Party. The Rat, 13 January 2006. http://therat.blogspot. com/2006_01_01_archive.html

p. 128   *The analysis by Gwen Robbins* ... Professor's research demonstrates starvation diet at the Donner Party's Alder Creek camp. Appalachian State University News, 23 April 2010. www.news.appstate.edu/2010/04/23/ professor%E2%80%99s-research-demonstrates-starvation-diet-at-the-donner-party%E2%80%99s-alder-creek-camp/

p. 129   *In 1990, anthropologist Donald Grayson* ... D. K. Grayson, Donner Party deaths: a demographic assessment, *Journal of Anthropological Research*, 46(3) (1990): 223–242.

p. 130   *Grayson later suggested a scenario* ... D. Grayson, The timing of Donner Party deaths, appendix 3, in Donald Hardesty (ed.), *The Archaeology of the Donner Party* (Reno: University of Nevada Press, 1997), p. 125.

p. 131   *In a 2010 study* ... D. Maestripieri, N. Baran, P. Sapienza and L. Zingales, Between- and within-sex variation in hormonal responses to psychological stress in a large sample of college students, *Stress*, 13(5) (2010): 413–424.

12   **Culture is King: Origins of the Western Cannibalism Taboo**

p. 133   *'Baby, baby, naughty baby ...'* The Oxford Dictionary of Nursery Rhymes, ed. Iona Opie and Peter Opie (Oxford: Oxford University Press, 1951), p. 59.

p. 134   *'They immediately shewed as much horror ...'* G. Obeyesekere, British cannibals: contemplation of an event in the death and resurrection of James Cook, explorer, in Gilles Bibeau and Ellen Corin (eds), *Beyond Textuality: Asceticism and Violence in Anthropological Interpretation* (Berlin: Mouton de Gruyter, 1994), p. 146.

p. 134   *'belief that a man needed his body after death ...'* Tannahill, *Flesh and Blood*, p. 45.

p. 134 *'an unprecedented and almost pathological ...'* ibid., p. 47.

p. 134 *'you are what you eat'* ... M. Kilgore, The function of cannibalism at the present time, in F. Baker, P. Hulme and M. Iversen (eds), *Cannibalism and the Colonial World* (Cambridge: Cambridge University Press, 1998), p. 239.

p. 135 *Homer's epic poem* ... Homer, *The Odyssey*, trans. Robert Fagles (New York: Penguin Books, 1996).

p. 136 *In Theogony, Homer's fellow poet Hesiod* ... Hesiod, *the Homeric Hymns and Homerica*, trans. Hugh G. Evelyn-White (Cambridge, MA, and London: Harvard University Press/William Heinemann, 1914); www.sacred-texts.com/cla/hesiod/theogony.htm

p. 136 *According to classicist Mary Knight* ... Mary Knight, personal communication.

p. 137 *In his* Histories ... Herodotus, *The History*, trans. David Grene (Chicago: University of Chicago Press, 1987), p. 228.

p. 137 *Herodotus was also the first writer* ... C. Avramescu, *An Intellectual History of Cannibalism*, trans. Alister Ian Blyth (Princeton, Princeton University Press, 2009), p. 33.

p. 138 *'some of them did something dreadful ...'* Herodotus, *The History*, p. 222.

p. 138 *The Father of History also wrote extensively about the Scythians* ... ibid., pp. 303–304.

p. 138 *the story of Astyages* ... ibid., pp. 84–90.

p. 140 *Seneca's first-century Roman tragedy* Thyestes ... *Seneca. Tragedies*, trans. F. J. Miller (Cambridge, MA, and London: Harvard University Press/William Heinemann, 1917); www.theoi.com/Text/SenecaThyestes.html

p. 142 *as translated by Paul Larue* ... J. Zipes, *Trials and Tribulations of Little Red Riding Hood* (New York: Routledge, 1993), p. 348.

p. 142 *In Perrault's 'Hop o' My Thumb'* ... Charles Perrault, Little Thumb, in *The Tales of Mother Goose*, trans. Charles Welsh (Boston, MA: D. C. Heath and Co., 1901), pp. 29–44.

p. 143 *The Brothers Grimm revisited a similar plot* ... The Brothers Grimm, *Hansel and Gretel and Other Tales* (London: Sovereign, 2013).

p. 143 *In his rendition, Jack is ... The Annotated Classic Fairy Tales*, ed. and trans. Maria Tatar (New York: W. W. Norton & Co., 2002).

p. 144 *In Joseph Jacob's revised epilogue ...* ibid., p. 143.

p. 145 *The plot of* Robinson Crusoe ... Daniel Defoe, *Robinson Crusoe* (New York: Paperview, 2004).

p. 147 *'Defoe's work is an effective contribution ...'* Lestringant, *Cannibals*, p. 141.

p. 148 *'judging the savage by the standard ...'* J. G. Frazer, *The Golden Bough: A Study in Magic and Religion* (New York: Macmillan, 1922), p. 342.

p. 148 *'the custom of tearing in pieces ...'* ibid., p. 454.

p. 149 *'The natives are superficially agreeable ...'* H. Lapsley, M. Mead and R. Benedict, *The Kinship of Women* (Amherst: University of Massachusetts Press, 2001), p. 217.

p. 149 *'Cannibal savages as they were ...'* Sigmund Freud, *Totem and Taboo* (New York: W. W. Norton & Co., 1950).

p. 149 *'mankind's earliest festival'* ... ibid., pp. x, 142.

13 China: Beyond the Western Taboo

p. 152 *'an institutionalized practice of consuming certain ...'* Key Ray Chong, *Cannibalism in China* (Wakefield, NH: Longwood Academic, 1990), p. 2.

p. 152 *publicly and culturally sanctioned ...* ibid.

p. 153 *Chong's investigation provides three examples of siege-related ...* ibid., pp. 45–46.

p. 153 *153 and 177 occurrences of cannibalism ...* ibid., pp. 160, 161.

p. 155 *Mao decided to install an 'improved' version ...* J. Becker, *Hungry Ghosts: Mao's Secret Famine* (New York: The Free Press, 1996), pp. 64–70.

p. 155 *Another of Mao's brainstorms ...* ibid., pp. 76–77.

p. 155 *in Mubei (Tombstone) ...* J. Yang, *Mubei (Tombstone)*, 8th edn (Hong King: Tiandi chubanshe, 2010[2008]).

p. 155 *'people ate tree bark, weeds, bird droppings ...'* Yang cited in China: from famine to Oslo, *The New York Times Review of Books*, 58(1) (13 January 2011), p. 52.

p. 156   *also believes that 36 million deaths* ... Yang cited in R.
MacFarquhar, The worst man-made catastrophe, ever, *The
New York Review of Books*, 10 February 2011, p. 28.

p. 156   *'Travelling around the region over thirty years later ...'*
Becker, *Hungry Ghosts*, pp. 118–119.

p. 156   *'hate, love, loyalty, filial piety ...'* Chong, *Cannibalism in
China*, p. 2.

p. 157   *Maggie Kilgore pointed out in 1998* ... Kilgore, The
function of cannibalism at the present time, p. 239.

p. 157   *'Methods of Cooking Human Flesh ...'* Chong,
Cannibalism in China, pp. 145–157.

p. 157   *'children's meat was the best food of all ...'* cited ibid.,
p. 137.

p. 157   *In Shui Hu Chuan (Outlaws of the Marsh)* ... Becker,
Hungry Ghosts, p. 216.

p. 157   *'five regional cuisines ...'* Chong, *Cannibalism in China*,
p. 145.

p. 157   *'many examples of steaming or boiling ...'* ibid., p. 153.

pp. 157–8   *Prisoners of war were preferred ingredients* ... ibid.

p. 158   *'Once victims had been subjected to criticism ...'* Zheng
Yi, The Slaughter at Wuxuan, from Scarlet Memorial ...
Tales of Cannibalism in Modern China, in Cummins (ed.),
Cannibals, p. 210.

p. 158   *'children would cut off parts of their body ...'* Chong,
Cannibalism in China, p. 154.

p. 159   *a total of 766 documented cases* ... ibid., pp. 100–101.

14   Skull Moss and Mummy Powder: Medicinal Cannibalism

p. 161   *The ancients were very eager* ... cited in Beth Conklin,
Consuming Grief.

p. 162   *'the gall bladder, bones, hair ...'* Korn, Radice and Hawes,
Cannibal – The History of the People-Eaters, p. 92.

p. 162   *'nail, hair, skin, milk ...'* Thomas S. Chen and Peter S.
Chen, Medical cannibalism in China: the case of ko-ku, *The
Pharos*, 61(2) (1998): 23–25.

p. 163   *So popular was this practice* ... K. Gordon-Grube,
Anthropophagy in post-Renaissance Europe: the tradition
of medicinal cannibalism, *American Anthropologist*, 90
(1988): 407.

p. 164 *'human liver ... oil distilled from human brains ...'* R. Sugg, *Mummies, Cannibals and Vampires: The History of Corpse Medicine from the Renaissance to the Victorians* (London and New York: Routledge, 2011).

p. 164 *'One thing we are rarely taught at school ...'* cited in Fiona Macrae, British royalty dined on human flesh (but don't worry it was 300 years ago), *Daily Mail*, 21 May 2011, www. dailymail.co.uk/news/article-1389142/British-royalty-dined-human-flesh-dont-worry-300-years-ago.html

p. 164 *Additional high-profile advocates of medicinal cannibalism included ...* Richard Sugg, The Aztecs, cannibalism and corpse medicine (1), Mexicolore, www.mexicolore.co.uk/aztecs/home/cannibalism-and-corpse-medicine-1

pp. 164–5 *Researcher Paolo Modinesi believes ...* P. Modinesi, Skull lichens: a curious chapter in the history of phytotherapy, *Fitoterapia*, 80 (2009): 145–148.

p. 165 *Ideally, the moss from the skulls ...* Gordon- Grube, Anthropophagy in post-Renaissance Europe, p. 406.

p. 165 *'the cranium of a carcass that had been broken ...'* Modinesi, Skull lichens, p. 147.

p. 165 *a bizarre medical treatment known as hoplochrisma ...* ibid.

p. 166 *'choose what is of a shining black ...'* A. Wootton, *Chronicles of Pharmacy*, 2 vols (New York: USV Pharmaceutical Corporation, 1972), vol. 2, p. 24.

p. 166 *'[The Paracelsist Oswald] Croll recommended ...'* Gordon-Grube, Anthropophagy in post-Renaissance Europe, p. 406.

p. 167 *Listed as Mumia vera aegyptica ...* Modinesi, Skull lichens, p. 148.

p. 168 *'the rise of Enlightenment attitudes ...'* Sugg, *Mummies, Cannibals and Vampires*, pp. 264–265.

p. 168 *'...after having Dad's ashes ...'* K. Richards, *Life* (New York: Little, Brown, 2010), p. 546.

15   Too Much to Swallow: Placentophagy

p. 169 *I read the title of the article ...* A. A. Abrahamian, The Placenta Cookbook, *New York*, 29 August 2011, pp. 46–49, 154.

p. 170 *A 2013 study ...* Jodi Selander, Allison Cantor, Sharon M. Young and Daniel C. Benyshek, Human maternal

placentophagy: a survey of self-reported motivations and
experiences associated with placenta consumption, *Ecology
of Food and Nutrition*, 52(2) (2013): 93–115.

p. 173   *In 1930, primatologist Otto Tinklepaugh* ... O. Tinklepaugh
and C. Hartman, Behavioral aspects of parturition in
the monkey (*Macacus rhesus*), *Journal of Comparative
Psychology*, 11(1) (1930): 63–98.

p. 173   *Kristal and his colleagues initially posited* ... M. B. Kristal,
J. Di Pirro and A. Thompson, Placentophagia in humans
and nonhuman mammals: causes and consequences,
Ecology of Food and Nutrition, 51 (2012): 179.

p. 174   *'voracious carnivorousness ...'* ibid.

p. 174   *and set out to investigate* ... M. B. Kristal, A. Thompson
and H. Grishkat, Placenta ingestion enhances opiate
analgesia in rats, *Physiology & Behavior*, 35 (1985):
481–486.

p. 175   *In 2010, researchers at the University of Nevada* ... S. Young
and D. Benyshek, In search of human placentophagy: a
cross-cultural survey of human placenta consumption,
disposal practices and cultural beliefs, *Ecology of Food and
Nutrition*, 49 (2010): 467–484.

p. 175   *the* Great Pharmacopoeia *of 1596* ... W. Ober, Notes on
placentophagy, *Bulletin of the New York Medical Academy*,
55(6) (1979): 596.

p. 176   *On a more recent note* ... S. Benet, *Song, Dance and
Customs of Peasant Poland* (New York: Roy, 1951),
pp. 196–197.

p. 179   *In a 1954 study, Czech researchers* ... E. Soyková-
Pachnerová, B. Golová and E. Zvolská, Placenta as a
lactagogon, *Gynaecologia*, 138 (1954): 617–627.

p. 182   *'The Somosomo people were fed ...'* From Online
Etymology Dictionary, www.etymonline.com/index.
php?term=long+pig&allowed_in_frame, Extract of a letter
from the Rev. John Watsford, dated October 6th 1846. In
'Wesleyan Missionary Notices', September 1847.

p. 183   *'I sautéed the steak of Bernd, with salt ...'* First TV
Interview With German Cannibal: 'Human flesh
tastes like pork'. Spiegel Online International, 16
October 2007, www.spiegel.de/international/zeitgeist/

first-tv-interview-with-german-cannibal-human-flesh-tastes-like-pork-a-511775.html

p. 184 *'It was good, fully developed veal ...'* W. Seabrook, *Jungle Ways* (New York: Harcourt, Brace, 1931), p. 272.

p. 184 *'Animals eat their placenta ...'* BBC News, Why eat a placenta? http://news.bbc.co.uk/2/hi/uk_news/magazine/4918290.stm

16 No Laughing Matter: Cannibalism and Kuru in the Pacific Islands

p. 186 *'Nothing it seems to me ...'* J. H. P. Murray (Lieutenant Governor/Chief Judicial Officer, British New Guinea 1908–1940), *Papua; or British New Guinea* (New York, Charles Scribner's Sons, 1912).

p. 187 *According to research biochemist Colm Kelleher ...* C. Kelleher, *Brain Trust* (New York: Paraview Pocket Books, 2004), p. 115.

p. 188 *By 1987 there were over 400 confirmed cases ...* ibid., p. 117.

p. 189 *Fore elders told the Australians ...* W. Anderson, *The Collectors of Lost Souls* (Baltimore: Johns Hopkins University Press, 2008), p. 14.

p. 190 *the locals were 'difficult people to deal with ...'* cited in Anderson, *The Collectors of Lost Souls*, pp. 21–22.

p. 190 *'Actually these people are "bestial" in many ways ...'* ibid., p. 25.

p. 190 *'Dead human flesh, to these people ...'* ibid., p. 24.

p. 191 *A decade later, the not-yet-controversial anthropologist Bill Arens commented ...* Arens, *The Man-Eating Myth*, p. 99.

p. 191 *'Now you have cut off my penis! ...'* R. Berndt, *Excess and Restraint* (Chicago: University of Chicago Press, 1962), p. 283.

p. 191 *He studied rabies and plague ...* R. Rhodes, *Deadly Feasts* (New York: Simon & Schuster, 1997), p. 32.

p. 192 *'I am in one of the most remote ...'* cited in Anderson, *The Collectors of Lost Souls*, p. 61.

p. 192 *But Gajdusek had never seen any actual cannibalism ...* ibid., pp. 62–80.

p. 192 *their initial findings were published ...* D. C. Gajdusek and V. Zigas, Degenerative disease of the central nervous system in New Guinea – the endemic occurrence of kuru in the native population, *New England Journal of Medicine*, 257 (1957): 974–978.

p. 193 *The closest condition he could think* ... Anderson, *The Collectors of Lost Souls*, p. 80.

p. 193 *Another NIH scientist noticed a similarity* ... Kelleher, *Brain Trust*, pp. 29–31.

p. 193 *Scrapie, which was present in European sheep* ... ibid., pp. 31–32.

p. 193 *At this point, Ronald Berndt stepped in* ... Anderson, *The Collectors of Lost Souls*, p. 81.

p. 194 *Bennett proposed that a mutant kuru gene* ... ibid., p. 124.

p. 194 *'In the eastern highlands of New Guinea ...'* Anonymous, The Laughing Death, *Time*, 11 November 1957, pp. 55–56.

p. 195 *For his part, Gajdusek hated the media coverage* ... Anderson, *The Collectors of Lost Souls*, p. 81.

p. 196 *Glasse published their hypothesis* ... R. M. Glasse, The social effects of kuru, *Papua New Guinea Medical Journal*, 7 (1964): 36–47.

p. 196 *In a later study, Glasse calculated that kuru* ... John D. Mathews, Robert Glasse and Shirley Lindenbaum, Kuru and cannibalism, *Lancet*, 292 (1968): 449–452.

p. 196 *Nearly fifty years after Glasse published* ... J. Whitfield, W. Pako, J. Collinge and M. Alpers, Mortuary rites of the South Fore and kuru, *Philosophical Transactions of the Royal Society B*, 363(1510) (2008): 3721–3724.

p. 198 *including reproductive organs and faeces* ... Rhodes, *Deadly Feasts*, pp. 22–23.

p. 198 *By tracing the path of the kuru reports* ... S. Lindenbaum, Cannibalism, kuru and anthropology, *Folia Neuropathologica*, 47(2) (2009): 139.

p. 199 *Whitfield, who conducted nearly 200 interviews* ... Shirley Lindenbaum and Jerome Whitfield, personal communications.

17 **Apocalypse Cow: The Origins of BSE**

p. 200 *'Unfortunately, the custom of consuming human flesh ...'* B. Fagan, *The Aztecs* (New York: W. H. Freeman & Co., 1984), p. 233.

p. 200 *meat and dairy industries in the UK* ... Kelleher, *Brain Trust*, p. 118.

p. 201 *In searching for answers, the British government enlisted* ... P. Yam, *The Pathological Protein* (New York: Copernicus Books, 2003), p. 110.

p. 201 *Previously, dangerous solvents had been used* ... Kelleher, *Brain Trust*, p. 120.

p. 202 *The first was a significant increase* ... Rhodes, *Deadly Feasts*, p. 180.

p. 203 *In 1947 an outbreak of what would become known* ... ibid., pp. 81–82.

p. 203 *they inoculated a trio of chimpanzees* ... ibid., p. 87.

p. 204 *In a February 1966 article* ... D. C. Gajdusek, C. Gibbs and M. Alpers, Experimental transmission of a kuru-like syndrome to chimpanzees, *Nature*, 209 (1966): 794–796.

p. 205 *'The mechanism of spread of kuru ...'* D. C. Gajdusek, Kuru in the New Guinea Highlands, in J. Spillane (ed.), *Tropical Neurology* (London: Oxford University Press, 1973), pp. 376–383.

p. 205 *In a radio interview, the NIH researcher* ... R. Uridge, *BSE – the untold story*, BBC Radio 4, 18 May 1999.

p. 207 *At the forefront of the mystery* ... Rhodes, *Deadly Feasts*, pp. 120–122.

p. 207 *In another set of experiments* ... T. Alper, D. Haig and M. Clarke, The exceptionally small size of the scrapie agent, *Biochemical and Biophysical Research Communications*, 22 (1966): 278–284.

p. 207 *After reading Alper's work* ... J. S. Griffith, Self-replication and scrapie, *Nature*, 215 (1967): 1043–1044.

p. 208 *But Stanley Prusiner, a young biochemist* ... Anderson, *The Collectors of Lost Souls*, pp. 190–194.

p. 208 *In 1982 Prusiner published his lab findings* ... S. Prusiner, Novel proteinaceous infectious particles cause scrapie, *Science*, 216(4542) (1982): 136–144.

p. 209 *'invaded and colonized the work ...'* Rhodes, *Deadly Feasts*, p. 203.

18   **Truth or Consequences: BSE, CJD and Human Health**

p. 211 *a 'blue ribbon' panel* ... Kelleher, *Brain Trust*, p. 125.

p. 211 *offering them only 50 per cent of market value* ... Yam, *The Pathological Protein*, p. 118.

p. 212 *'Spongiform Fear Grows ...'* Farming News, 22 April 1988.

p. 212 *'Raging Madness Attacks Cattle ...'* Sunday Telegraph, 24 April 1988.

p. 212 *An earlier paper in* Nature *also demonstrated* ... C. Gibbs, Jr. and D. C. Gajdusek, Transmission of scrapie to the cynomolgus monkey (*Macaca fascicularis*), *Nature*, 236 (1972): 73–74.

p. 212 *'the risk of transmission of BSE ...'* The BSE Inquiry: The Report, The National Archives, http://collections. europarchive.org/tna/20090505194948/http://bseinquiry.gov. uk/report/volume4/chapt102.htm#888456

p. 212 *The authors of the Southwood report* ... Kelleher, *Brain Trust*, p. 140.

p. 213 *she and her colleagues have performed* ... L. Manuelidis, Y. Zhoa-Xue, N. Barquero and B. Mullins, Cells infected with scrapie and Creutzfeldt-Jakob disease agents produce intracellular 25-nm virus-like particles, *Proceedings of the National Academy of Sciences*, 104(6) (2007): 1965–1970.

p. 214 *In 1993, two British dairy farmers died* ... Rhodes, *Deadly Feasts*, p. 187.

p. 214 *In May of the same year, fifteen-year-old British schoolgirl Victoria Rimmer* ... ibid., pp. 187–188.

p. 214 *think of the consequences* ... ibid., p. 188.

p. 214 *In 1994, a sixteen-year-old schoolgirl* ... ibid., pp. 188–189.

p. 215 *On 8 March 1996 the hammer fell* ... Kelleher, *Brain Trust*, p. 165.

p. 215 *The new disease was initially* ... J. Ironside and J. Bell, Florid plaques and new variant Creutzfeldt-Jakob disease, *The Lancet*, 350 (1997): 1475.

p. 215 *By October 2013 the number of definite* ... One in 2,000 people in the UK carry 'abnormal proteins' linked to mad cow disease, *Daily Mail*, 15 October 2013, www.dailymail. co.uk/health/article-2461354/Mad-cow-disease-One-2-000-people-UK-carry-abnormal-proteins-linked-vCJD.html

p. 215 *'anonymous appendix samples ...'* Researchers estimate one in 2,000 people in the UK carry variant CJD proteins, press release, *British Medical Journal*, 14 October 2013, www.

bmj.com/press-releases/2013/10/14/researchers-estimate-one-2000-people-uk-carry-variant-cjd-proteins

p. 216 *The researchers and their colleagues ...* S. Mead, J. Whitfield, M. Poulter, P. Shah, J. Uphill, J. Beck, T. Campbell, Al-H. Dujaily, M. Alpers and J. Collinge, Genetic susceptibility, evolution and the kuru epidemic, *Philosophical Transactions of the Royal Society, B*, 363 (2008): 3741–3746.

p. 216 *In 2015 Collinge and his research team ...* E. Asante, M. Smidak, A. Grimshaw, R. Houghton, A. Tomlinson, A. Jeelani, T. Jakubcova, S. Hamdan, A. Richard-Londt, J. Linehan, S. Brandner, M. Alpers, J. Whitfield, S. Mead, J. Wadsworth and J. Collinge, A naturally occurring variant of the human prion protein completely prevents prion disease, *Nature*, 522 (2015): 478–481.

Epilogue One Step Beyond

p. 219 *'Viewing anything that involves violence ...'* F. Rice, Whodunnit then? Here's why we're all so obsessed with violent crime, *Marie Claire*, 9 March 2015, www.marieclaire.co.uk/blogs/548712/whodunnit-then-here-s-why-we-re-all-so-obsessed-with-violent-crime.html

p. 219 *'an older homosexual tramp ...'* J. Green, *Cassell's Dictionary of Slang* (London: Orion, 2005), p. 240.

p. 219 *'are people who have a tremendous desire to destroy ...'* Why killers cannibalize, ABC News, 22 May 2002, http://abcnews.go.com/US/story?id=90012

p. 220 *where researchers Daniel Griffin and Kevin Anchukaitis used soil ...* D. Griffin and K. Anchukaitis, How unusual is the 2012–2014 California drought?, *Geophysical Research Letters*, 41 (2014): 9017–9023.

FURTHER READING

Warwick Anderson, *The Collectors of Lost Souls* (Baltimore: Johns
    Hopkins University Press, 2008)
William Arens, *The Man-Eating Myth* (Oxford: Oxford University
    Press, 1979)
Hans Askenasy, *Cannibalism – From Sacrifice to Survival* (New
    York: Prometheus Books, 1994)
Catalin Avramescu, *An Intellectual History of Cannibalism*, trans.
    Alister Ian Blyth (Princeton: Princeton University Press, 2009)
John Barber and Andrei Dzeniskevich (eds), *Life and Death in
    Besieged Leningrad, 1941–44* (Basingstoke: Macmillan, 2005)
Francis Barker, Peter Hulme and Margaret Iversen (eds),
    Cannibalism and the Colonial World (Cambridge: Cambridge
    University Press, 1998)
Jasper Becker, *Hungry Ghosts: Mao's Secret Famine* (New York:
    The Free Press, 1996)
Ronald M. Berndt, *Excess and Restraint* (Chicago: University of
    Chicago Press, 1962)
James Gillespie Blaine, James William Buel, John Clark Ridpath
    and Benjamin Butterworth, *Columbus and Columbia: A
    Pictorial History of the Man and the Nation* (Richmond, VA:
    B. F. Johnson & Co., 1892)
Robert Bloch, *Psycho* (New York: Random House, 1958)
Daniel James Brown, *The Indifferent Stars Above* (New York:
    William Morrow, 2009)
Robert Chambers, *Vestiges of the Natural History of Creation*
    (London: John Churchill, 1844)
Key Ray Chong, *Cannibalism in China* (Wakefield, NH: Longwood
    Academic, 1990)

Beth A. Conklin, *Consuming Grief: Compassionate Cannibalism in an Amazonian Society* (Austin: University of Texas Press, 2001)

Nathan Constantine, *A History of Cannibalism: From Ancient Cultures to Survival Stories and Modern Psychopaths* (Edison, NJ: Cartwell Books, 2006)

Homer Croy, *Wheels West* (New York: Hastings House, 1955)

Joseph S. Cummins (ed.), *Cannibals: Shocking True Tales of the Last Taboo on Land and Sea* (Guilford, CT: The Lyons Press, 2001)

Francis Darwin (ed.), *The Life and Letters of Charles Darwin, Including an Autobiographical Chapter* (London: John Murray, 1887)

Patricia de Fuentes (ed.), *The Conquistadores* (New York: Orion, 1963)

Daniel Defoe, *Robinson Crusoe*, New York Post Family Classics Library (New York: Paperview, 2004)

Daniel Diehl and Mark P. Donnelly, *Eat Thy Neighbor – A History of Cannibalism* (Stroud: Sutton, 2006)

Niles Eldredge and Ian Tattersall, *The Myths of Human Evolution* (New York: Columbia University Press, 1982)

Mark Elgar and Bernard Crespi (eds), *Cannibalism: Ecology and Evolution Among Diverse Taxa* (New York: Oxford University Press, 1992)

Brian M. Fagan, *The Aztecs* (New York: W. H. Freeman & Co., 1984)

James George Frazer, *The Golden Bough: A Study in Magic and Religion* (New York: Macmillan, 1922)

David M. Glantz, *The Siege of Leningrad* (London: Cassell Military Paperbacks, 2001)

Laurence R. Goldman (ed.), *The Anthropology of Cannibalism* (Westport, CT: Bergin & Garvey, 1999)

Leon Gouré, *The Siege of Leningrad* (Stanford: Stanford University Press, 1962)

Donald Hardesty, *Archaeology of the Donner Party* (Reno: University of Nevada Press, 1997)

Lansford W. Hastings, *The Emigrants' Guide to Oregon and California* (Bedford, MA: Applewood Books, 1994)

Glenn Hausfater and Sarah Blaffer Hrdy (eds), *Infanticide: Comparative and Evolutionary Perspectives* (Hawthorne, NY: Aldine, 1984)

Herodotus, *The History*, trans. David Grene (Chicago: University of Chicago Press, 1987)

Homer, *The Odyssey*, trans. Robert Fagles (New York: Penguin Books, 1996)

Peter Hulme and Neil Whitehead (eds), *Wild Majesty: Encounters with Caribs from Columbus to the Present Day* (Oxford: Clarendon Press, 1992)

Irving, Washington, *The Complete Works of Washington Irving*, ed. John Harmon McElroy, vol. 9 (Boston, MA: Twayne, 1981)

Jisheng, Yang, *Mubei (Tombstone)*, 8th edn (Hong Kong: Tiandi chubanshe, 2010[2008])

Kristin Johnson (ed.), *'Unfortunate Emigrants': Narratives of the Donner Party* (Logan: Utah State University Press, 1996)

Michael Jones, *Leningrad: State of Siege* (New York: Basic Books, 2008)

Colm A. Kelleher, *Brain Trust* (New York: Paraview Pocket Books, 2004)

Joseph King, *Winter of Entrapment* (Toronto: P. D. Meany, 1992)

Robert Klitzman, *The Trembling Mountain* (New York: Plenum Trade, 1998)

Daniel Korn, Mark Radice and Charlie Hawes, *Cannibal – The History of the People-Eaters* (London: Channel 4 Books, 2001)

Janet Leonard and Alex Córdoba-Aguilar (eds), *The Evolution of Primary Sexual Characters in Animals* (New York: Oxford University Press, 2010)

Frank Lestringant, *Cannibals: The Discovery and Representation of the Cannibal from Columbus to Jules Verne* (Berkeley: University of California Press, 1997)

Francis Augustus MacNutt, *De Orbe Novo; The Eight Decades of Peter Martyr D'Anghera*, vol. 1 (New York and London: G. P. Putnam's Sons, 1912)

Moira Martingale, *Cannibal Killers: The History of Impossible Murders* (New York: Carroll & Graf, 1993)

C. F. McGlashan, *History of the Donner Party: A Tragedy of the Sierra* (Stanford: Stanford University Press, 1947)

J. H. P. Murray, *Papua or British New Guinea* (London, T. Fisher Unwin, 1912)

Linda A. Newson, *Aboriginal and Spanish Colonial Trinidad* (London: Academic Press, 1976)

Ganeth Obeyesekere, *Cannibal Talk: The Man-Eating Myth and Human Sacrifice in the South Seas* (Berkeley: University of California Press, 2005)

Lewis Petrinovich, *The Cannibal Within* (Piscataway, NJ: Transaction Books, 2000)

Sheldon Rampton and John Stauber, *Mad Cow U.S.A.* (Monroe, MA: Common Courage Press, 2004)

Richard Rhodes, *Deadly Feasts* (New York: Simon & Schuster, 1997)

Irving Rouse, *The Tainos: Rise and Decline of the People Who Greeted Columbus* (Hartford, CT: Yale University Press, 1992)

Sharman Apt Russell, *Hunger: An Unnatural History* (New York: Basic Books, 2005)

Harrison Salisbury, *The 900 Days: The Siege of Leningrad* (New York: Harper & Row, 1969)

Carl O. Sauer, *The Early Spanish Main* (Berkeley: University of California Press, 1966)

Bill Schutt, *Dark Banquet: Blood and the Curious Lives of Blood-Feeding Creatures* (New York: Harmony Books, 2008)

Ralph S. Solecki, *Shanidar: The First Flower People* (New York: Knopf, 1971)

David E. Stannard, *American Holocaust: Conquest of the New World* (New York: Oxford University Press, 1992)

George R. Stewart, *Ordeal by Hunger: The Story of the Donner Party* (New York: Houghton Mifflin, 1992)

Reay Tannahill, *Flesh and Blood: A History of the Cannibal Complex* (New York: Little, Brown, 1975)

Maria Tatar, *Off With Their Heads* (Princeton: Princeton University Press, 1992)

Ian Tattersall, *The Fossil Trail* (New York: Oxford University Press, 2009)

Carole A. Travis-Henikoff, *Dinner with a Cannibal* (Santa Monica, CA: Santa Monica Press, 2008)

Philip Yam, *The Pathological Protein: Mad Cow, Chronic Wasting, and Other Deadly Prion Diseases* (New York: Copernicus Books, 2003)

Zheng Yi, *Scarlett Memorial: Tales of Cannibalism in Modern China* (Boulder, CO: Westview Press, 1996)

Jack Zipes, *The Brothers Grimm: From Enchanted Forests to the Modern World* (London: Routledge, Kegan & Paul, 1988)

INDEX